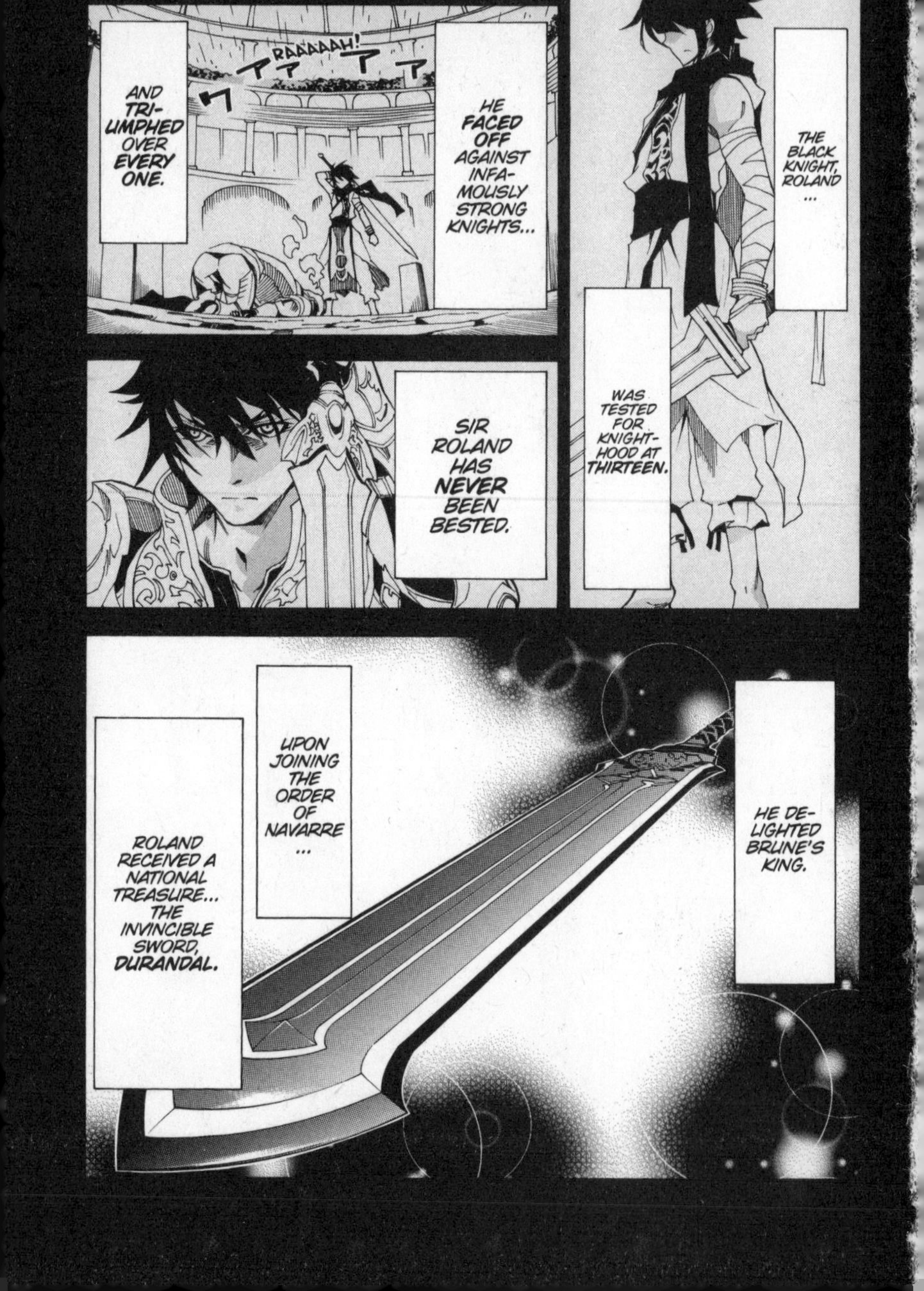
THE BLACK KNIGHT, ROLAND ...
WAS TESTED FOR KNIGHTHOOD AT THIRTEEN.
HE FACED OFF AGAINST INFAMOUSLY STRONG KNIGHTS...
ワアアアア RAAAAAH!
AND TRIUMPHED OVER EVERY ONE.
SIR ROLAND HAS NEVER BEEN BESTED.
HE DELIGHTED BRUNE'S KING.
UPON JOINING THE ORDER OF NAVARRE ...
ROLAND RECEIVED A NATIONAL TREASURE... THE INVINCIBLE SWORD, DURANDAL.

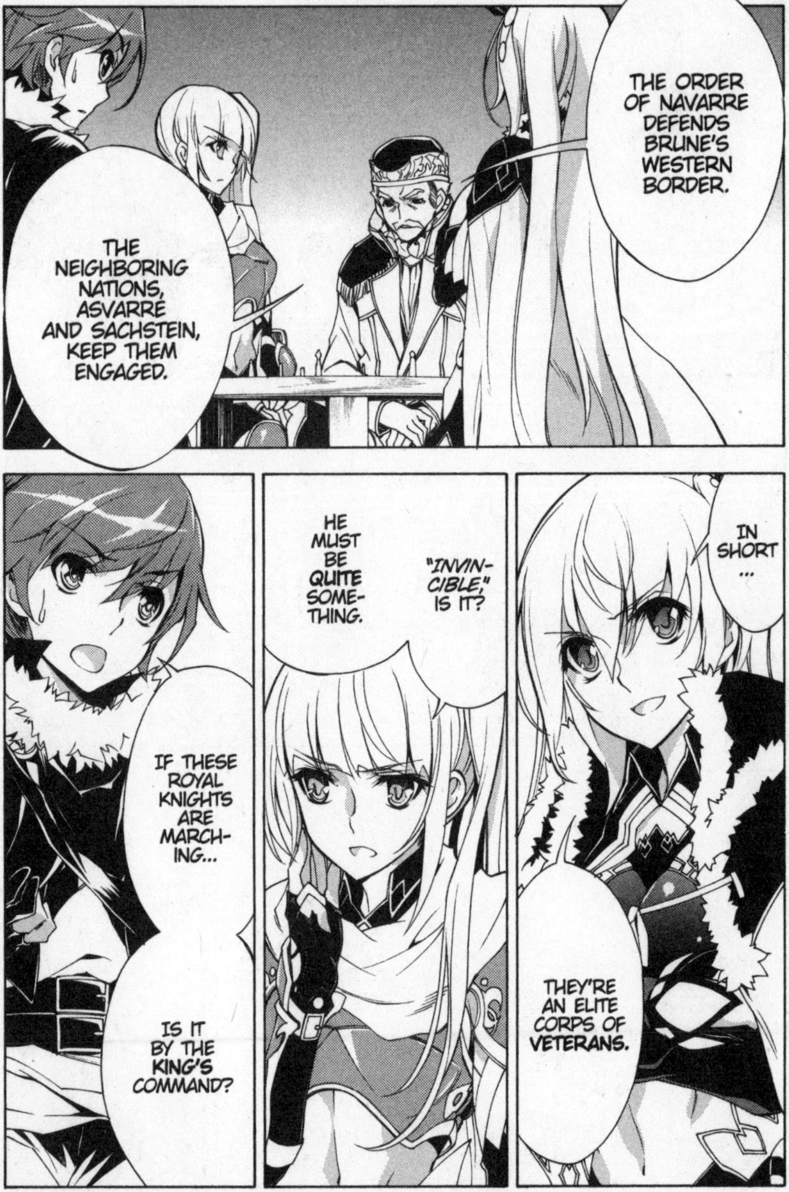
THE ORDER OF NAVARRE DEFENDS BRUNE'S WESTERN BORDER.
THE NEIGHBORING NATIONS, ASVARRE AND SACHSTEIN, KEEP THEM ENGAGED.
IN SHORT ...
THEY'RE AN ELITE CORPS OF VETERANS.
"INVIN-CIBLE," IS IT?
HE MUST BE QUITE SOME-THING.
IF THESE ROYAL KNIGHTS ARE MARCH-ING...
IS IT BY THE KING'S COMMAND?

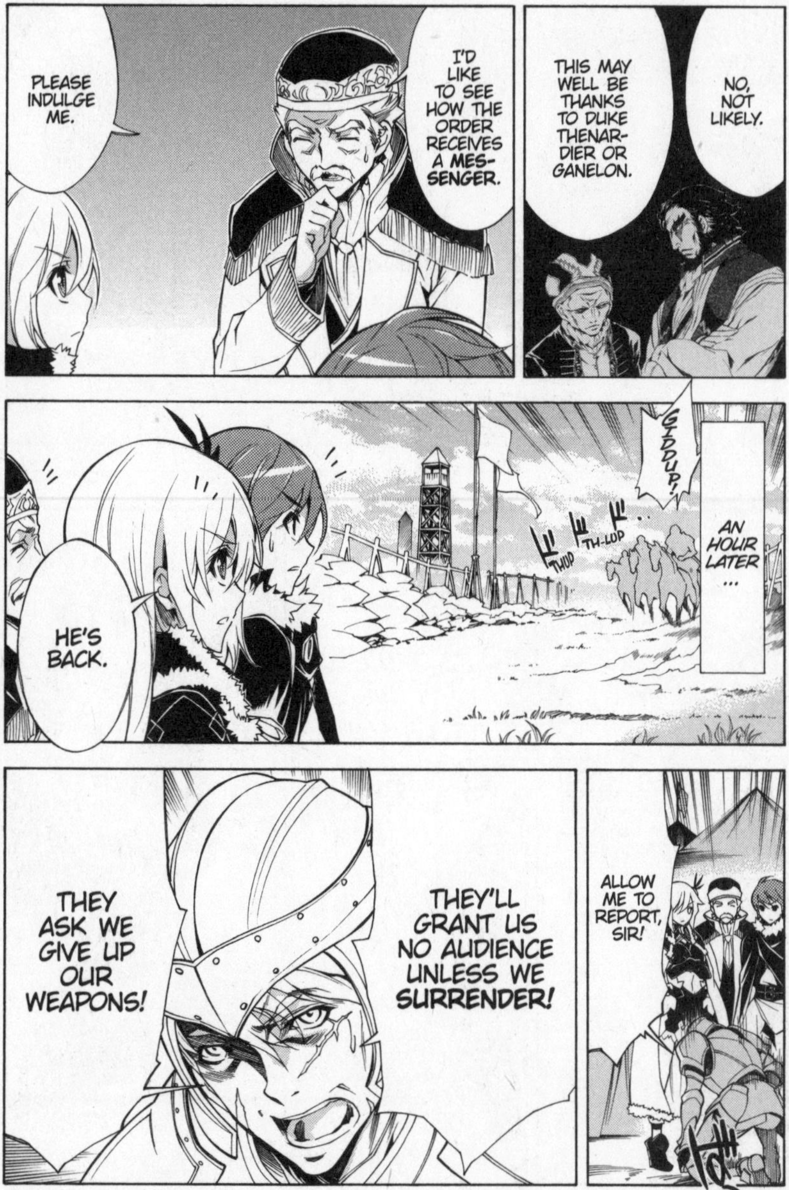
NO, NOT LIKELY.
THIS MAY WELL BE THANKS TO DUKE THENARDIER OR GANELON.
I'D LIKE TO SEE HOW THE ORDER RECEIVES A MESSENGER.
PLEASE INDULGE ME.
AN HOUR LATER...
GIDDUP!
TH-LUP
THUP
HE'S BACK.
ALLOW ME TO REPORT, SIR!
BWAK
THEY'LL GRANT US NO AUDIENCE UNLESS WE SURRENDER!
THEY ASK WE GIVE UP OUR WEAPONS!

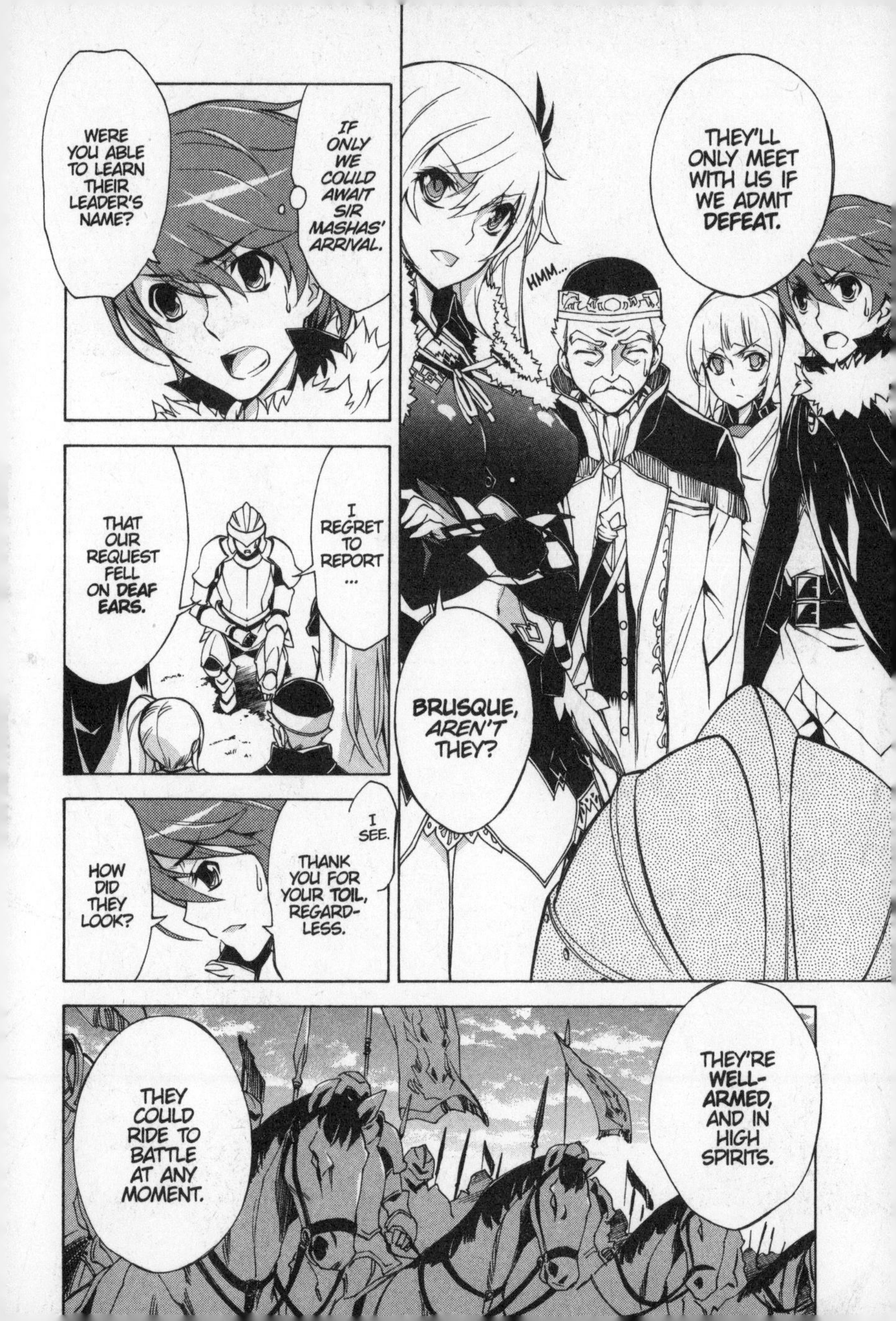
THEY'LL ONLY MEET WITH US IF WE ADMIT DEFEAT.
HMM...
BRUSQUE, AREN'T THEY?
IF ONLY WE COULD AWAIT SIR MASHAS' ARRIVAL.
WERE YOU ABLE TO LEARN THEIR LEADER'S NAME?
I REGRET TO REPORT ...
THAT OUR REQUEST FELL ON DEAF EARS.
I SEE.
THANK YOU FOR YOUR TOIL, REGARDLESS.
HOW DID THEY LOOK?
THEY'RE WELL-ARMED, AND IN HIGH SPIRITS.
THEY COULD RIDE TO BATTLE AT ANY MOMENT.

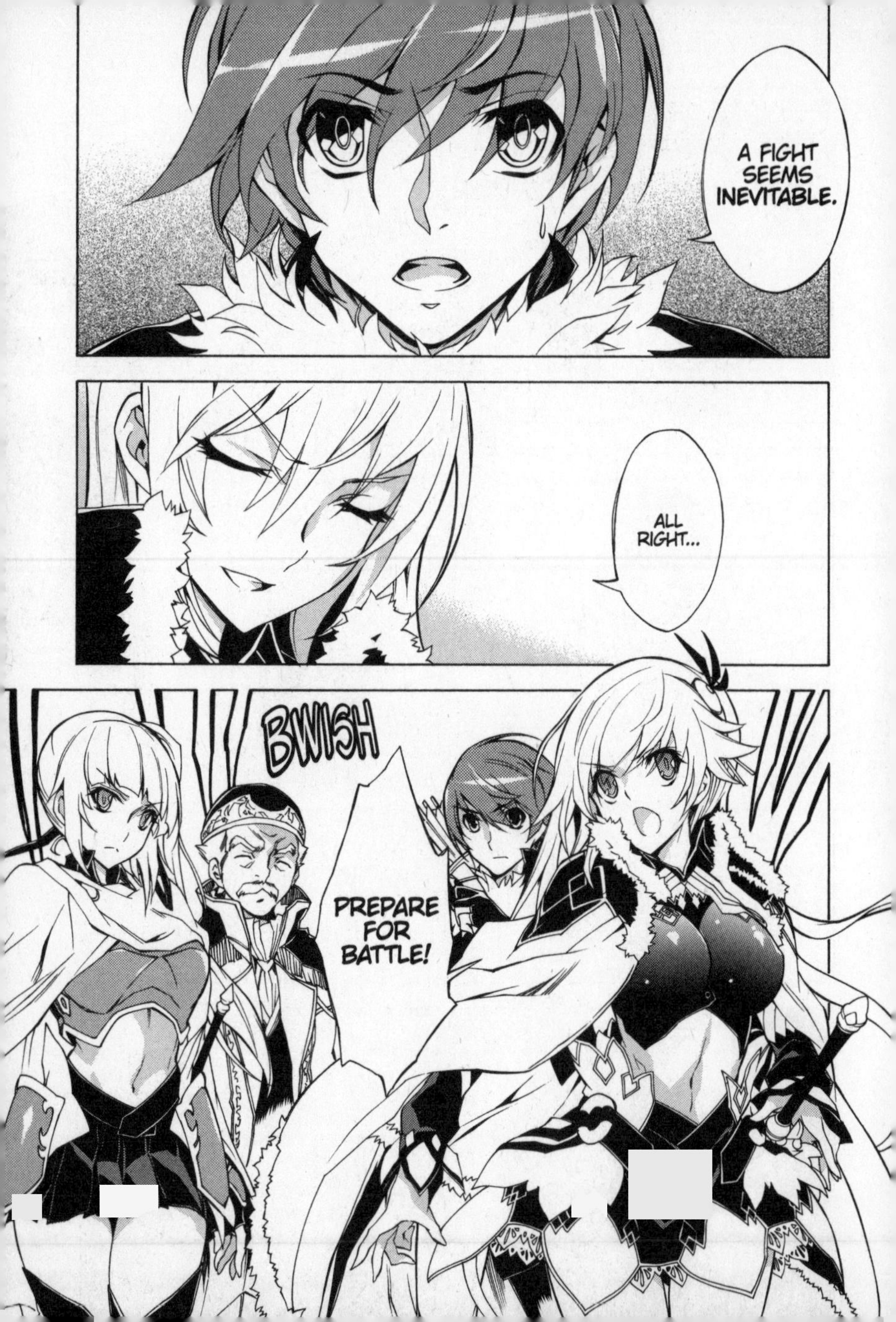
A FIGHT SEEMS INEVITABLE.
ALL RIGHT...
PREPARE FOR BATTLE!
BWISH

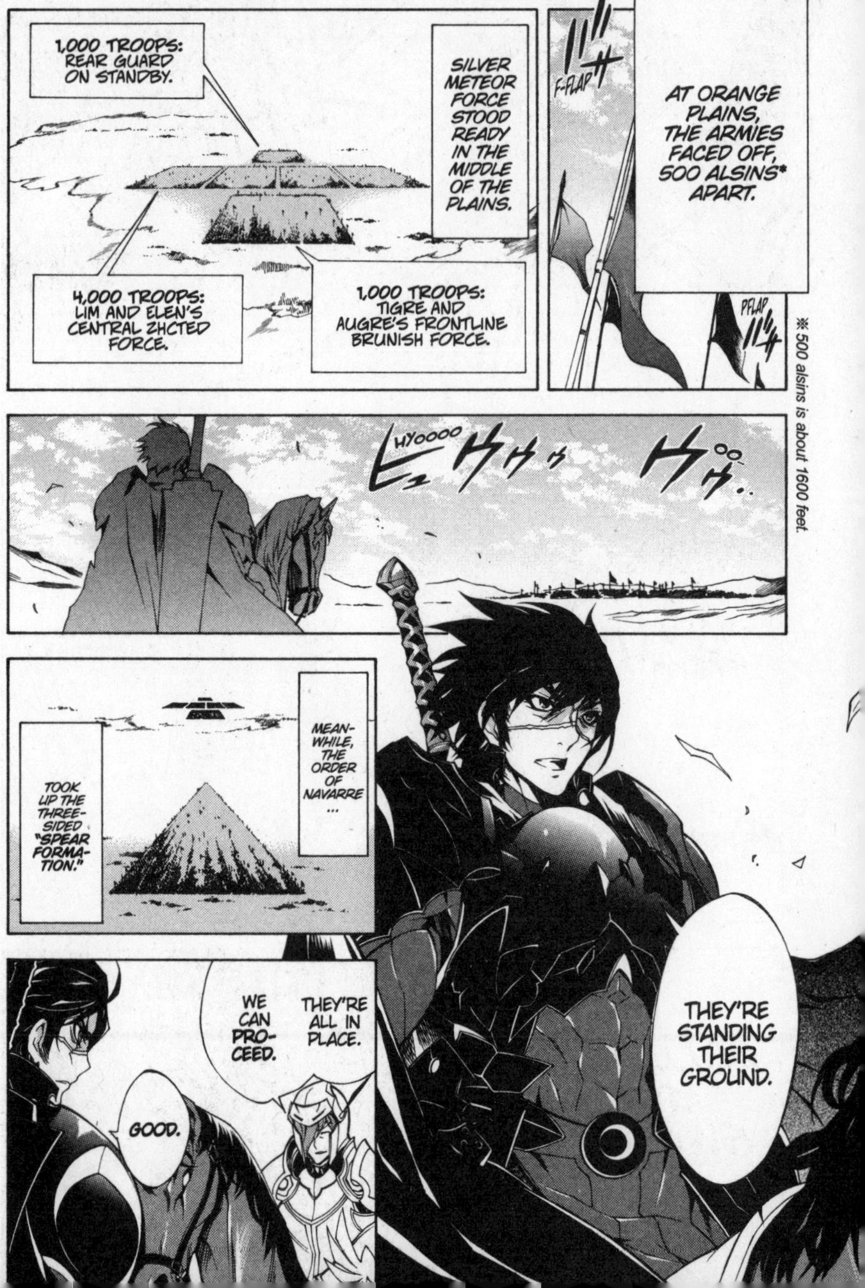
AT ORANGE PLAINS, THE ARMIES FACED OFF, 500 ALSINS* APART.
F-FLAP
PFLAP
SILVER METEOR FORCE STOOD READY IN THE MIDDLE OF THE PLAINS.
1,000 TROOPS: REAR GUARD ON STANDBY.
1,000 TROOPS: TIGRE AND AUGRE'S FRONTLINE BRUNISH FORCE.
4,000 TROOPS: LIM AND ELEN'S CENTRAL ZHCTED FORCE.
HYOOOO
MEAN-WHILE, THE ORDER OF NAVARRE ...
TOOK UP THE THREE-SIDED "SPEAR FORMATION."
THEY'RE STANDING THEIR GROUND.
THEY'RE ALL IN PLACE.
WE CAN PRO-CEED.
GOOD.

※ 500 alsins is about 1600 feet.

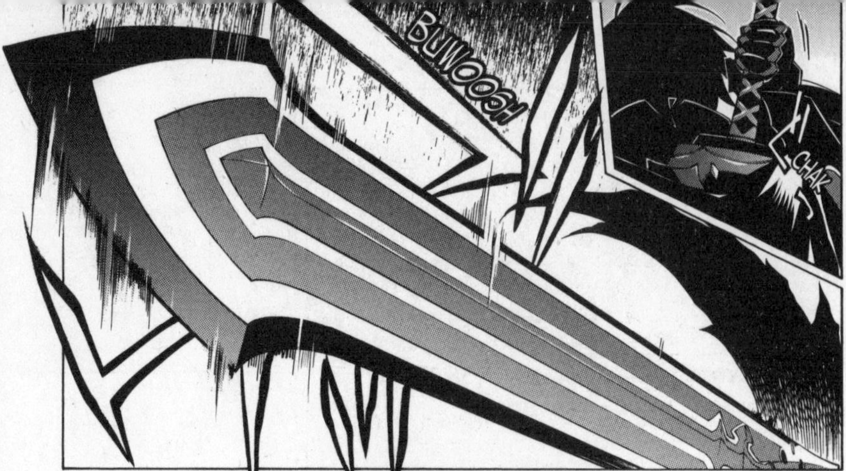
CHAK
BUWOOSH

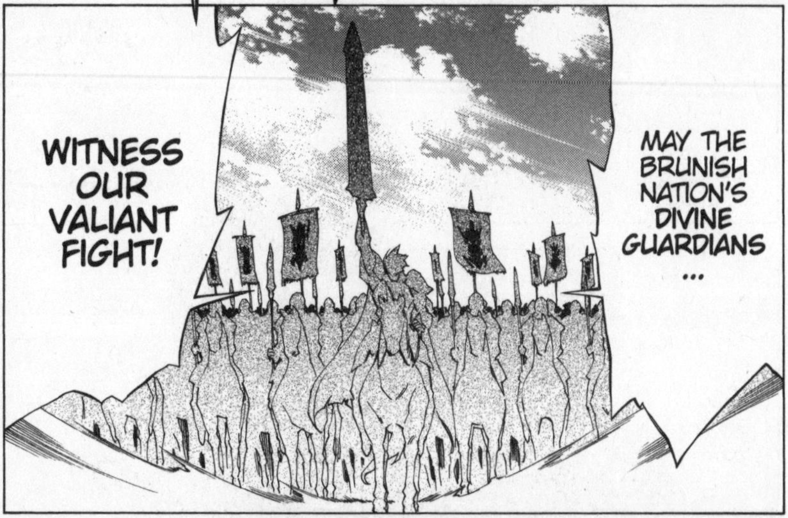
MAY THE BRUNISH NATION'S DIVINE GUARDIANS ...
WITNESS OUR VALIANT FIGHT!

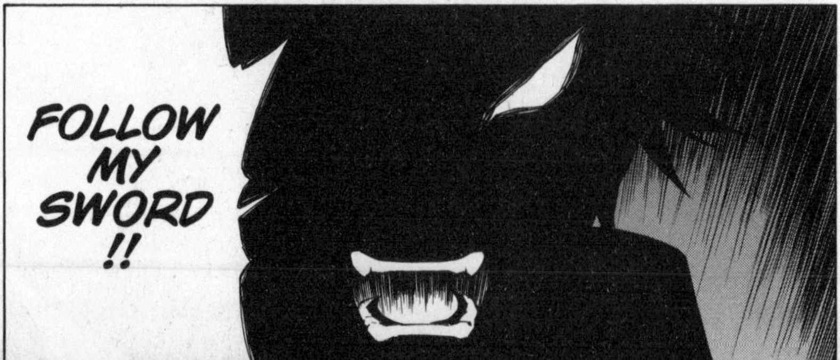
FOLLOW MY SWORD !!

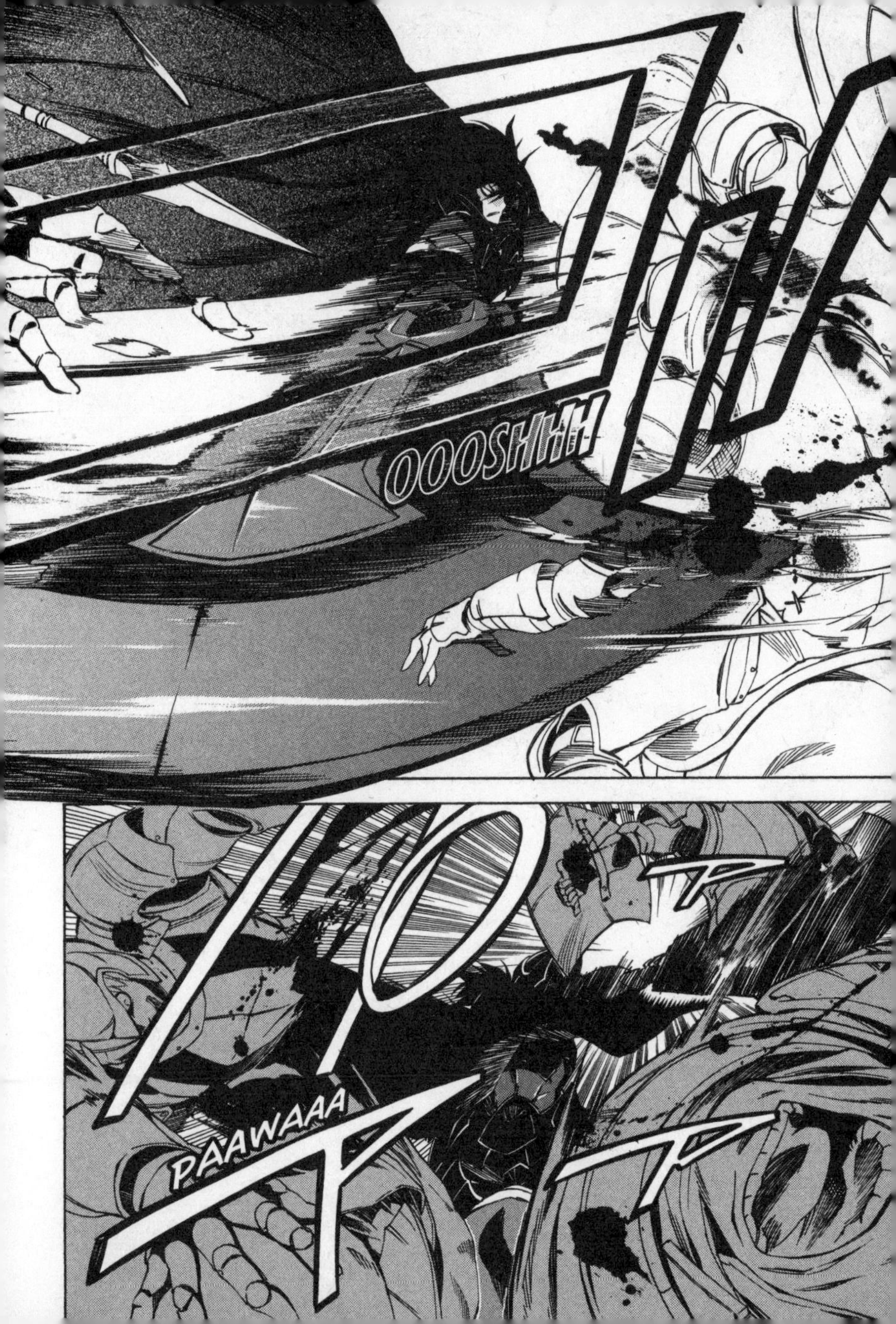
OOOSHHH
PAAWAAA

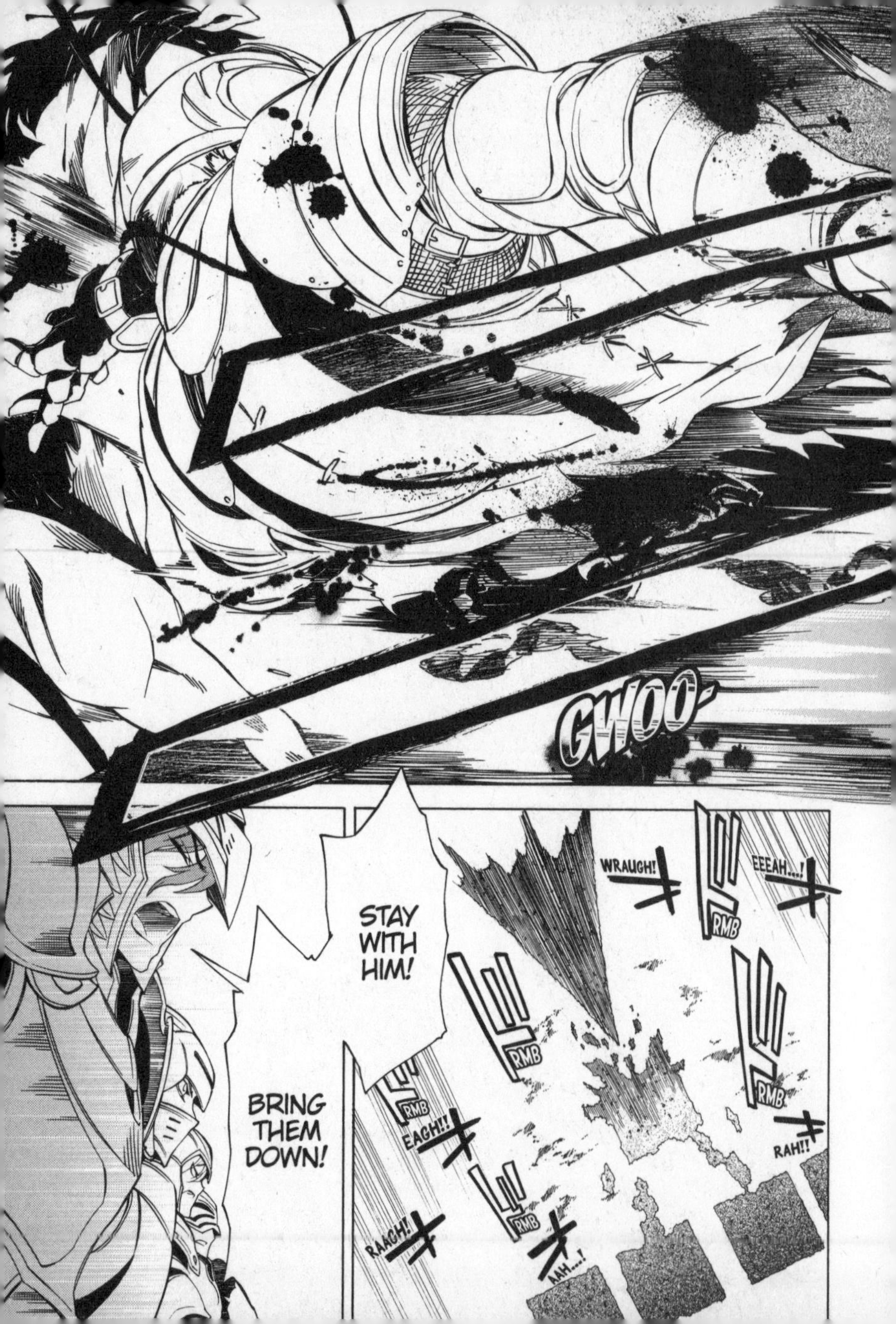
GWOO-
EEEAH...!
RMB
WRAUGH!
RMB
RMB
RAH!!
RMB
EAGH!!
RMB
RAACH!
AAH...!
STAY WITH HIM!
BRING THEM DOWN!

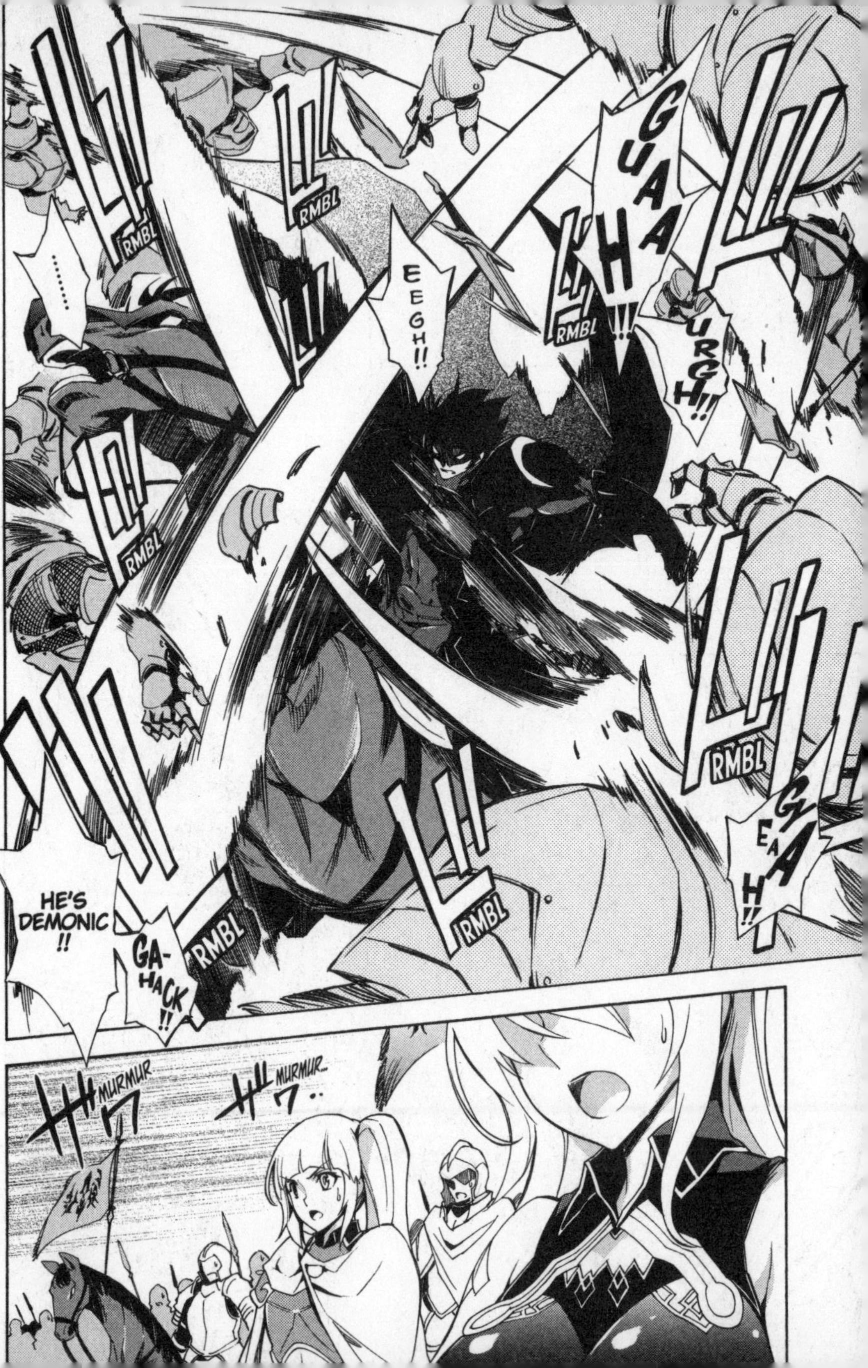
RMBL
GUAAH!!
URGH!!
RMBL
EEGH!!
RMBL
RMBL
......
RMBL
RMBL
GYEAAH!!
RMBL
RMBL
GA-HACK!!
HE'S DEMONIC!!
MURMUR...
MURMUR

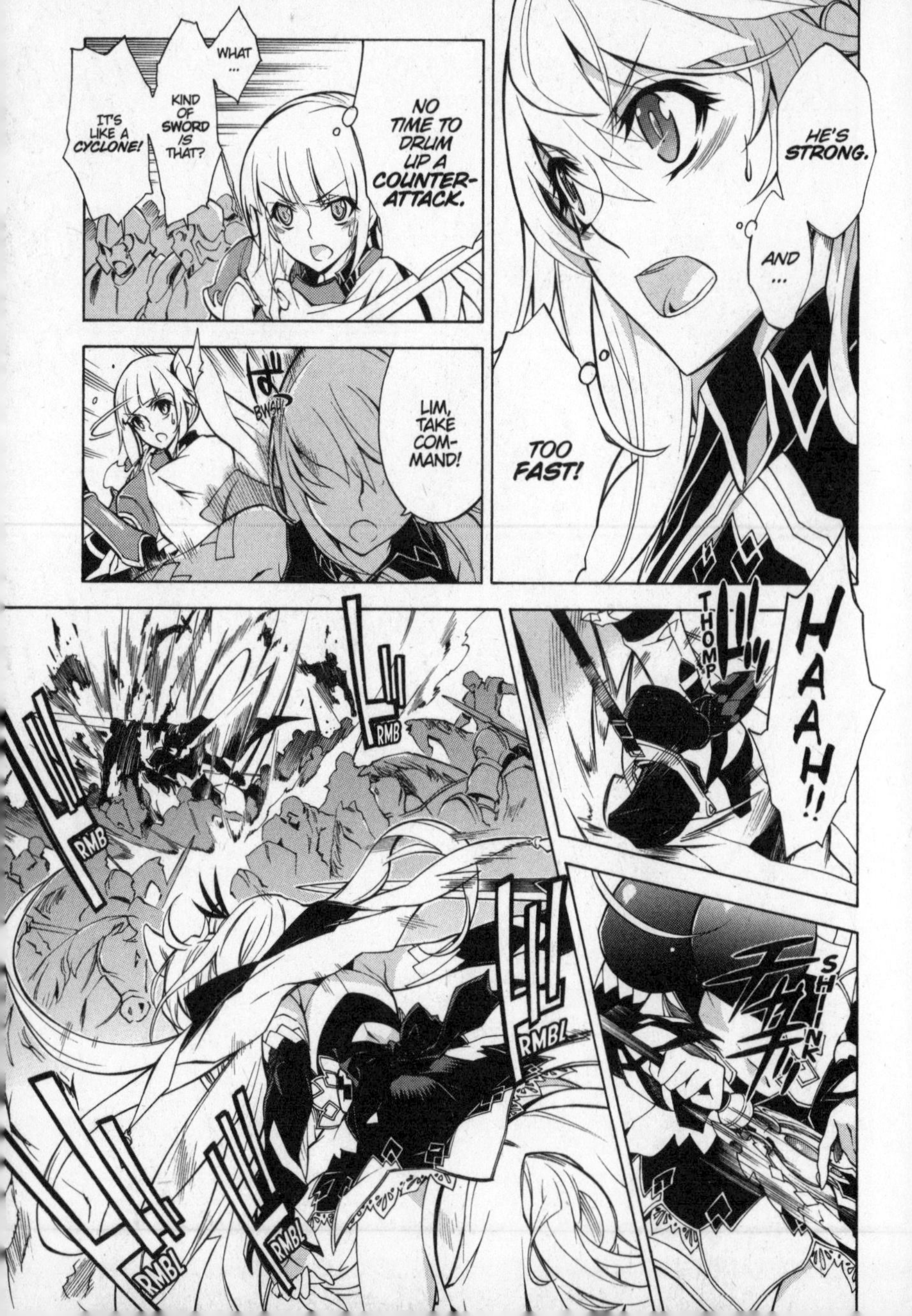
HE'S STRONG.
AND ...
TOO FAST!
NO TIME TO DRUM UP A COUNTER-ATTACK.
WHAT ...
KIND OF SWORD IS THAT?
IT'S LIKE A CYCLONE!
LIM, TAKE COM-MAND!
BWSH
HAAH!!
THOMP
RMB
RMB
SHIINK
RMBL
RMBL
RMBL

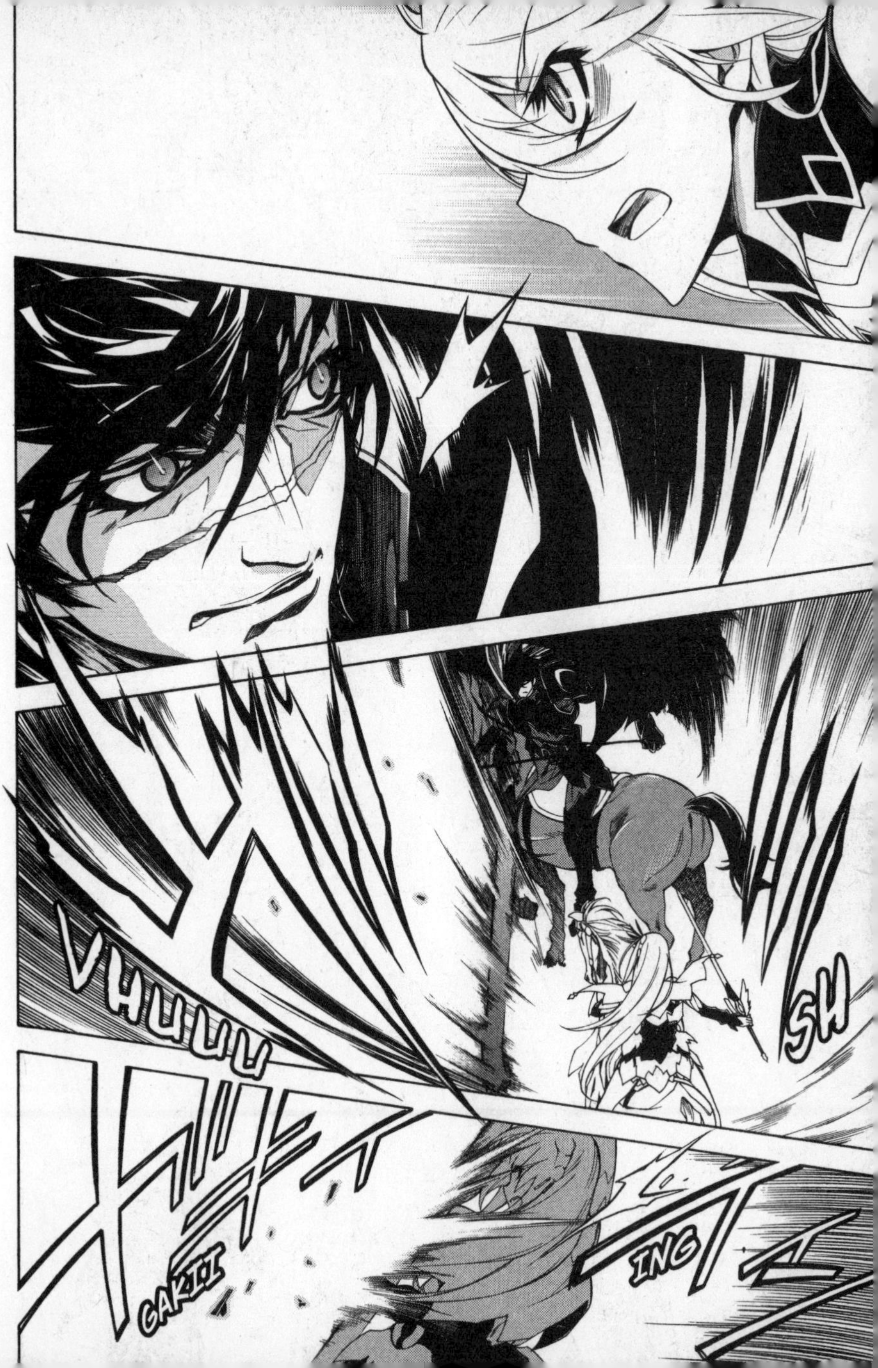
SH
VHUUUU
ING
GAKIII

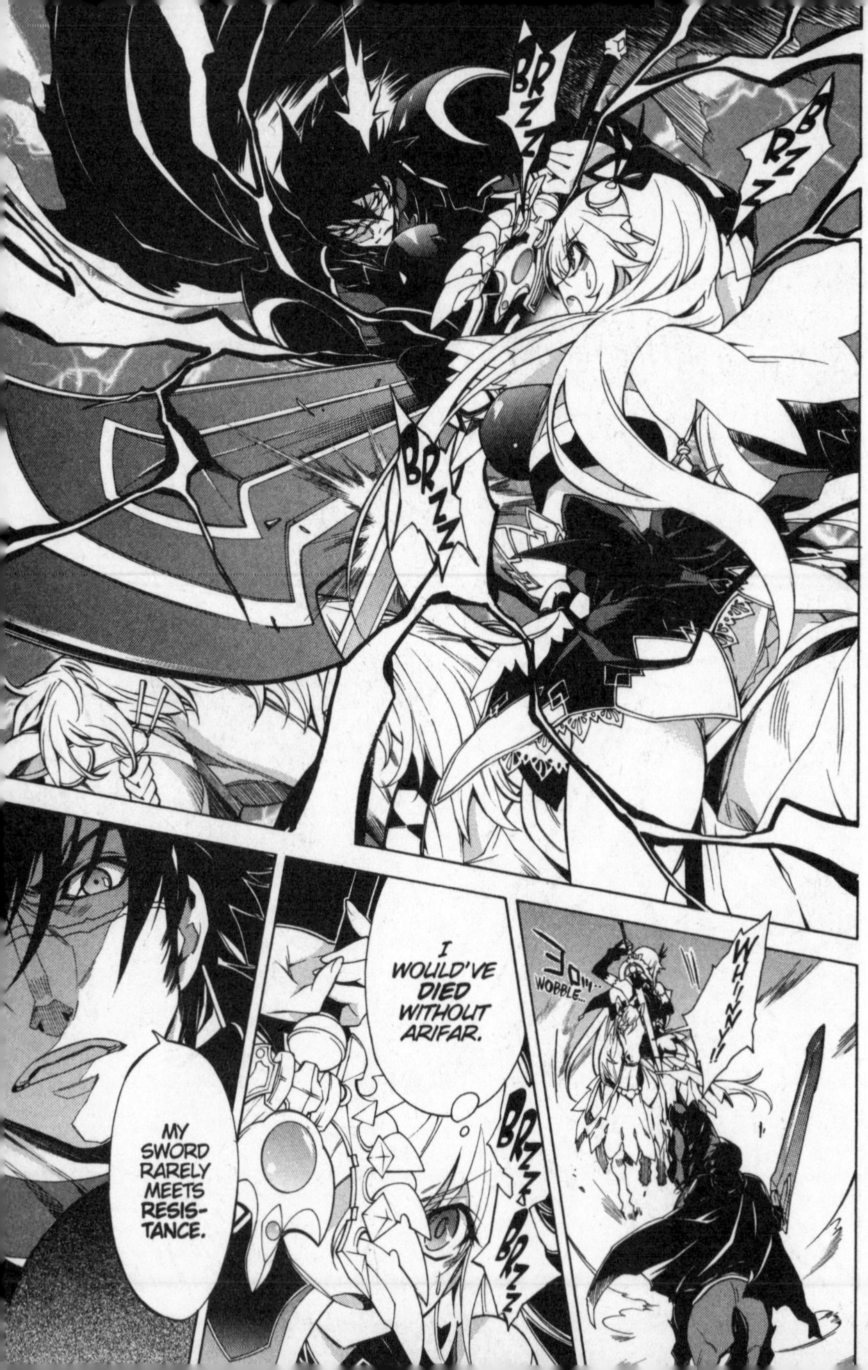
BRZZ
BRZZ
BRZZ
WHINNY!!
WOBBLE...
BRZZ BRZZ BRZZ
I WOULD'VE DIED WITHOUT ARIFAR.
MY SWORD RARELY MEETS RESIS-TANCE.

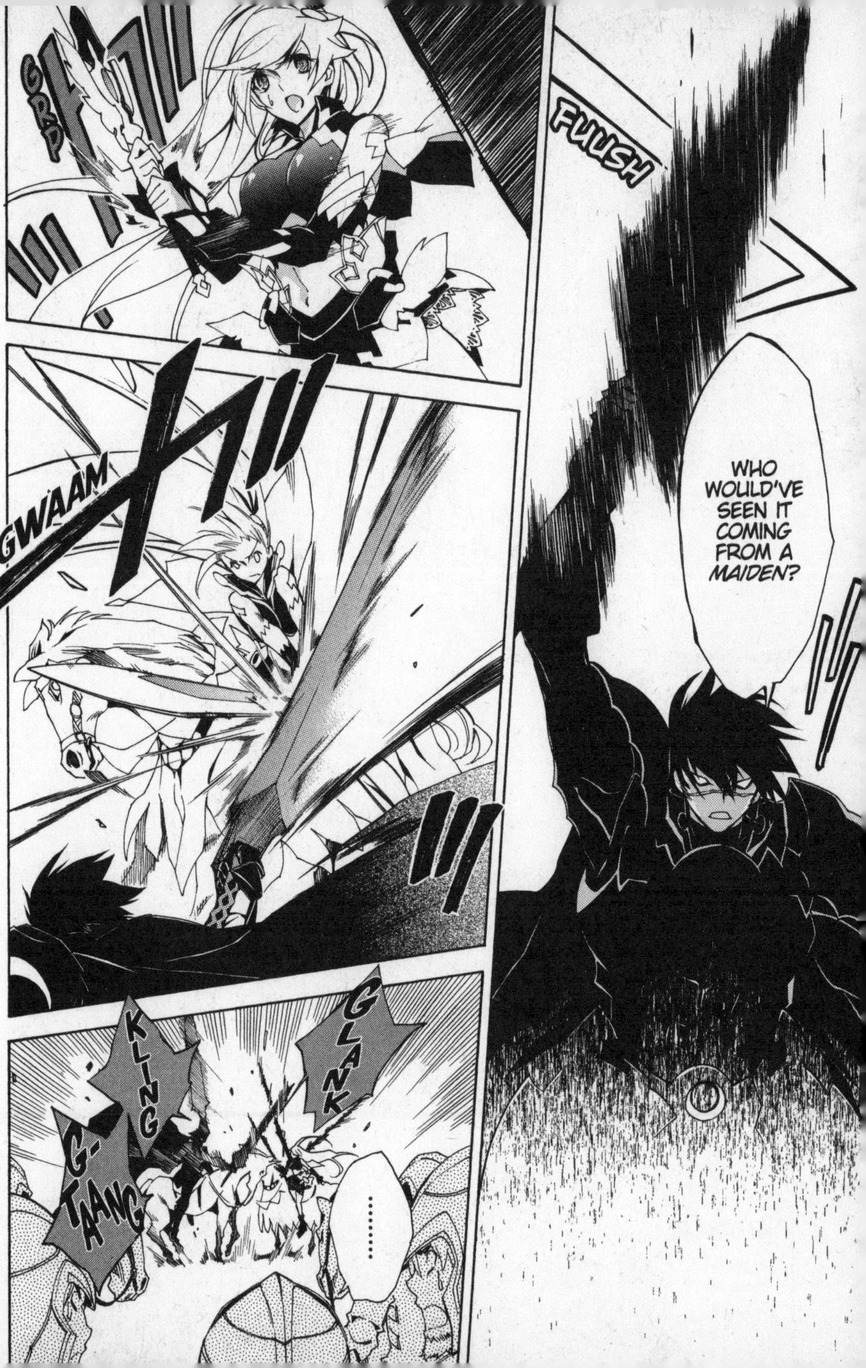
FUUSH
WHO WOULD'VE SEEN IT COMING FROM A MAIDEN?
GRP
GWAAM
GLANK
KLING
G-TAANG
......

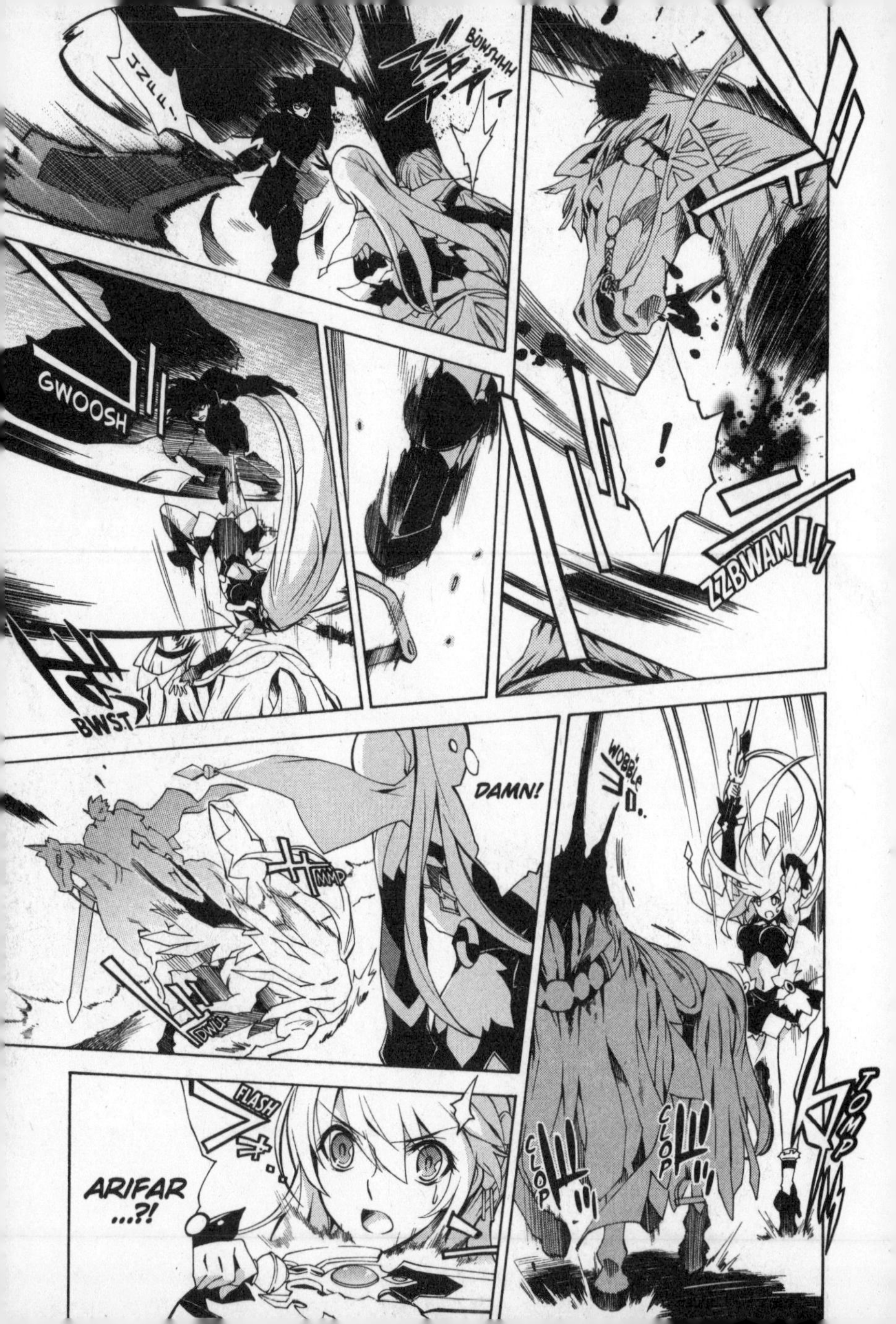
!
ZZBWAM!!
BÜWSHHH
GWOOSH
BWST
WOBBLE
TOMP
CLOP
CLOP
DAMN!
MMP
FLASH
ARIFAR ...?!

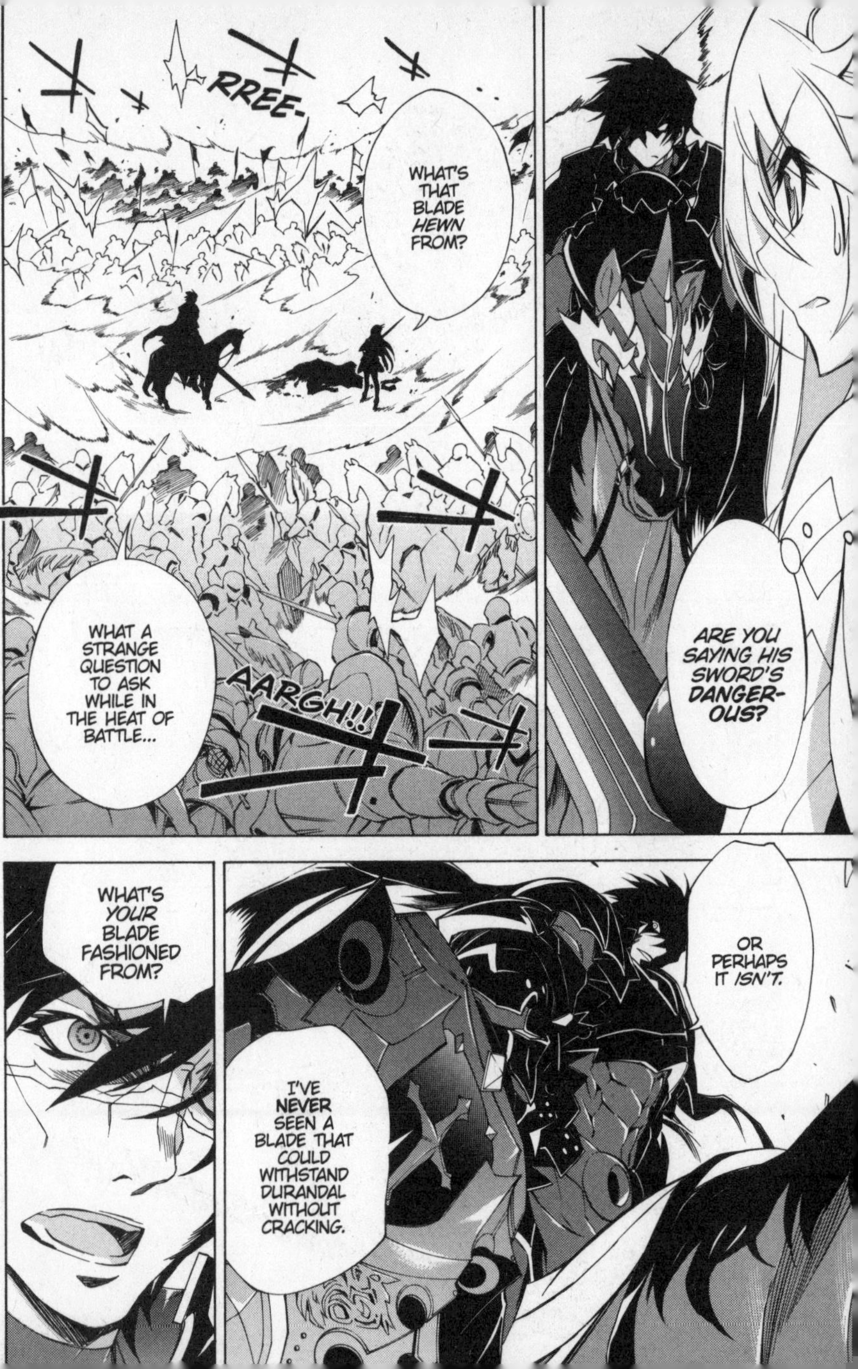
ARE YOU SAYING HIS SWORD'S DANGER-OUS?
RREE-
WHAT'S THAT BLADE HEWN FROM?
WHAT A STRANGE QUESTION TO ASK WHILE IN THE HEAT OF BATTLE...
AARGH!!
OR PERHAPS IT ISN'T.
I'VE NEVER SEEN A BLADE THAT COULD WITHSTAND DURANDAL WITHOUT CRACKING.
WHAT'S YOUR BLADE FASHIONED FROM?

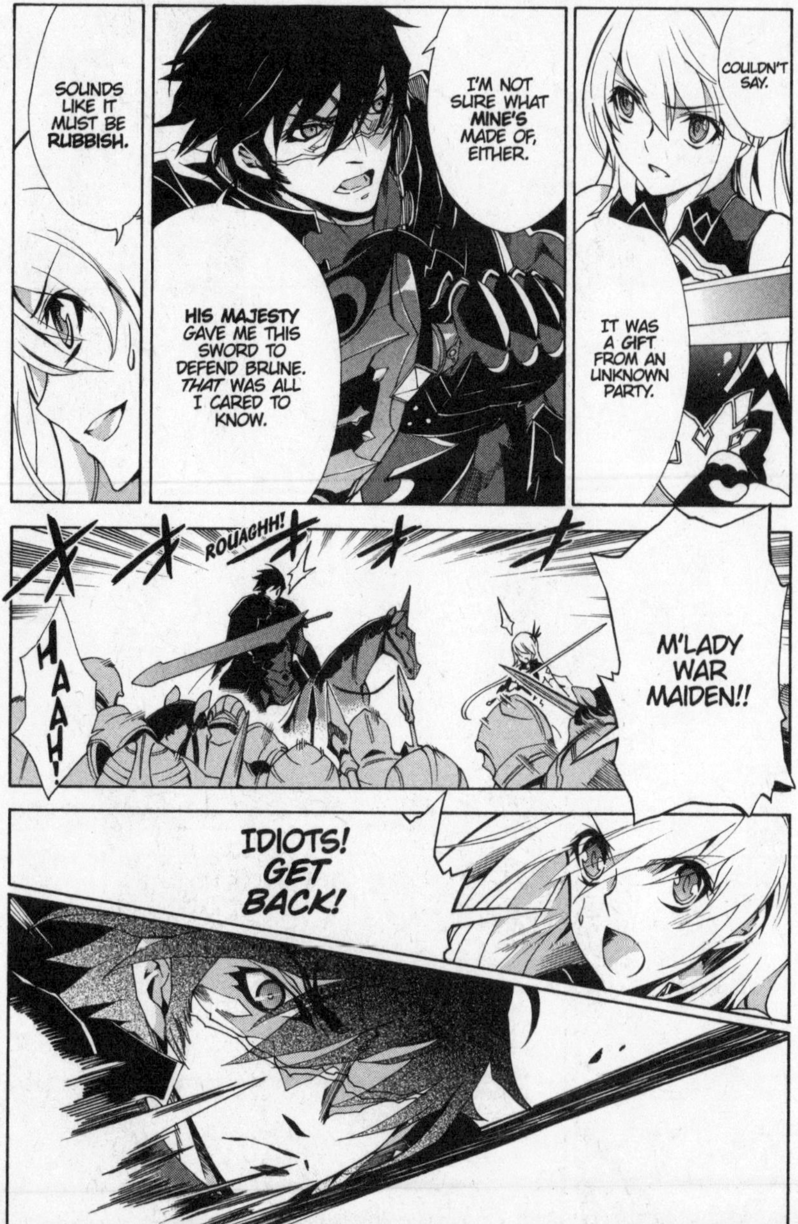
COULDN'T SAY.
IT WAS A GIFT FROM AN UNKNOWN PARTY.
I'M NOT SURE WHAT MINE'S MADE OF, EITHER.
HIS MAJESTY GAVE ME THIS SWORD TO DEFEND BRUNE. THAT WAS ALL I CARED TO KNOW.
SOUNDS LIKE IT MUST BE RUBBISH.
M'LADY WAR MAIDEN!!
ROUAGHH!
HAAH!
IDIOTS! GET BACK!

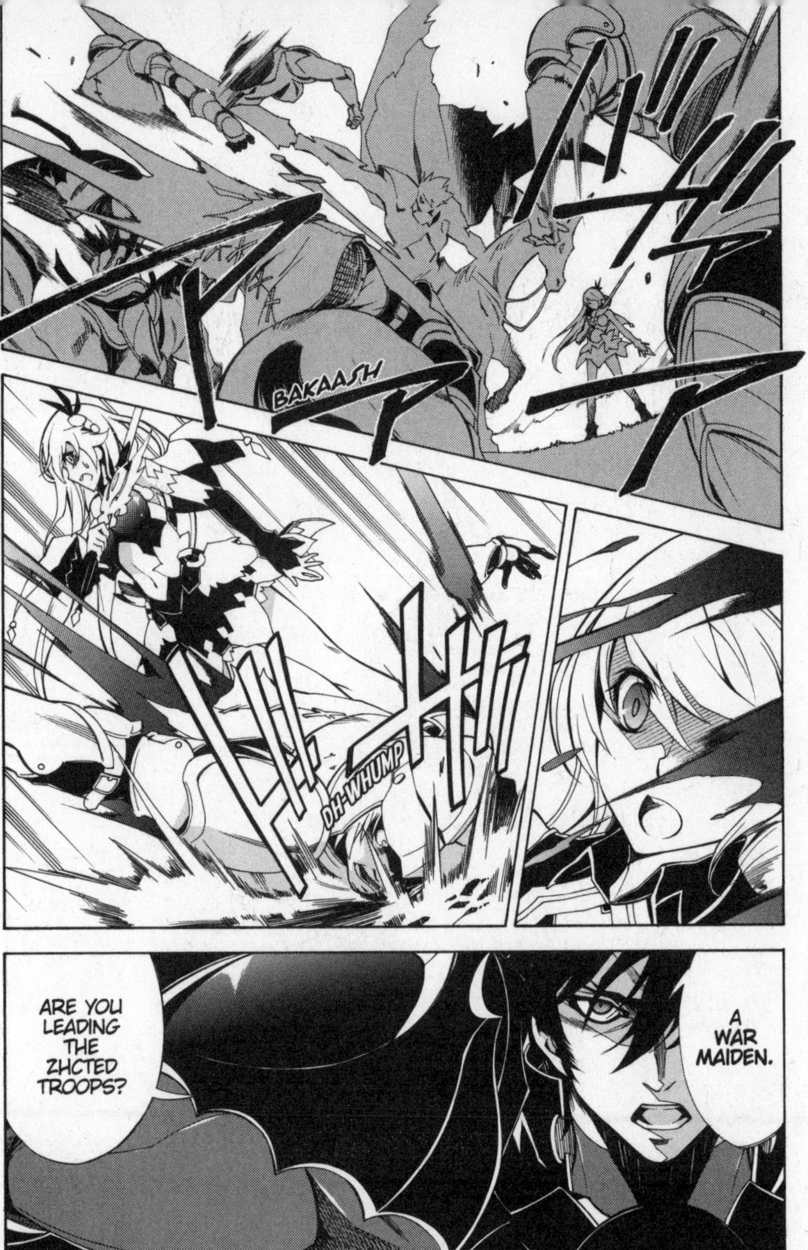
BAKAASH
DH-WHUMP
A WAR MAIDEN.
ARE YOU LEADING THE ZHCTED TROOPS?

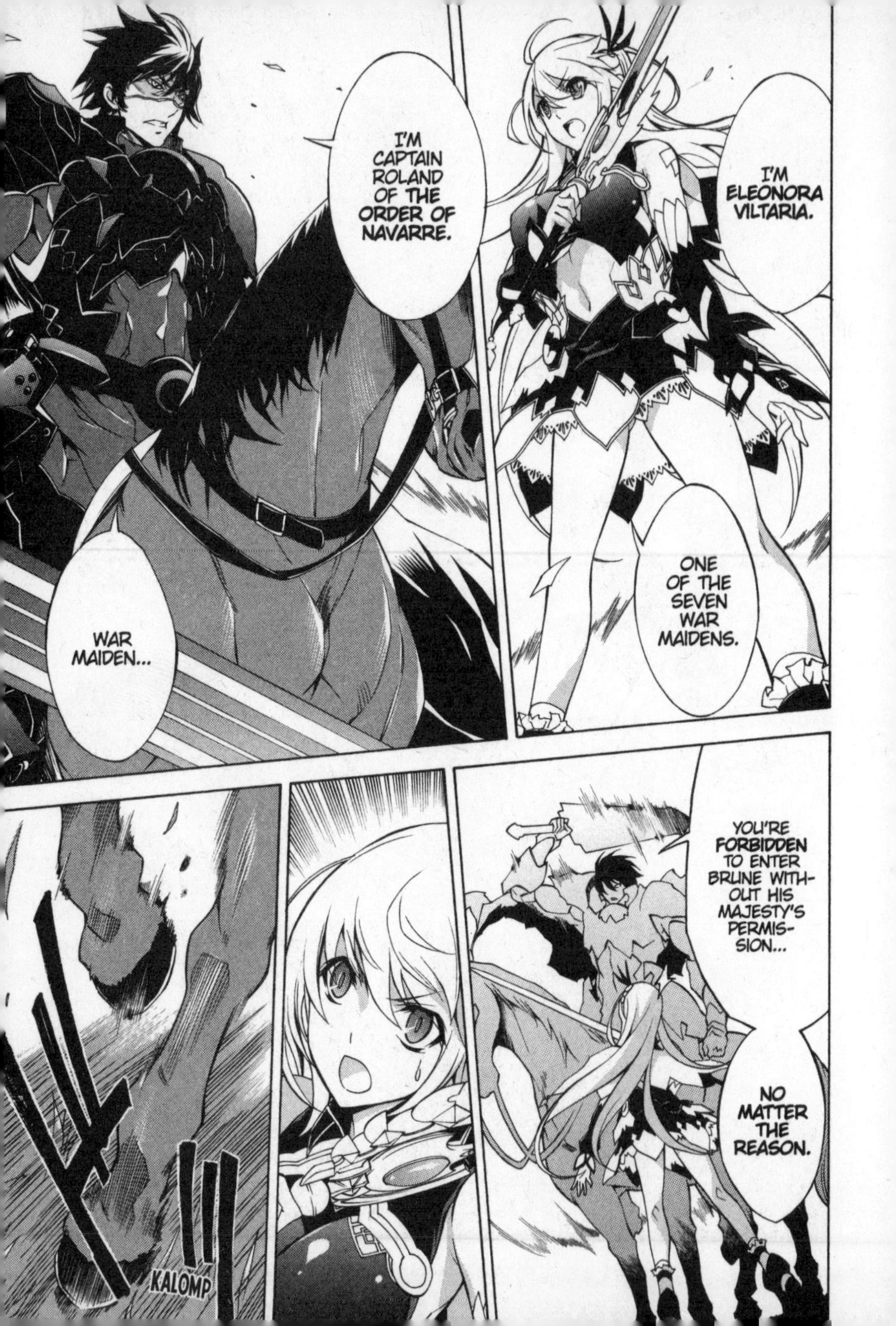
I'M ELEONORA VILTARIA.
ONE OF THE SEVEN WAR MAIDENS.
I'M CAPTAIN ROLAND OF THE ORDER OF NAVARRE.
WAR MAIDEN...
YOU'RE FORBIDDEN TO ENTER BRUNE WITH-OUT HIS MAJESTY'S PERMIS-SION...
NO MATTER THE REASON.
KALOMP

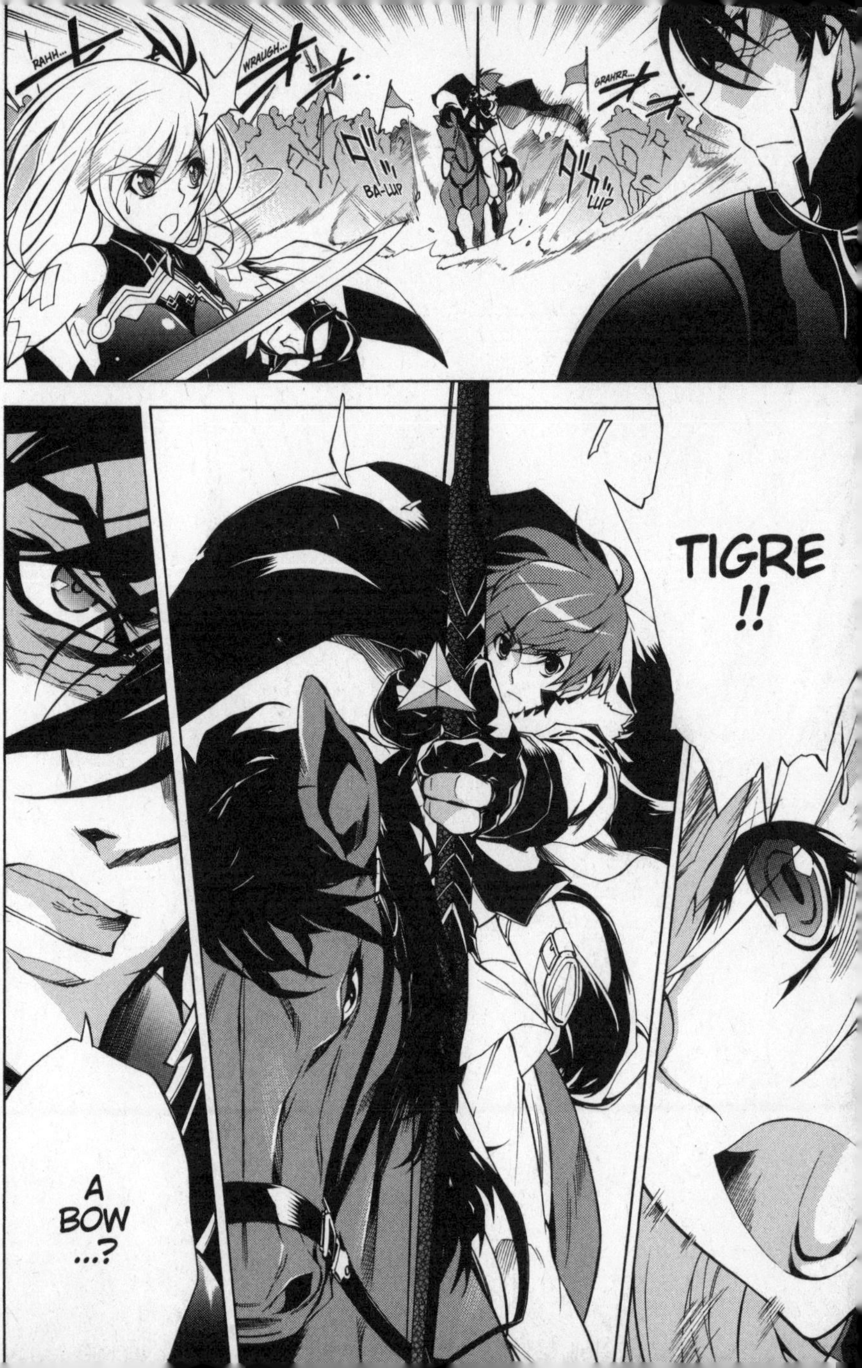
GRAHRR...
LUP
BA-LUP
WRAUGH...
RAHH...
TIGRE !!
A BOW ...?

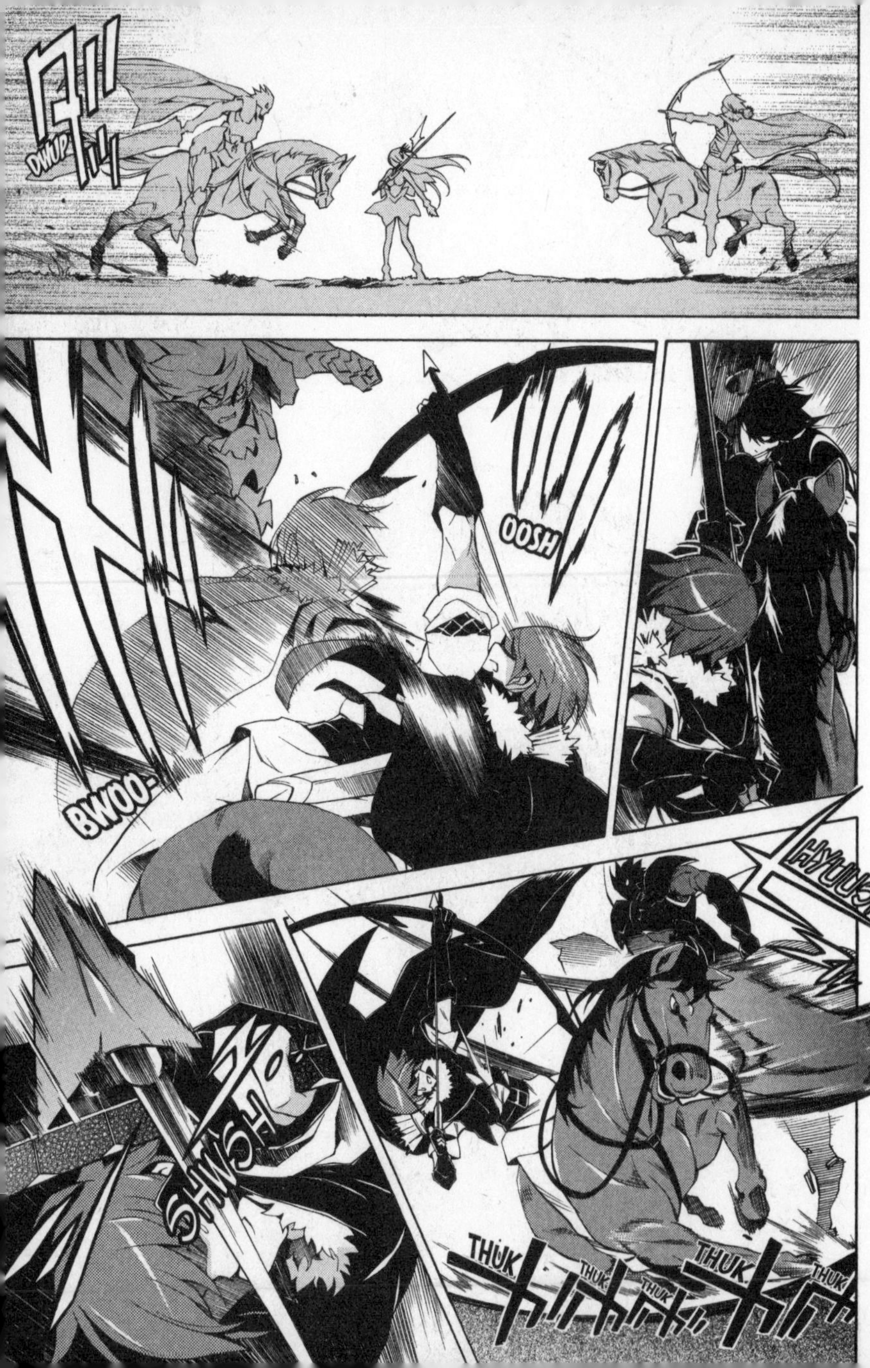
DWUP
OOSH
BWOO-
HYUUSH
THUK
THUK
THUK
THUK
THUK
SHWOOSH

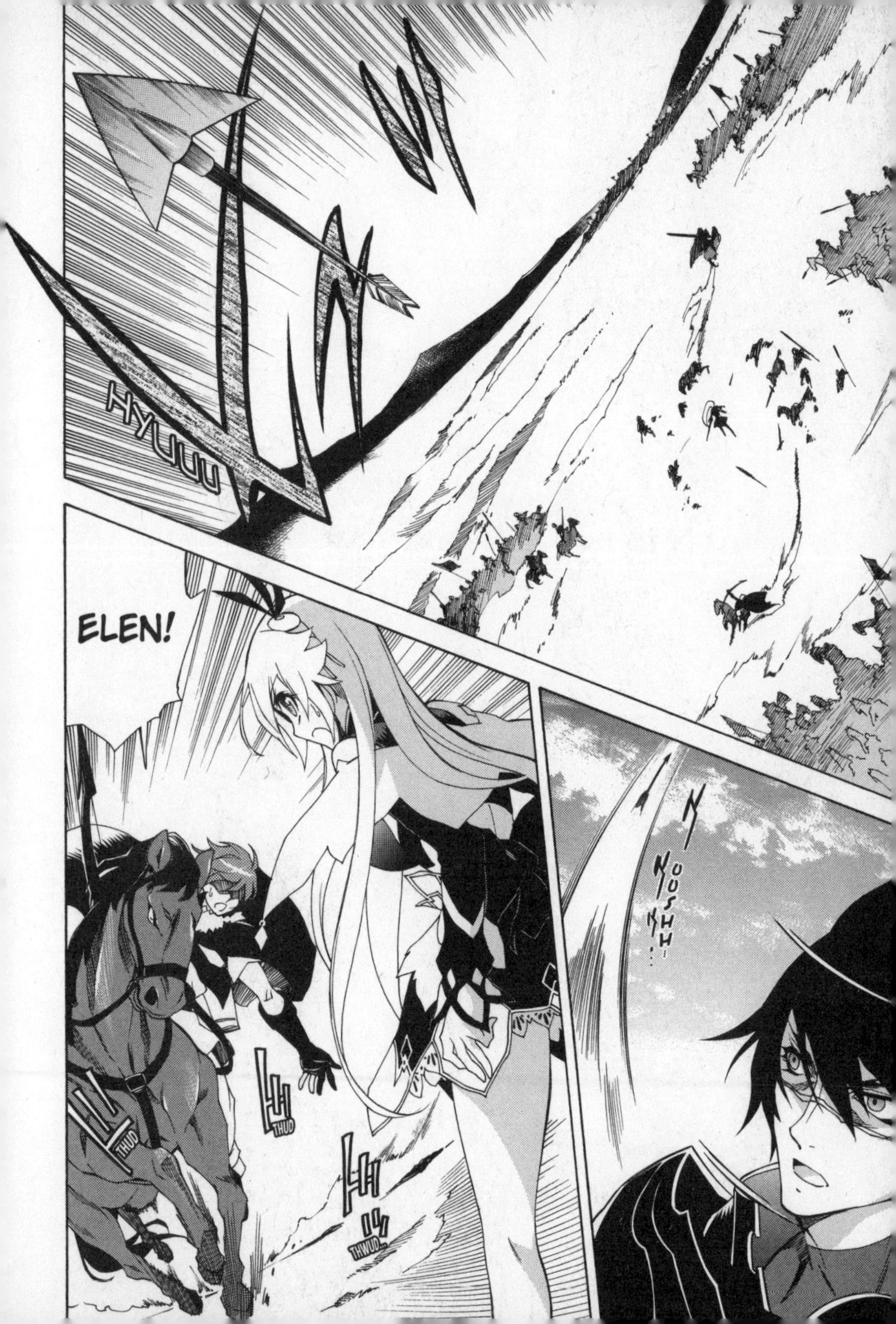
HYUUU
WOUSHH...
ELEN!
THUD
THUD
THWUD...

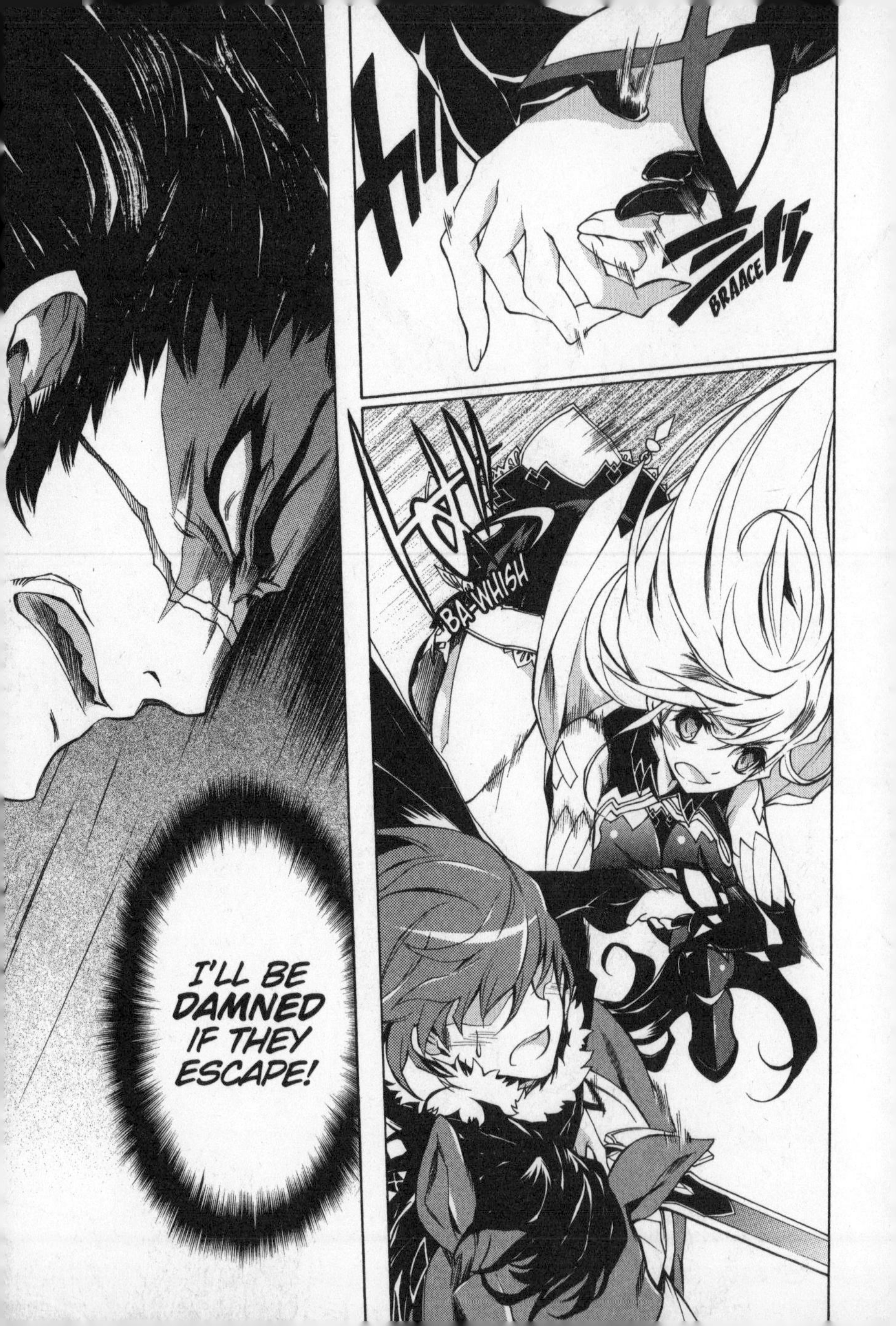
BRAACE
BA-WHISH
I'LL BE DAMNED IF THEY ESCAPE!

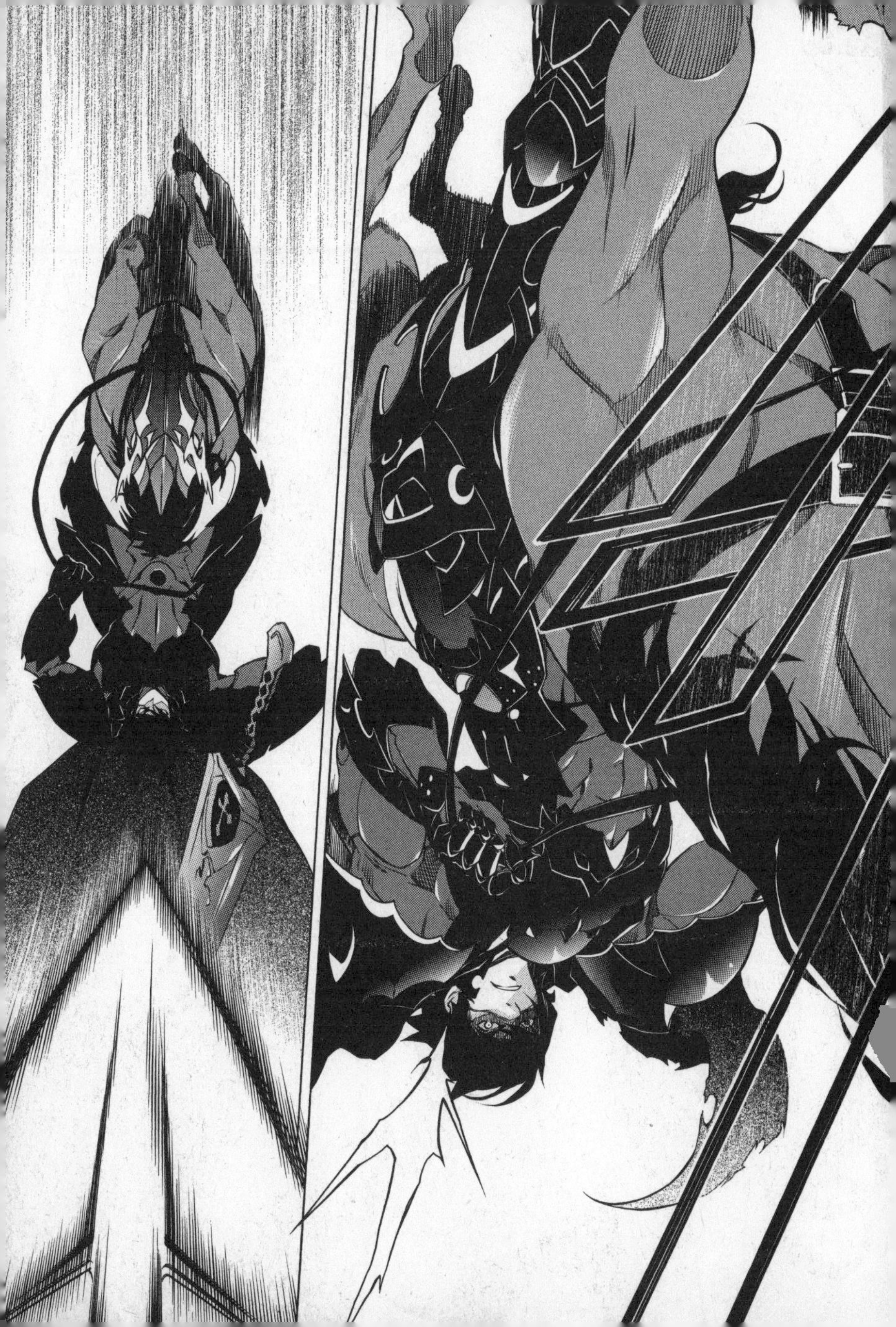

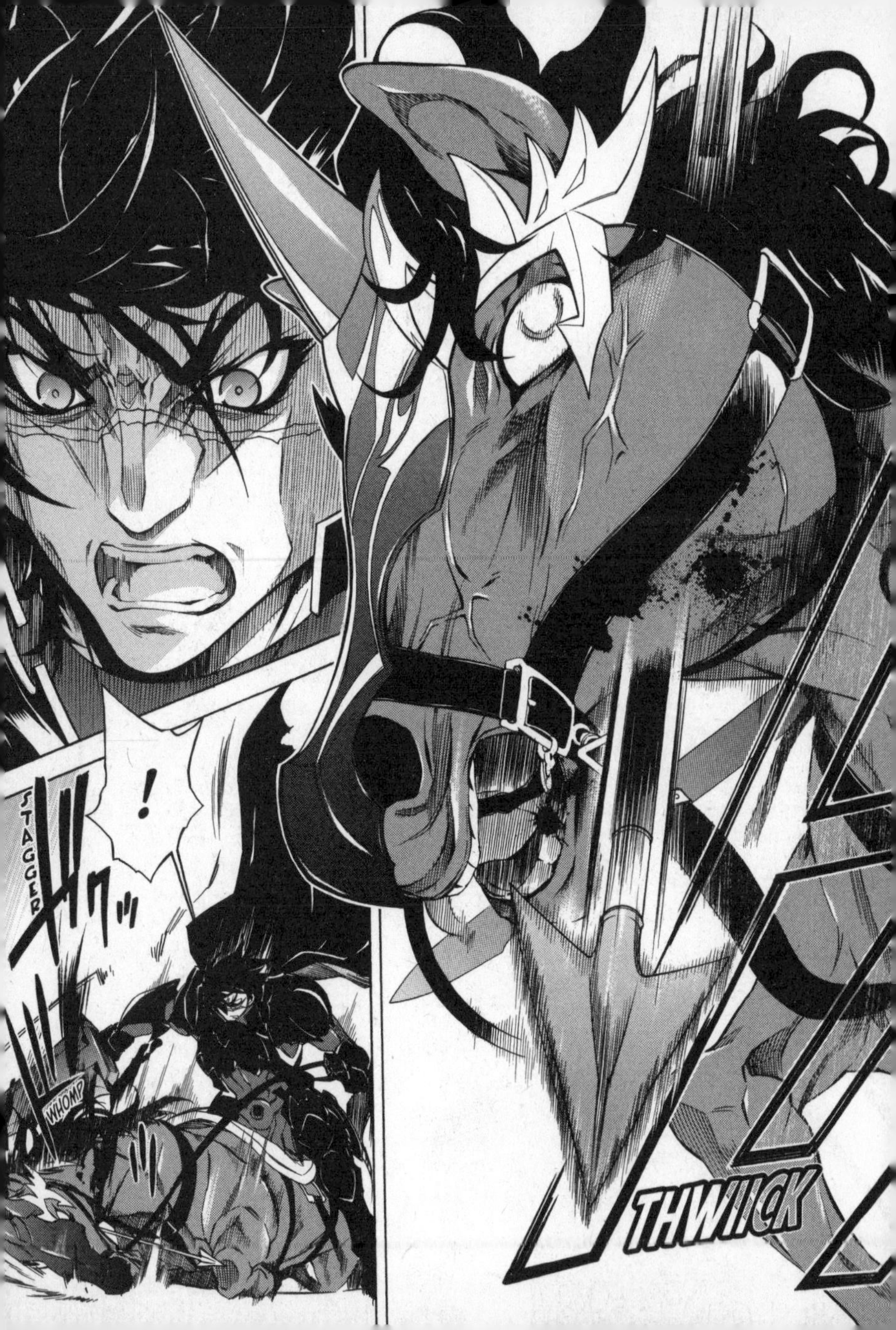
THWIICK
!
STAGGER
WHOMP

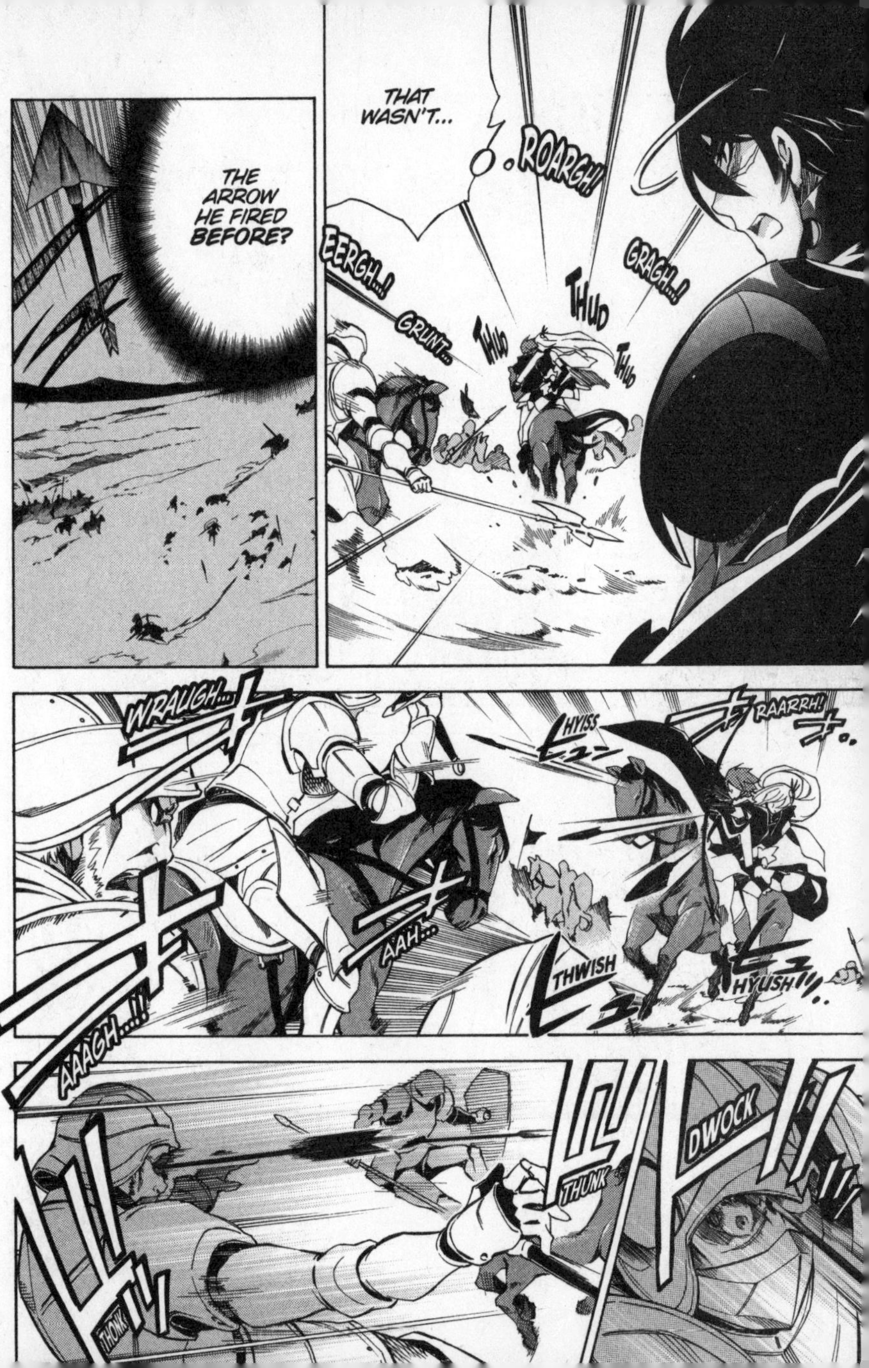
THAT WASN'T...
ROARGH!
GRAGH...!
THUD
THUD
THUD
GRUNT...
EERGH...!
THE ARROW HE FIRED BEFORE?
RAARRH!
HYISS
WRAUGH...!
HYUSH
THWISH
AAH...
AAAGH...!!
DWOCK
THUNK
THUNK

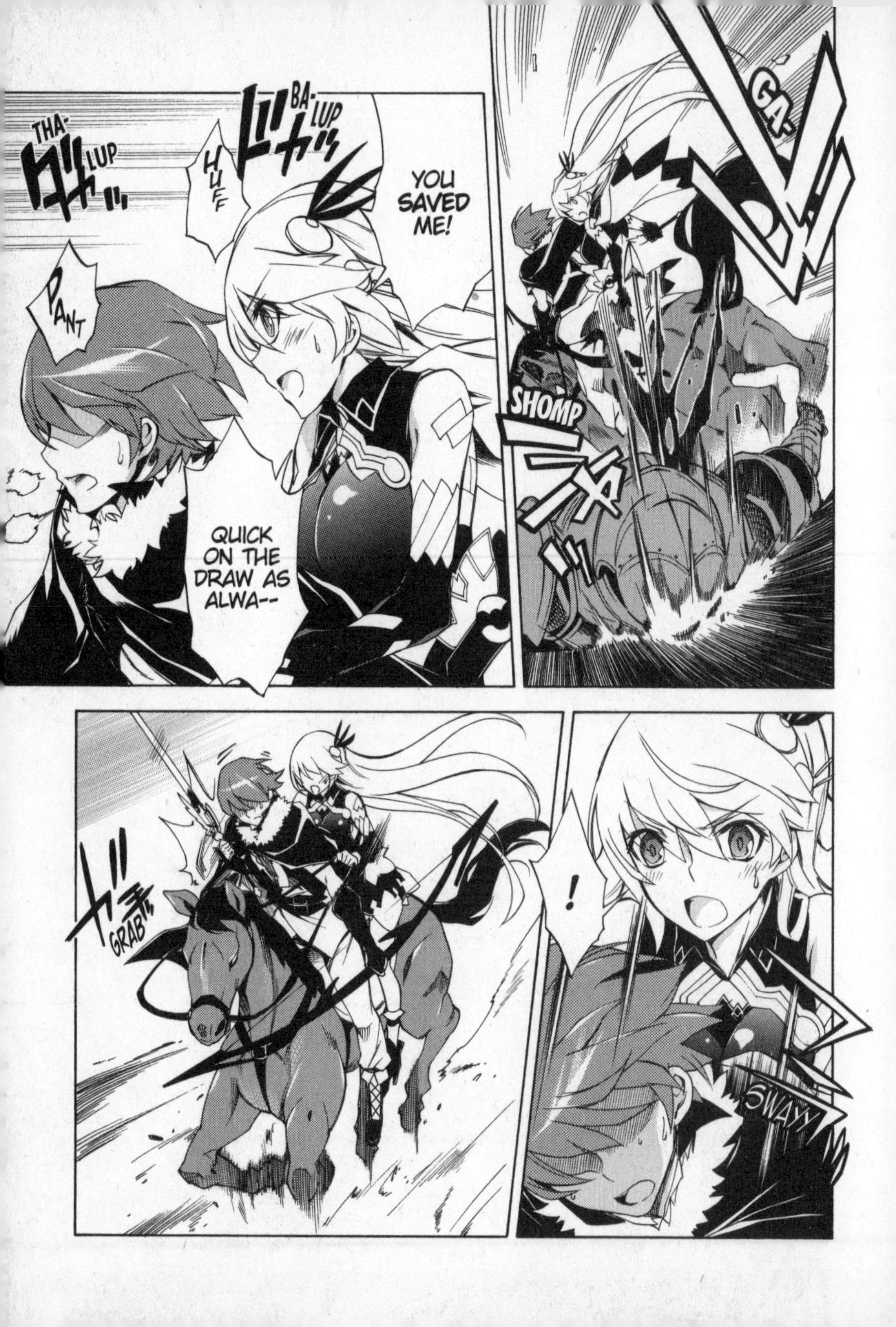
GA-
SHOMP
THA-LUP
BA-LUP
HUFF
YOU SAVED ME!
PANT
QUICK ON THE DRAW AS ALWA--
!
SWAYY
GRAB

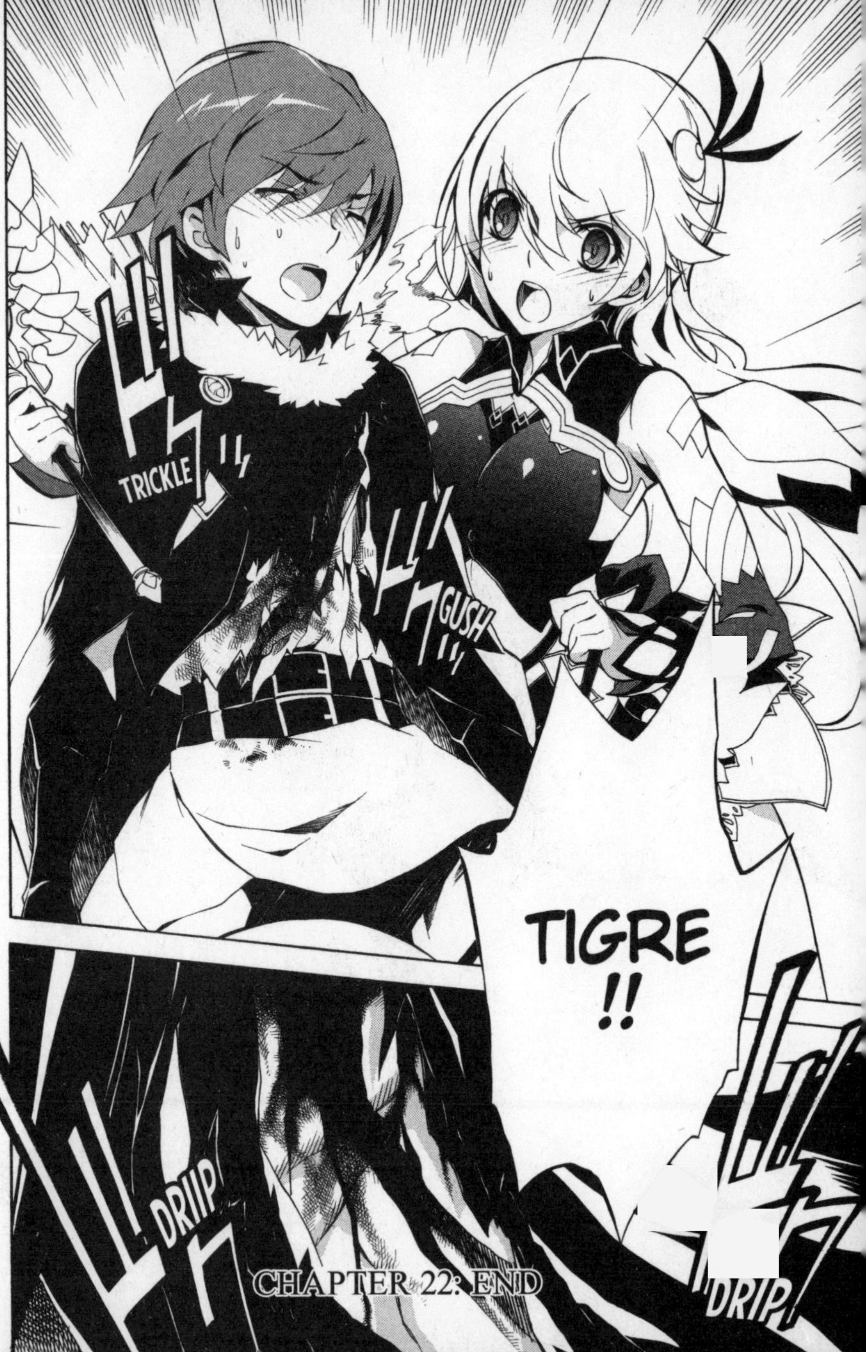
TRICKLE
GUSH
TIGRE !!
DRIP
DRIIP
CHAPTER 22: END

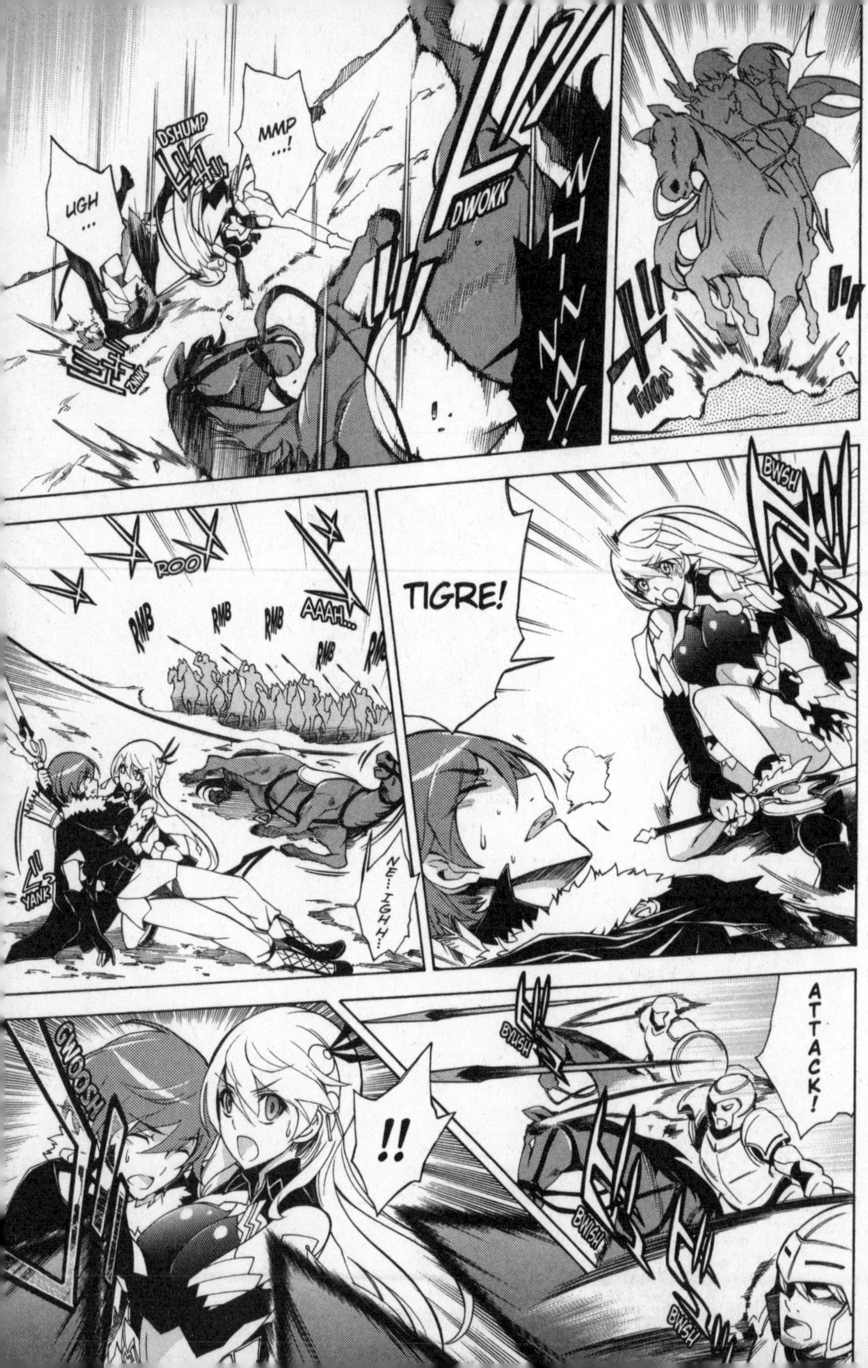
THOK
WHINNY!
DWOKK
MMP ...!
DSHUMP
UGH ...
ZNNK
BWSH
TIGRE!
NE... IGHH...
ROO
AAAH...
RMB
RMB
RMB
RMB
YANK
ATTACK!
BVUSH
BWSH
BWSH
!!
GWOOSH

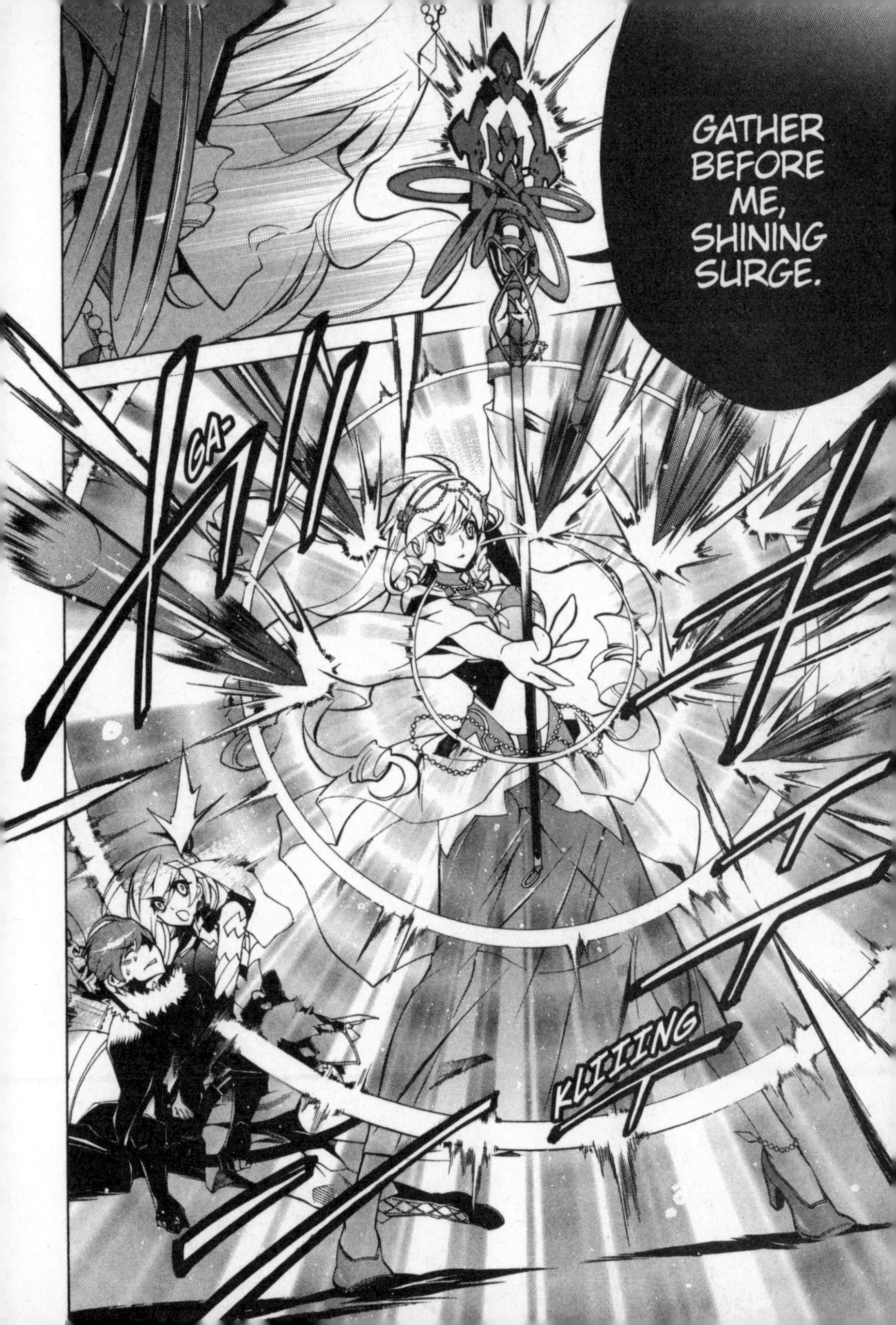
GATHER BEFORE ME, SHINING SURGE.
GA-
KLI-I-I-ING

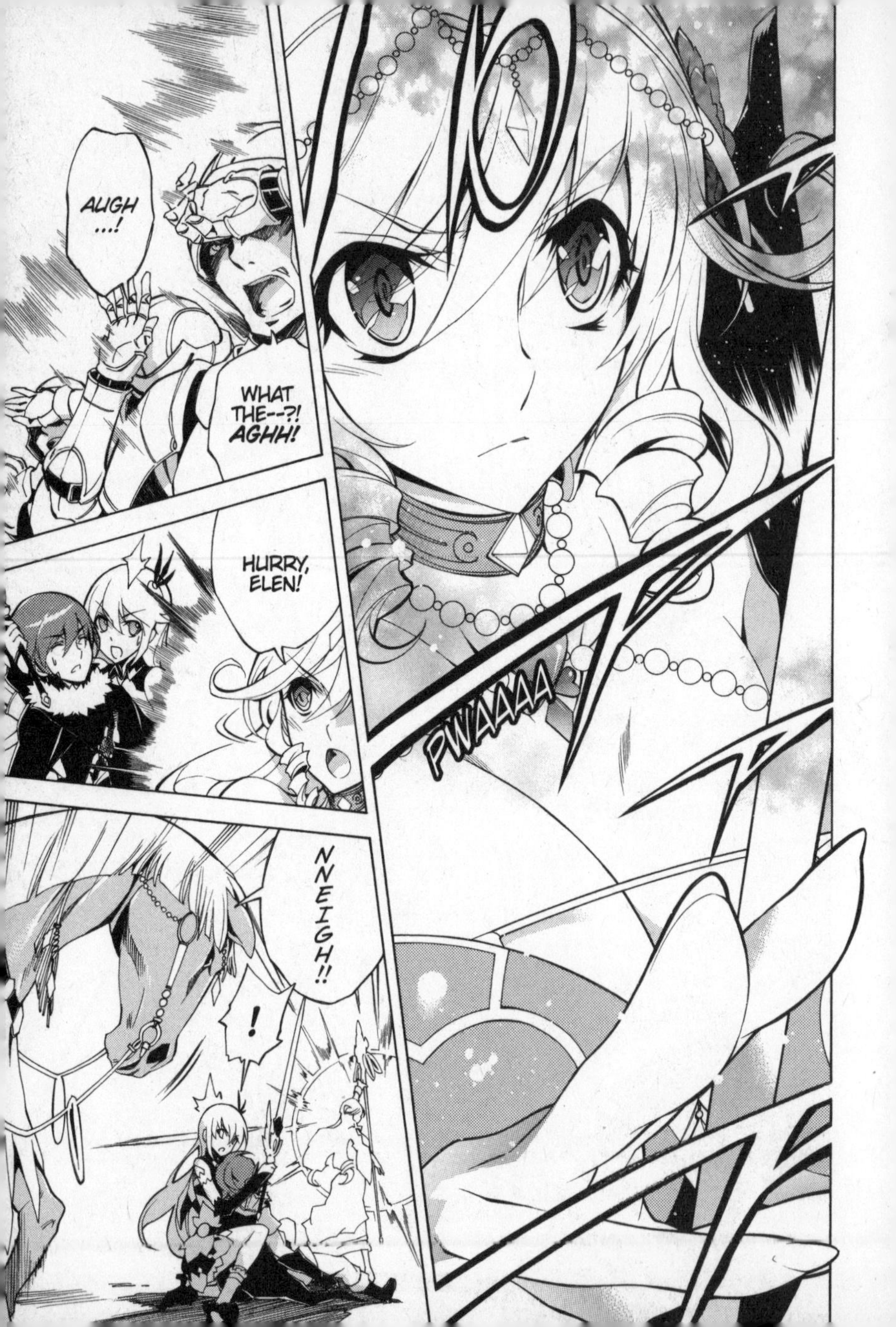
PWAAAA
AUGH ...!
WHAT THE--?! AGHH!
HURRY, ELEN!
NNEIGH!!
!

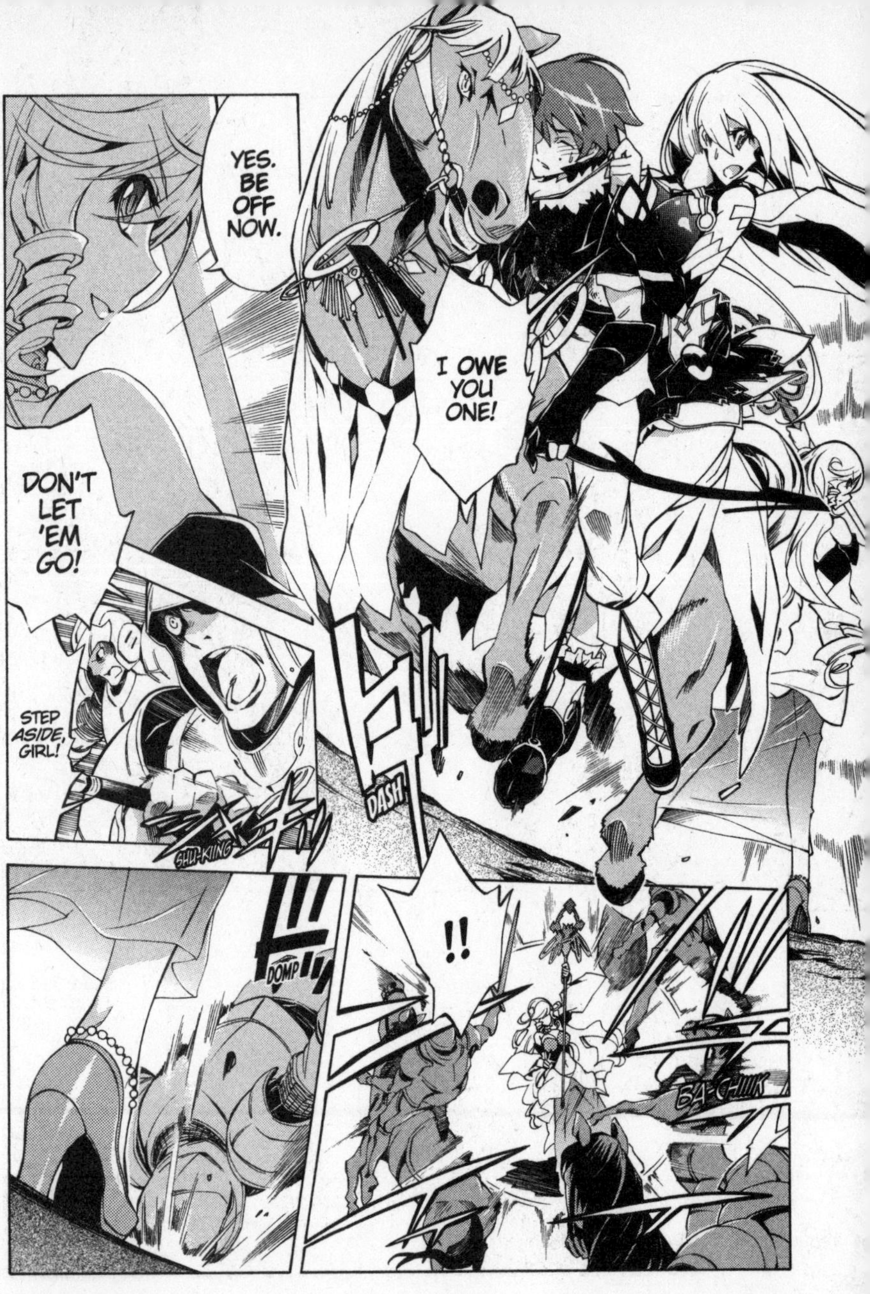
I OWE YOU ONE!
DASH
YES. BE OFF NOW.
DON'T LET 'EM GO!
STEP ASIDE, GIRL!
SHU-KIING
!!
BA-CHIIK
DOMP

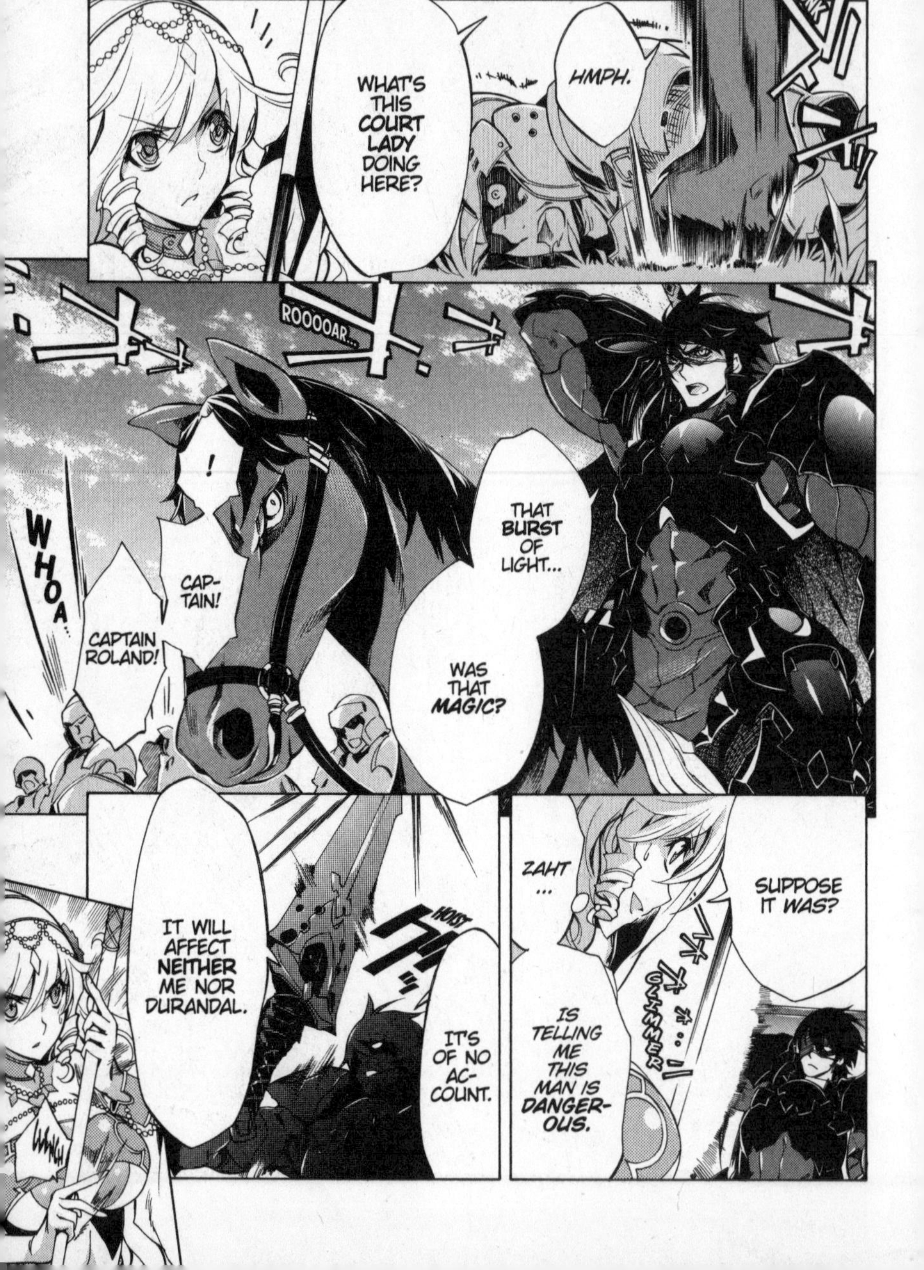
ZUNK
HMPH.
WHAT'S THIS COURT LADY DOING HERE?
ROOOOAR...
THAT BURST OF LIGHT...
WAS THAT MAGIC?
!
CAP-TAIN!
CAPTAIN ROLAND!
WHOA...
SUPPOSE IT WAS?
ZAHT...
GLIMMER
IS TELLING ME THIS MAN IS DANGER-OUS.
HOIST
IT'S OF NO AC-COUNT.
IT WILL AFFECT NEITHER ME NOR DURANDAL.

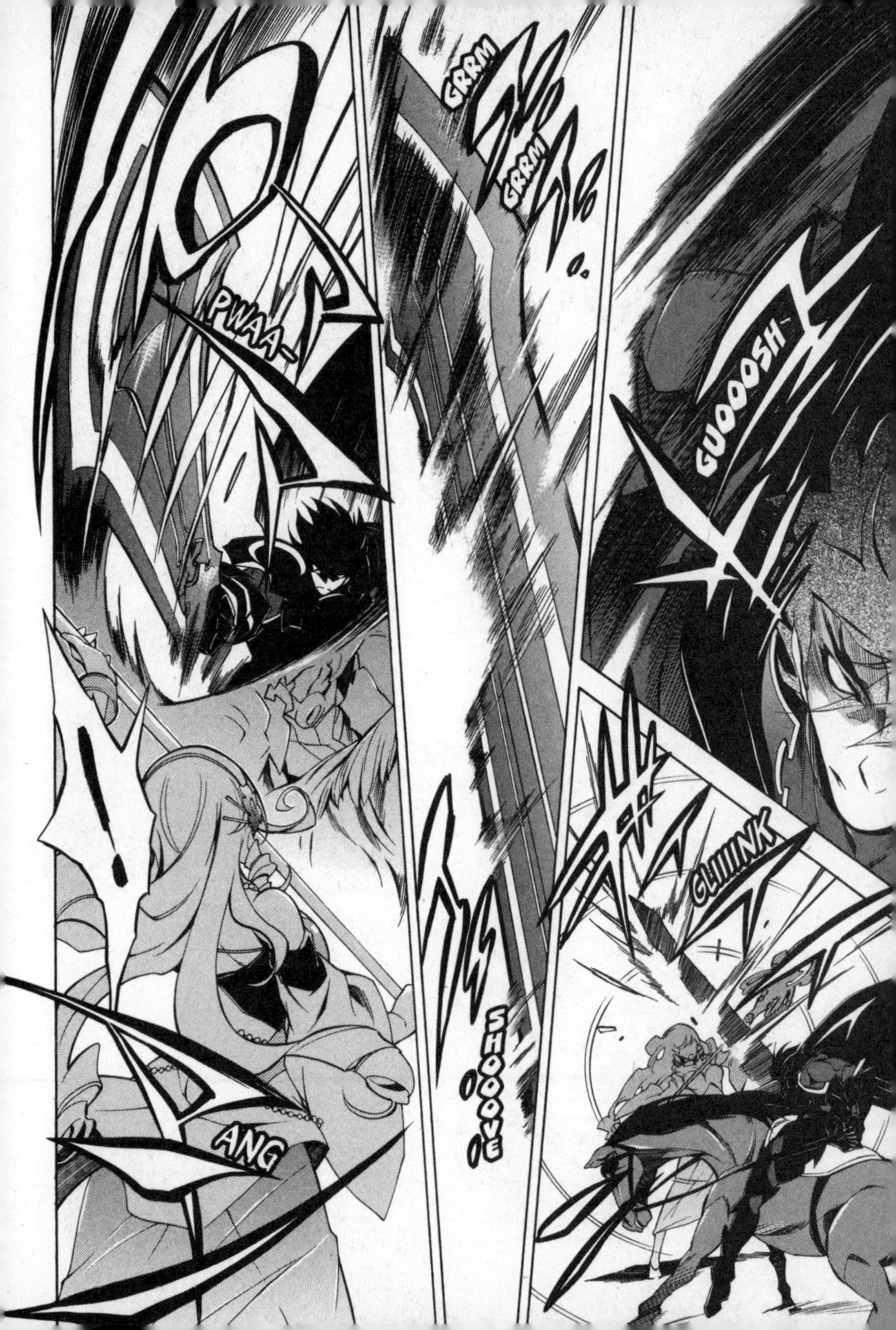
GUOOOSH-
CLIIIINK
GRRM
GRRM
SHOOOOVE
PWAA-
!
ANG

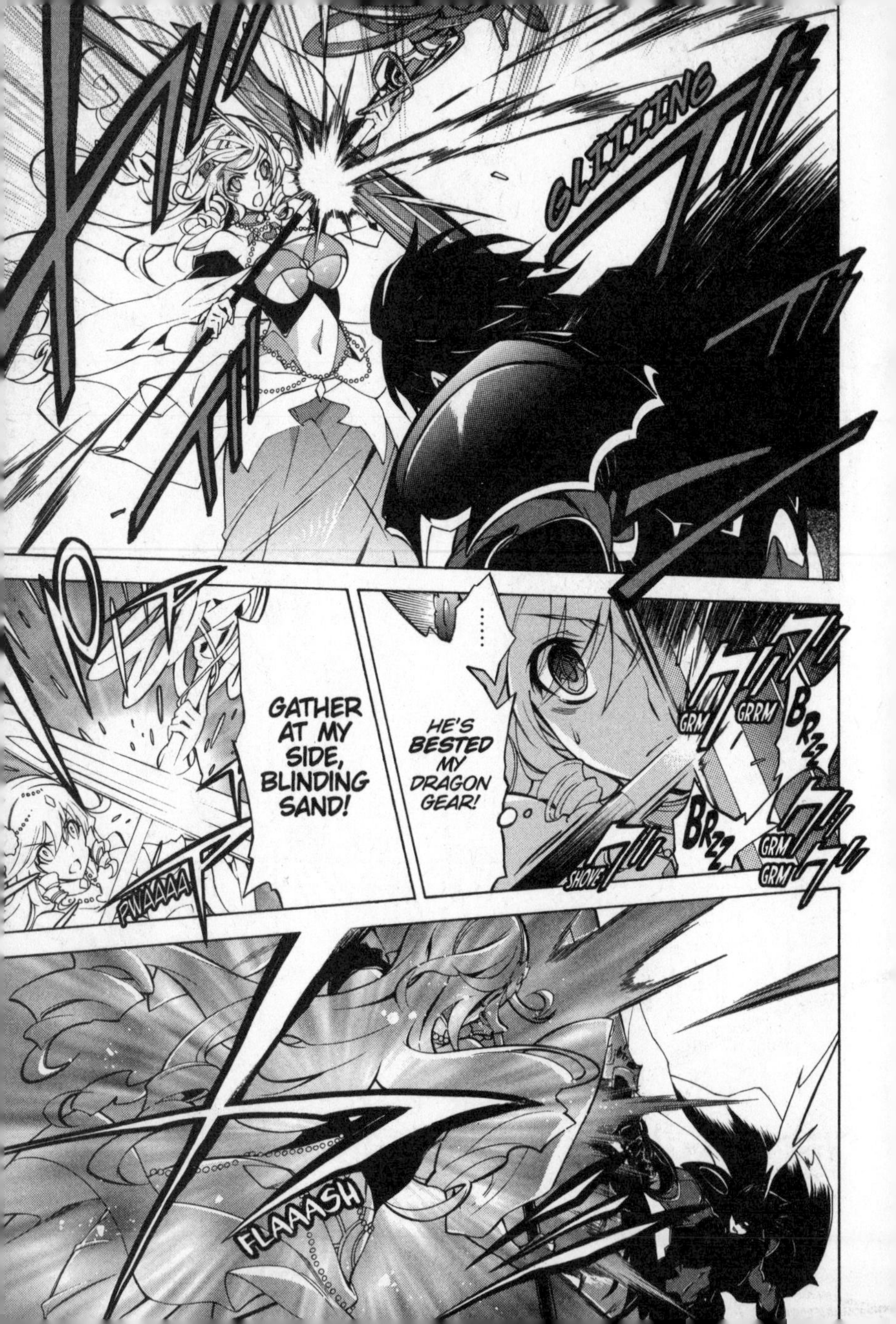
GLIIIING
GRM
GRRM
BRZZ
BRZZ
GRM
GRM
SHOVE
HE'S BESTED MY DRAGON GEAR!
......
GATHER AT MY SIDE, BLINDING SAND!
PWAAAAT
FLAAASH

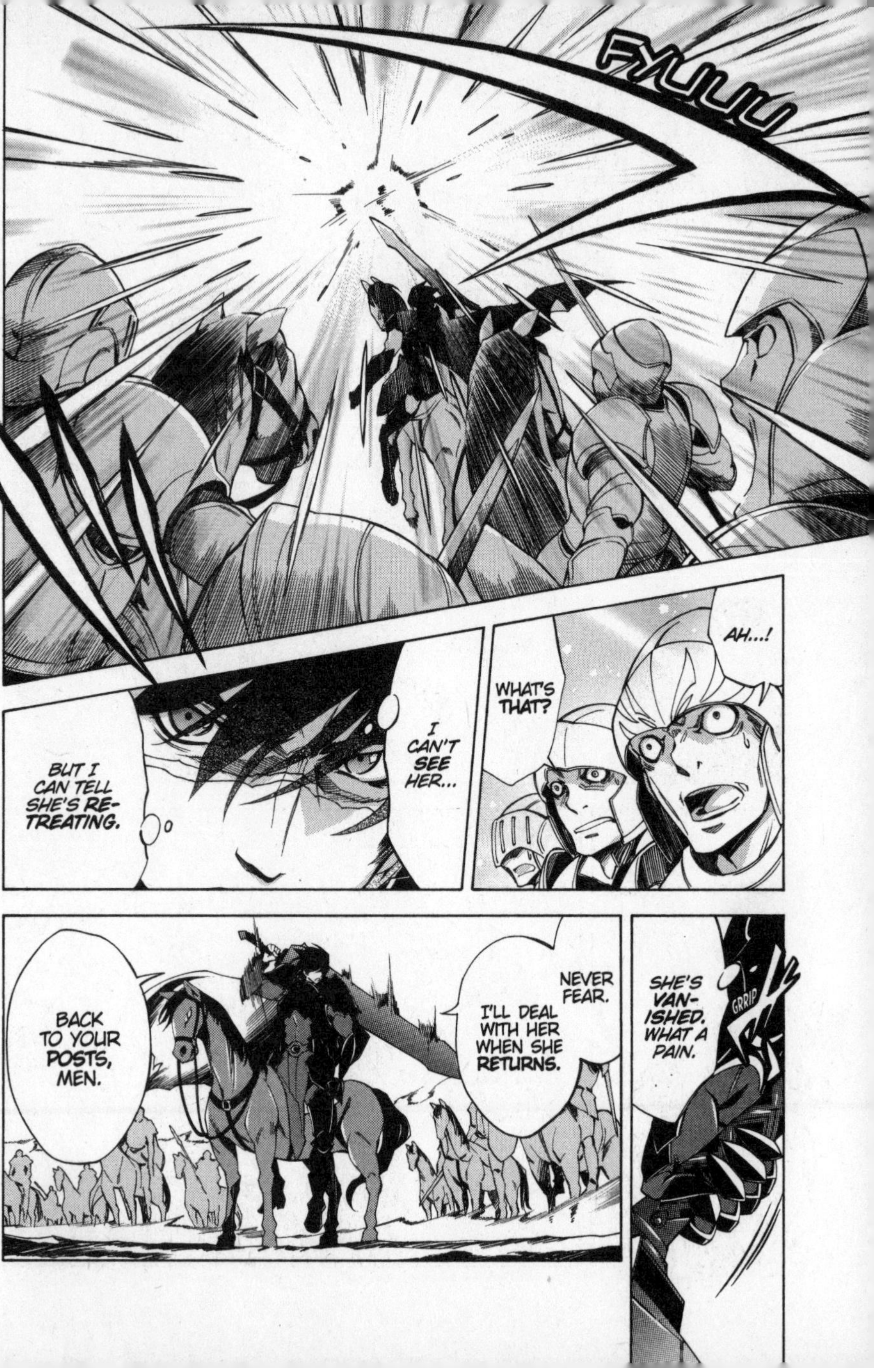
FYUUU
AH...!
WHAT'S THAT?
I CAN'T SEE HER...
BUT I CAN TELL SHE'S RE-TREATING.
SHE'S VAN-ISHED. WHAT A PAIN.
GRRIP
NEVER FEAR.
I'LL DEAL WITH HER WHEN SHE RETURNS.
BACK TO YOUR POSTS, MEN.

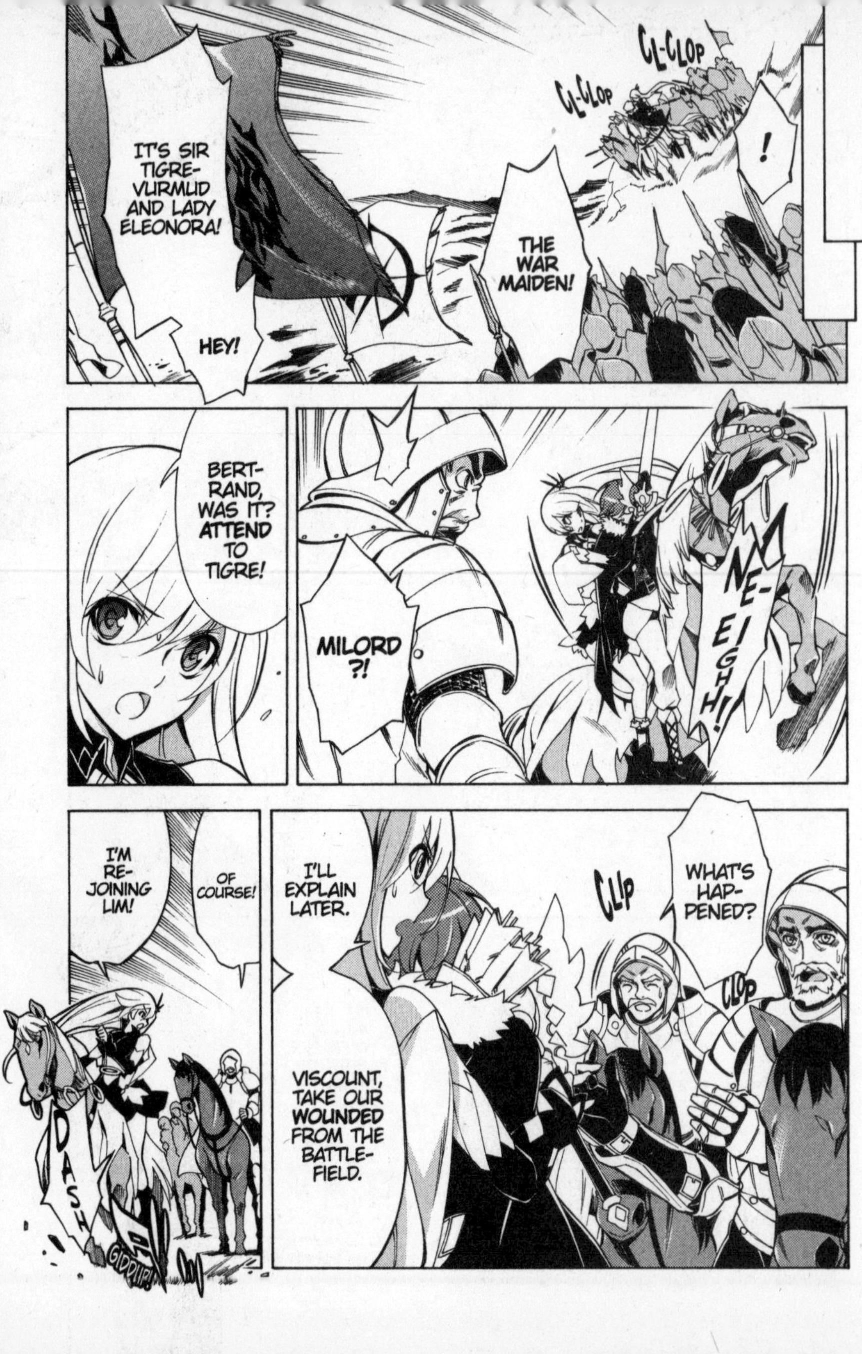
CL-CLOP
CL-CLOP
!
THE WAR MAIDEN!
IT'S SIR TIGRE-VURMUD AND LADY ELEONORA!
HEY!
NE-EIGHH!!
MILORD ?!
BERT-RAND, WAS IT? ATTEND TO TIGRE!
WHAT'S HAP-PENED?
CLIP
CLOP
I'LL EXPLAIN LATER.
VISCOUNT, TAKE OUR WOUNDED FROM THE BATTLE-FIELD.
I'M RE-JOINING LIM!
OF COURSE!
DASH
GIDDIUP!

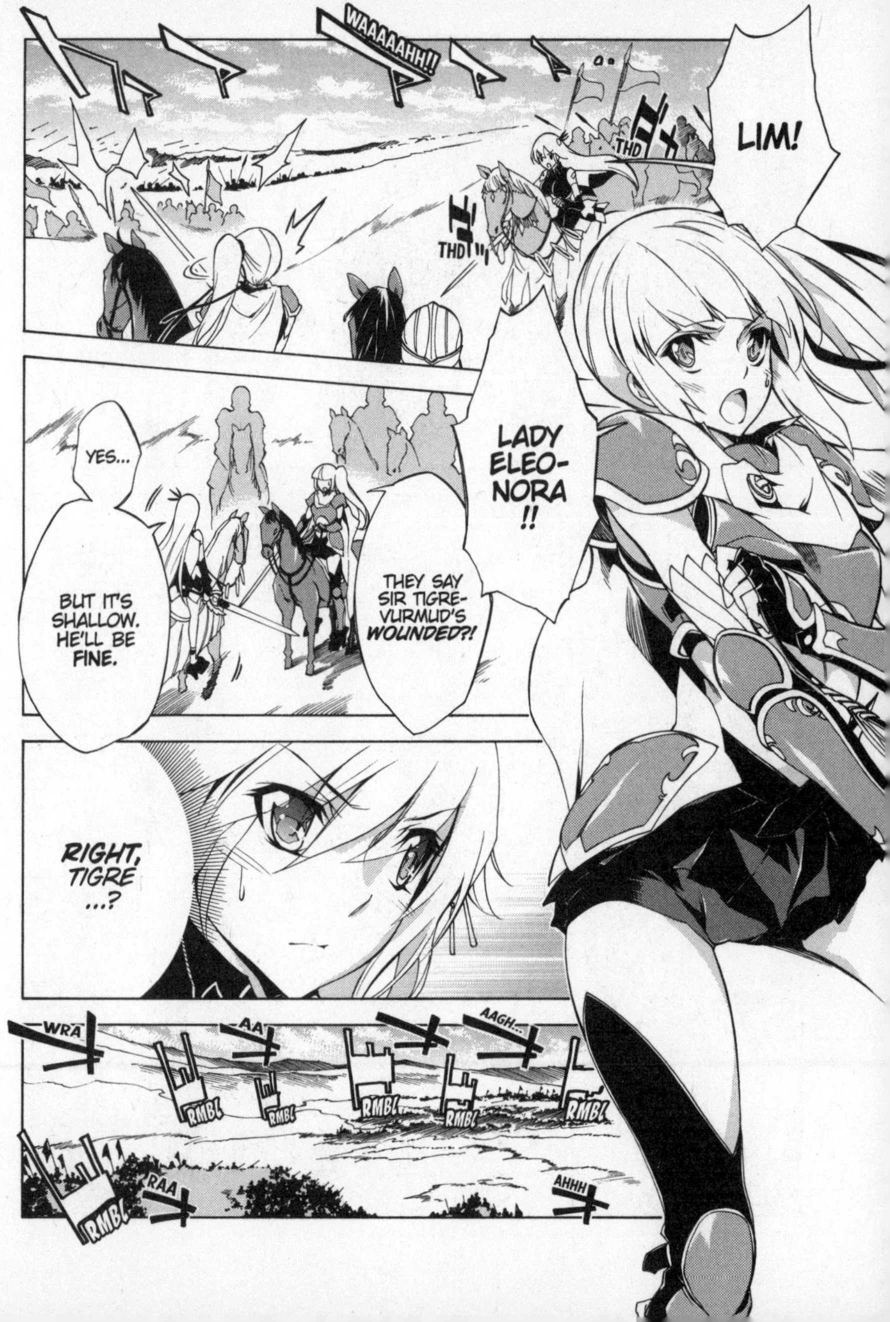
WAAAAAHH!!
THD
LIM!
THD
LADY ELEO-NORA!!
THEY SAY SIR TIGRE-VURMUD'S WOUNDED?!
YES...
BUT IT'S SHALLOW. HE'LL BE FINE.
RIGHT, TIGRE...?
WRA
AA
AAGH...
RMBL
RMBL
RMBL
RMBL
RMBL
AHHH
RAA
RMBL

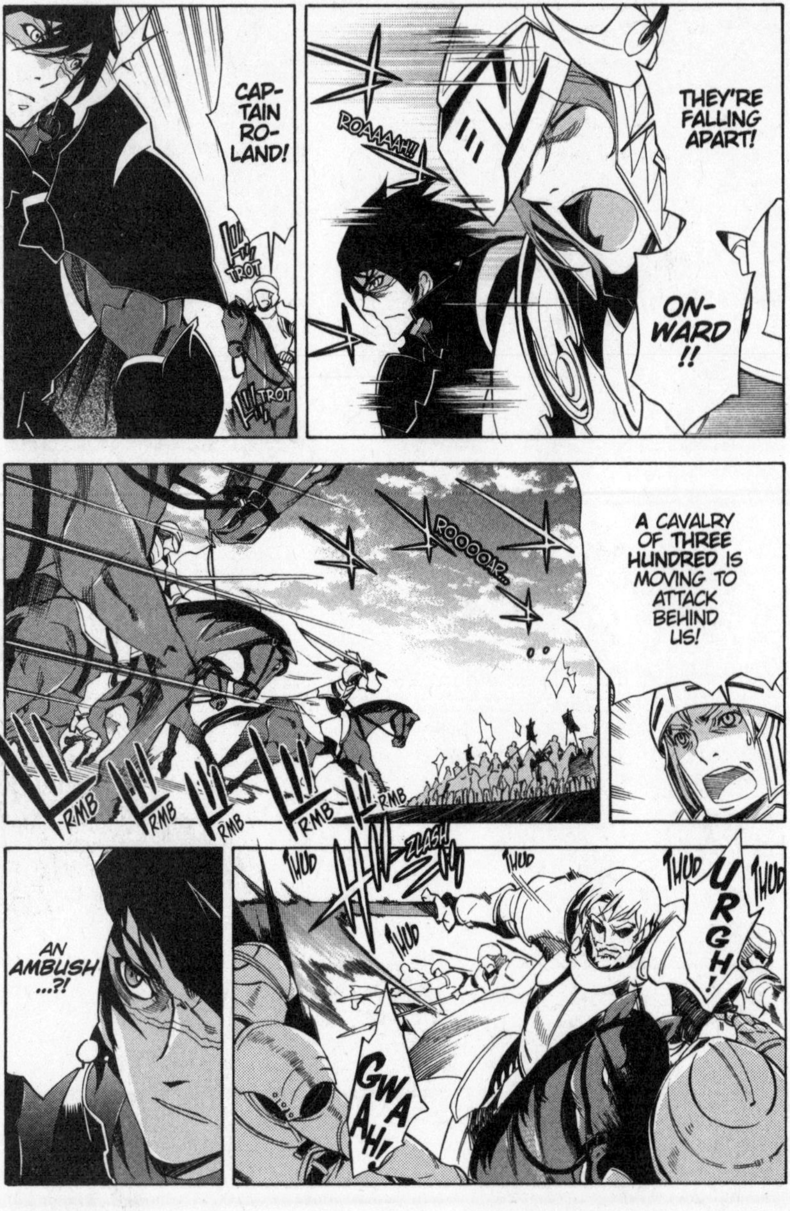
THEY'RE FALLING APART!
ROAAAAH!!
ON-WARD !!
CAP-TAIN RO-LAND!
TROT
TROT
A CAVALRY OF THREE HUNDRED IS MOVING TO ATTACK BEHIND US!
ROOOOAR...
RMB
RMB
RMB
RMB
RMB
THUD
URGH!
THUD
THUD
ZLASH
THUD
THUD
GWAAH!
AN AMBUSH ...?!

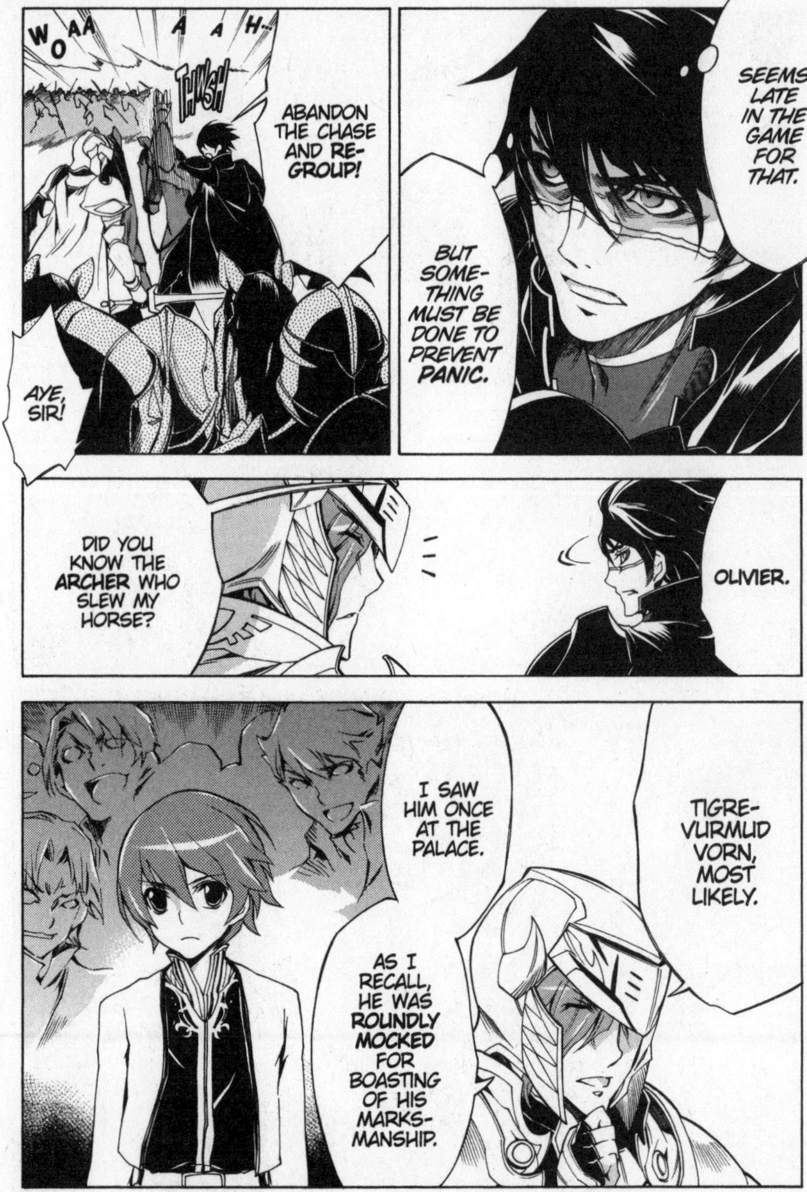
SEEMS LATE IN THE GAME FOR THAT.
BUT SOMETHING MUST BE DONE TO PREVENT PANIC.
ABANDON THE CHASE AND REGROUP!
WOAAAAH...
THWSH
AYE, SIR!
OLIVIER.
DID YOU KNOW THE ARCHER WHO SLEW MY HORSE?
TIGREVURMUD VORN, MOST LIKELY.
I SAW HIM ONCE AT THE PALACE.
AS I RECALL, HE WAS ROUNDLY MOCKED FOR BOASTING OF HIS MARKSMANSHIP.

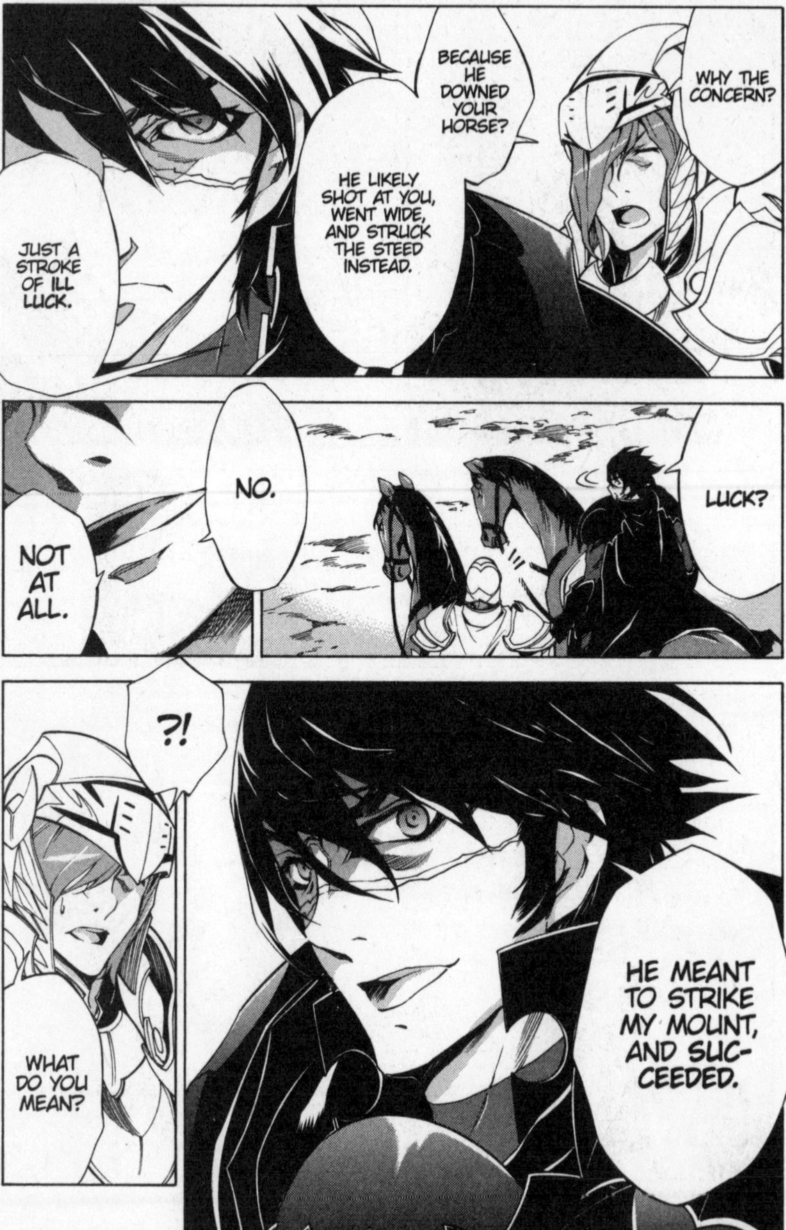
WHY THE CONCERN?
BECAUSE HE DOWNED YOUR HORSE?
HE LIKELY SHOT AT YOU, WENT WIDE, AND STRUCK THE STEED INSTEAD.
JUST A STROKE OF ILL LUCK.
LUCK?
NO.
NOT AT ALL.
HE MEANT TO STRIKE MY MOUNT, AND SUC-CEEDED.
?!
WHAT DO YOU MEAN?

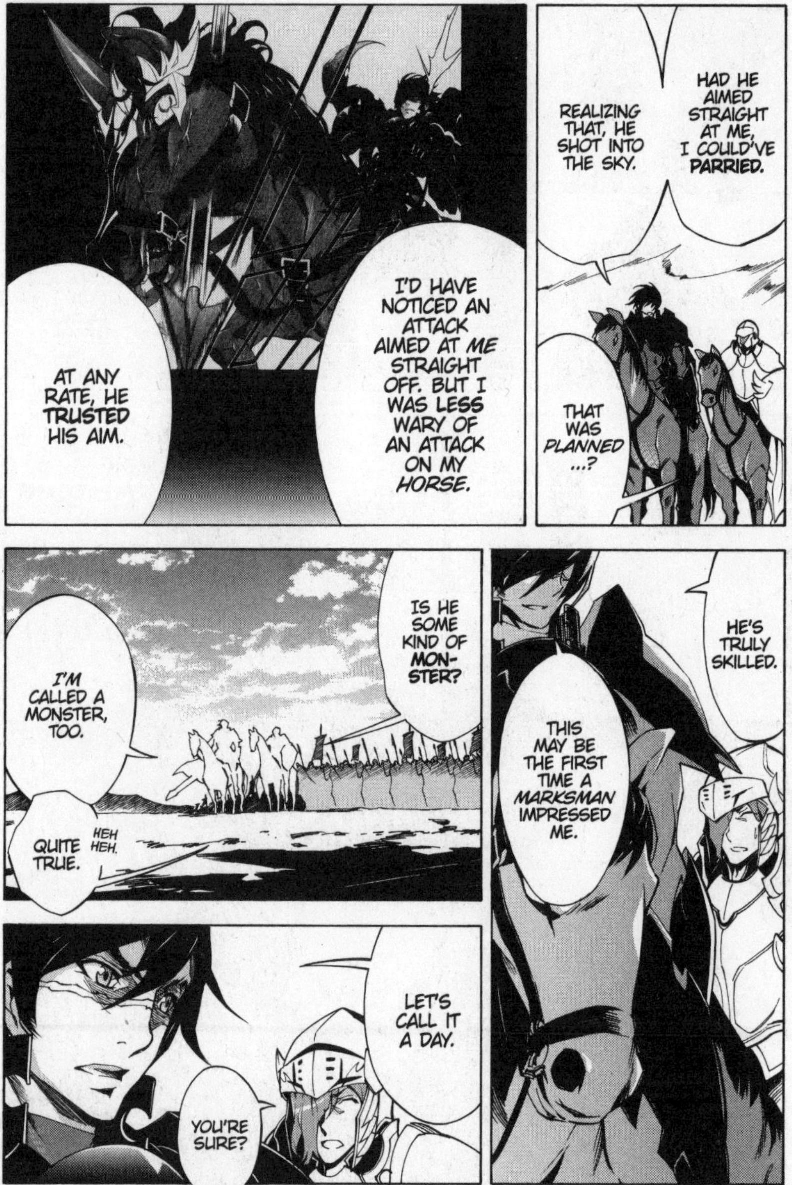
HAD HE AIMED STRAIGHT AT ME, I COULD'VE PARRIED.
REALIZING THAT, HE SHOT INTO THE SKY.
THAT WAS PLANNED ...?
I'D HAVE NOTICED AN ATTACK AIMED AT ME STRAIGHT OFF. BUT I WAS LESS WARY OF AN ATTACK ON MY HORSE.
AT ANY RATE, HE TRUSTED HIS AIM.
HE'S TRULY SKILLED.
THIS MAY BE THE FIRST TIME A MARKSMAN IMPRESSED ME.
IS HE SOME KIND OF MON-STER?
I'M CALLED A MONSTER, TOO.
HEH HEH.
QUITE TRUE.
LET'S CALL IT A DAY.
YOU'RE SURE?

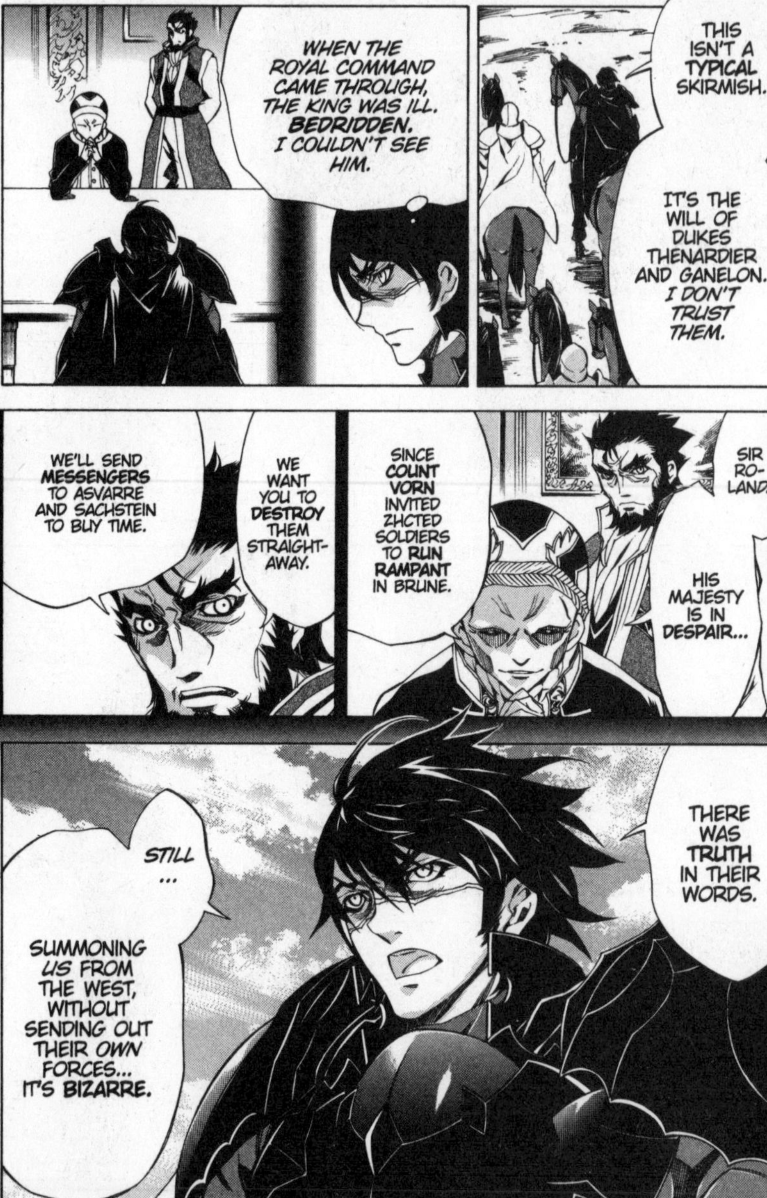
THIS ISN'T A TYPICAL SKIRMISH.
IT'S THE WILL OF DUKES THENARDIER AND GANELON. I DON'T TRUST THEM.
WHEN THE ROYAL COMMAND CAME THROUGH, THE KING WAS ILL. BEDRIDDEN. I COULDN'T SEE HIM.
SIR RO-LAND.
HIS MAJESTY IS IN DESPAIR...
SINCE COUNT VORN INVITED ZHCTED SOLDIERS TO RUN RAMPANT IN BRUNE.
WE WANT YOU TO DESTROY THEM STRAIGHT-AWAY.
WE'LL SEND MESSENGERS TO ASVARRE AND SACHSTEIN TO BUY TIME.
THERE WAS TRUTH IN THEIR WORDS.
STILL ...
SUMMONING US FROM THE WEST, WITHOUT SENDING OUT THEIR OWN FORCES... IT'S BIZARRE.

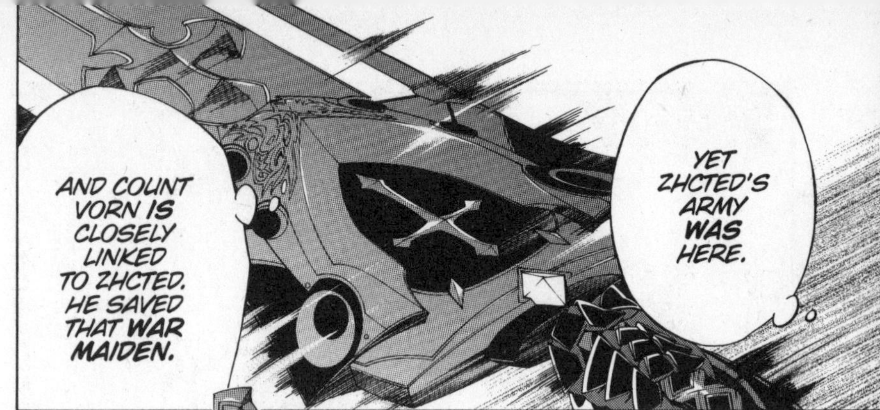
YET ZHCTED'S ARMY WAS HERE.
AND COUNT VORN IS CLOSELY LINKED TO ZHCTED. HE SAVED THAT WAR MAIDEN.
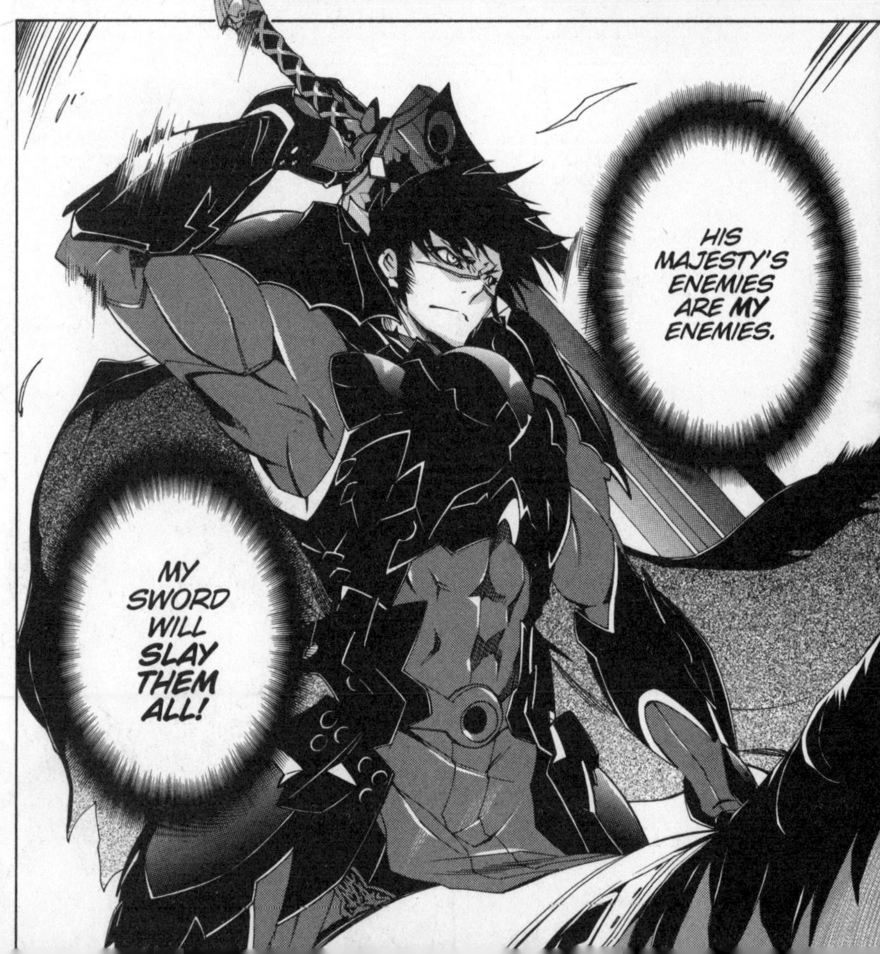
HIS MAJESTY'S ENEMIES ARE MY ENEMIES.
MY SWORD WILL SLAY THEM ALL!

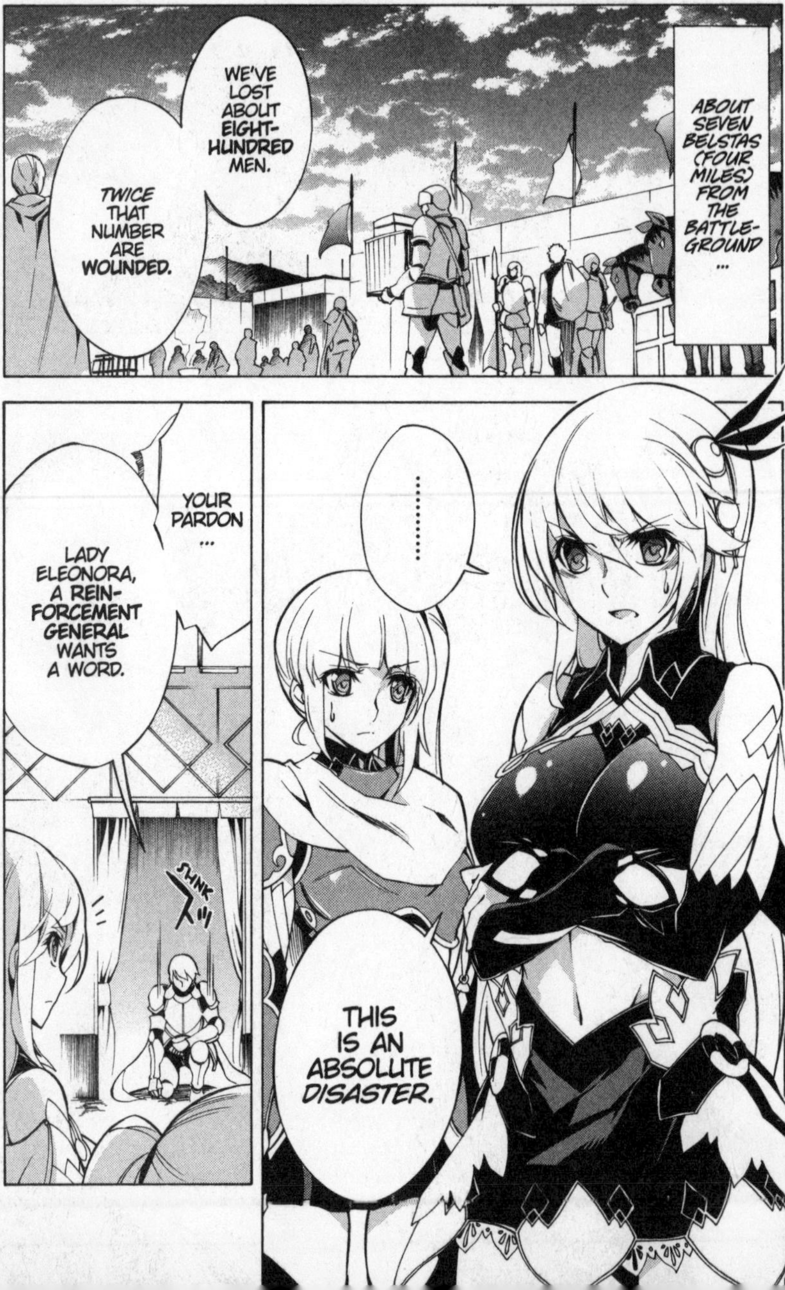
ABOUT SEVEN BELSTAS (FOUR MILES) FROM THE BATTLE-GROUND ...
WE'VE LOST ABOUT EIGHT-HUNDRED MEN.
TWICE THAT NUMBER ARE WOUNDED.
THIS IS AN ABSOLUTE DISASTER.
....
SHNK
YOUR PARDON ...
LADY ELEONORA, A REIN-FORCEMENT GENERAL WANTS A WORD.

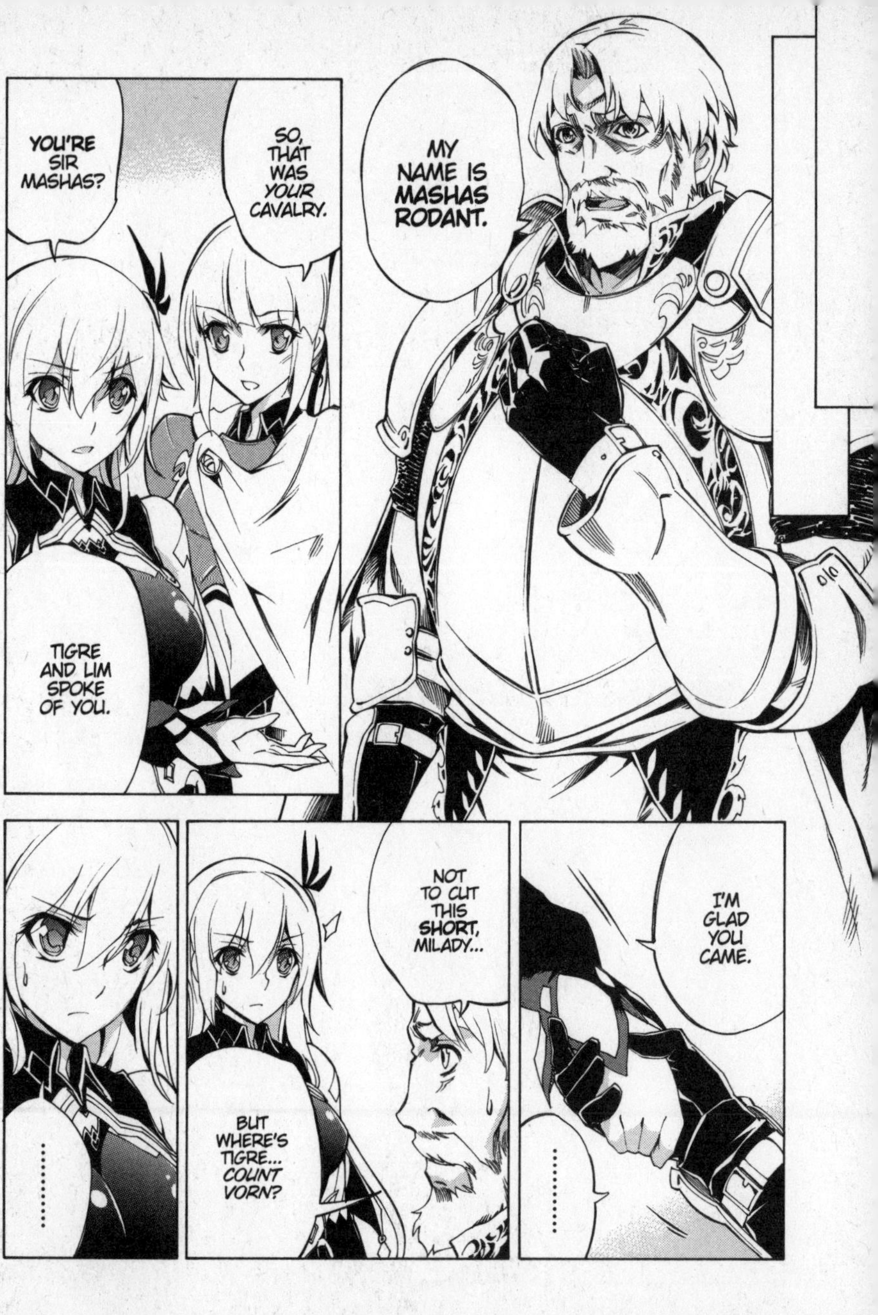
MY NAME IS MASHAS RODANT.
SO, THAT WAS YOUR CAVALRY.
YOU'RE SIR MASHAS?
TIGRE AND LIM SPOKE OF YOU.
I'M GLAD YOU CAME.
......
NOT TO CUT THIS SHORT, MILADY...
BUT WHERE'S TIGRE... COUNT VORN?
......

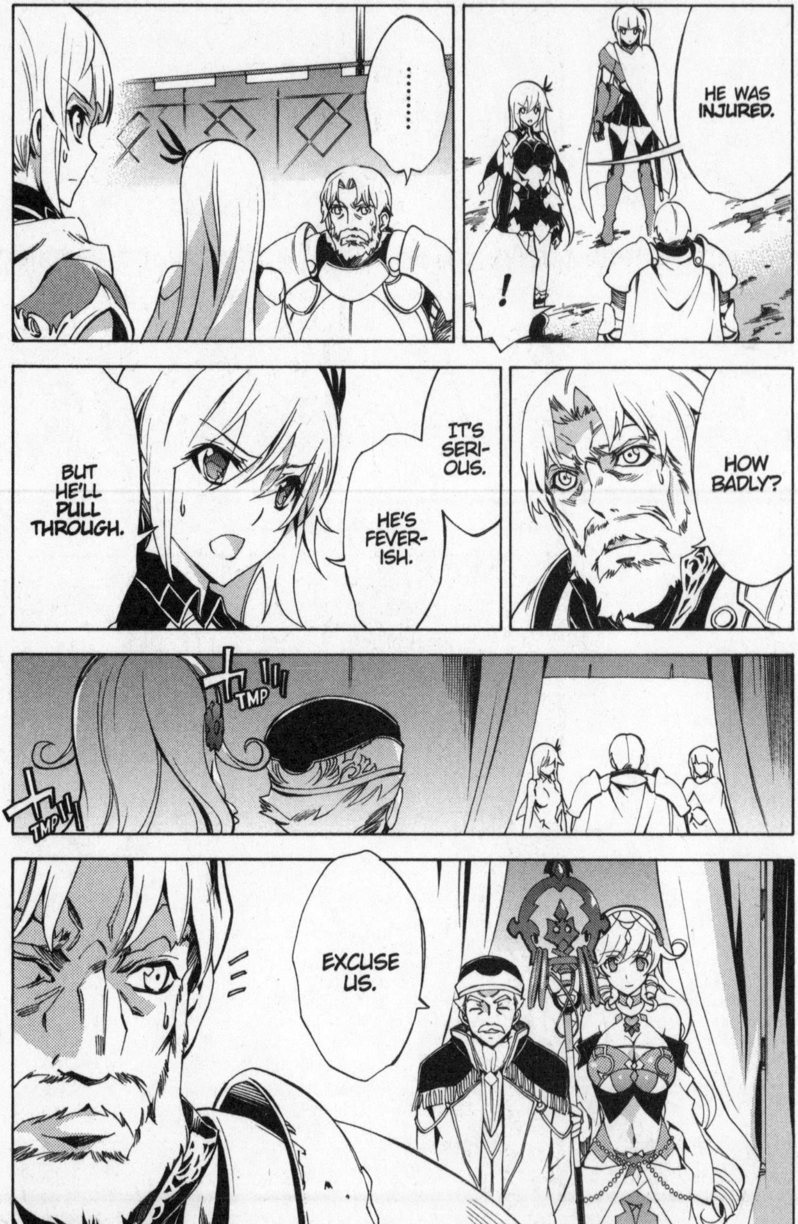
HE WAS INJURED.
!
......
HOW BADLY?
IT'S SERI-OUS.
HE'S FEVER-ISH.
BUT HE'LL PULL THROUGH.
TMP
TMP
EXCUSE US.

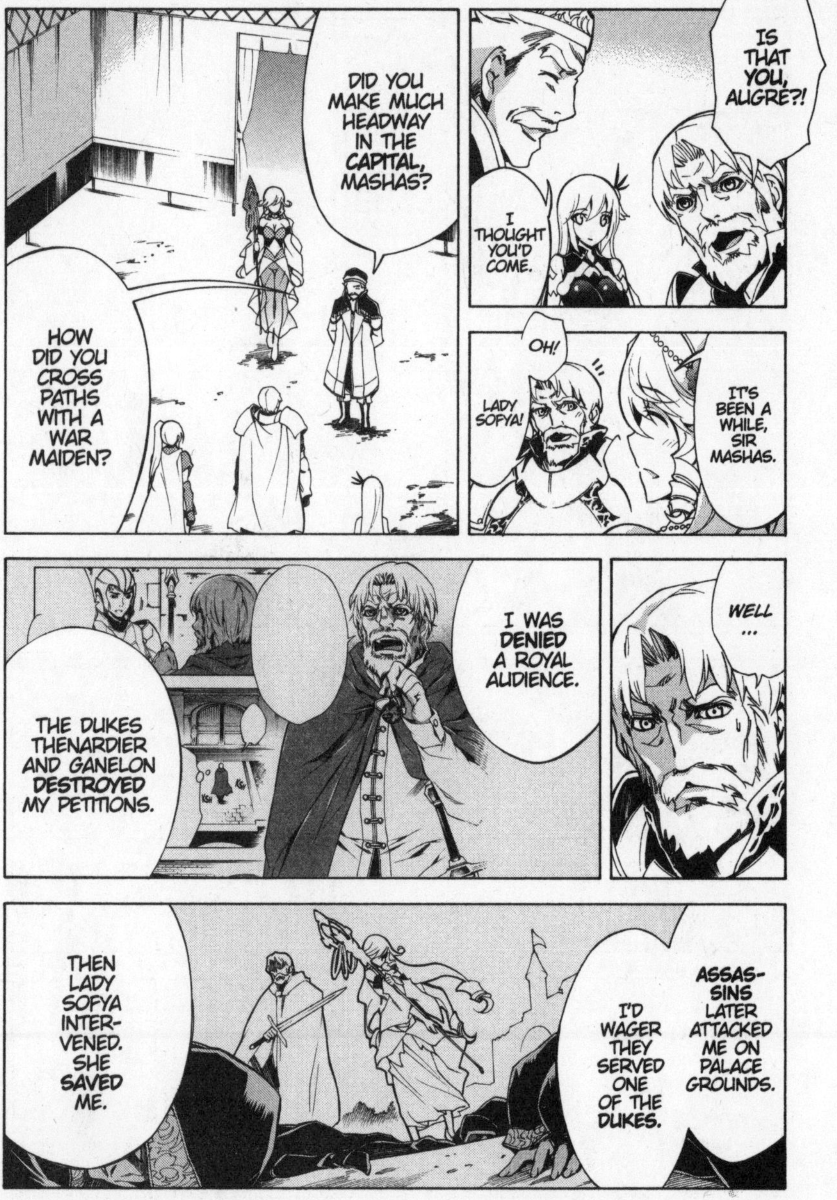
IS THAT YOU, AUGRE?!
I THOUGHT YOU'D COME.
DID YOU MAKE MUCH HEADWAY IN THE CAPITAL, MASHAS?
HOW DID YOU CROSS PATHS WITH A WAR MAIDEN?
OH!
LADY SOFYA!
IT'S BEEN A WHILE, SIR MASHAS.
WELL ...
I WAS DENIED A ROYAL AUDIENCE.
THE DUKES THENARDIER AND GANELON DESTROYED MY PETITIONS.
ASSAS-SINS LATER ATTACKED ME ON PALACE GROUNDS.
I'D WAGER THEY SERVED ONE OF THE DUKES.
THEN LADY SOFYA INTER-VENED. SHE SAVED ME.

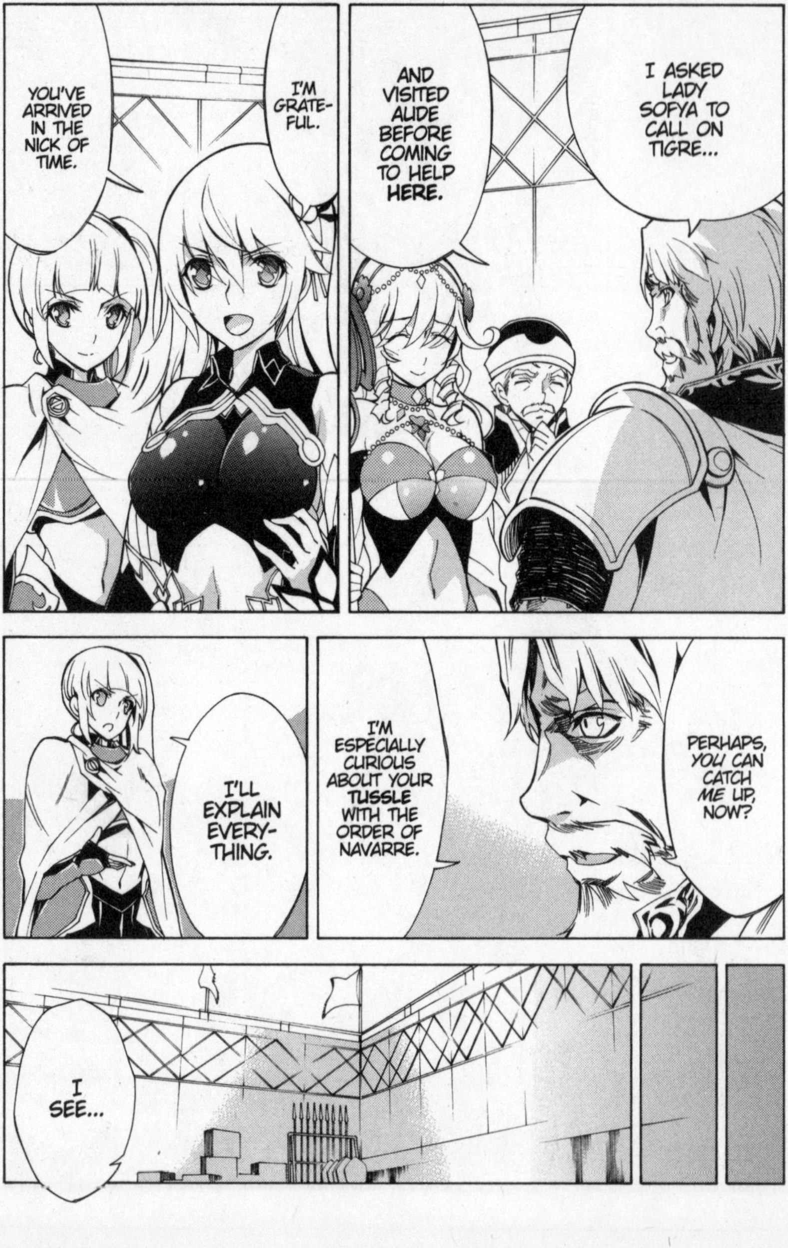
I ASKED LADY SOFYA TO CALL ON TIGRE...
AND VISITED AUDE BEFORE COMING TO HELP HERE.
I'M GRATE-FUL.
YOU'VE ARRIVED IN THE NICK OF TIME.
PERHAPS, YOU CAN CATCH ME UP, NOW?
I'M ESPECIALLY CURIOUS ABOUT YOUR TUSSLE WITH THE ORDER OF NAVARRE.
I'LL EXPLAIN EVERY-THING.
I SEE...

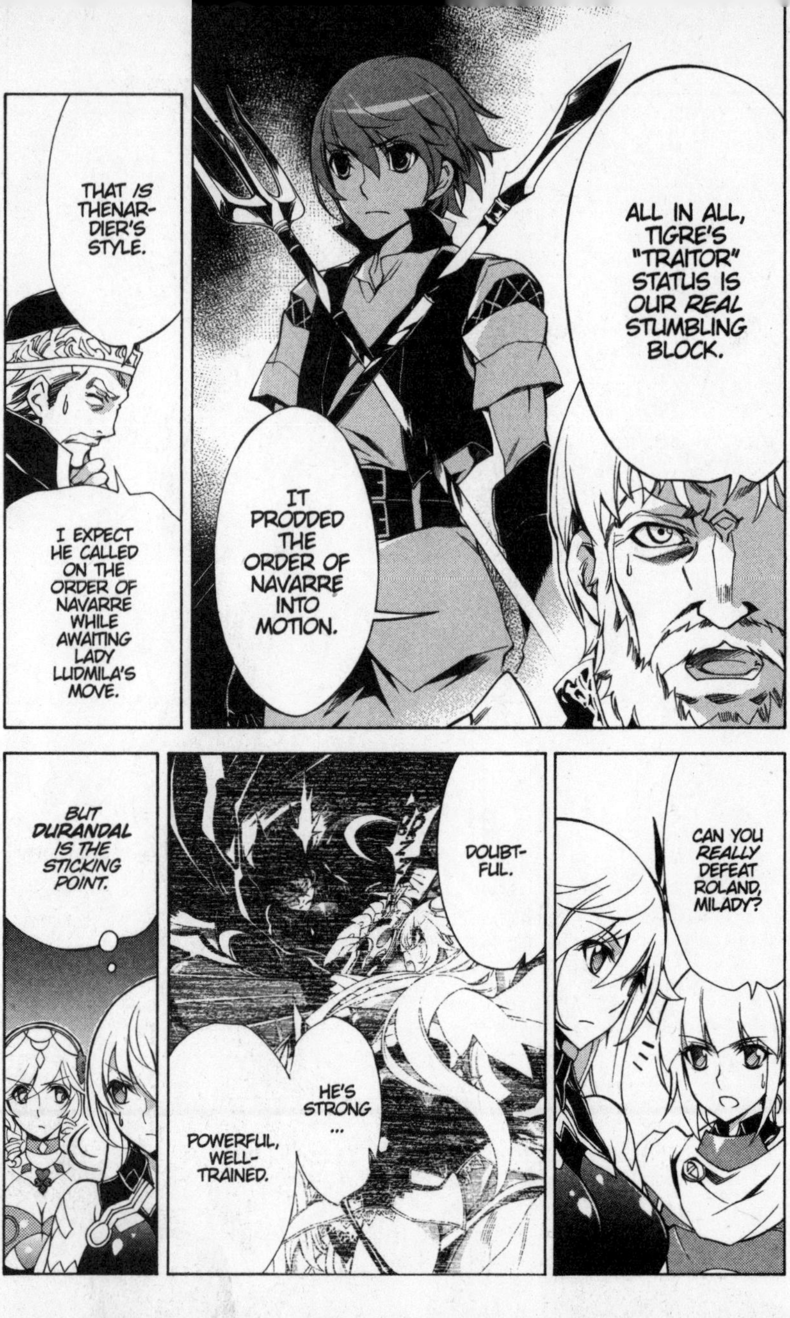
ALL IN ALL, TIGRE'S "TRAITOR" STATUS IS OUR *REAL* STUMBLING BLOCK.
IT PRODDED THE ORDER OF NAVARRE INTO MOTION.
THAT *IS* THENARDIER'S STYLE.
I EXPECT HE CALLED ON THE ORDER OF NAVARRE WHILE AWAITING LADY LUDMILA'S MOVE.
CAN YOU *REALLY* DEFEAT ROLAND, MILADY?
DOUBT-FUL.
HE'S STRONG ...
POWERFUL, WELL-TRAINED.
BUT DURANDAL IS THE STICKING POINT.

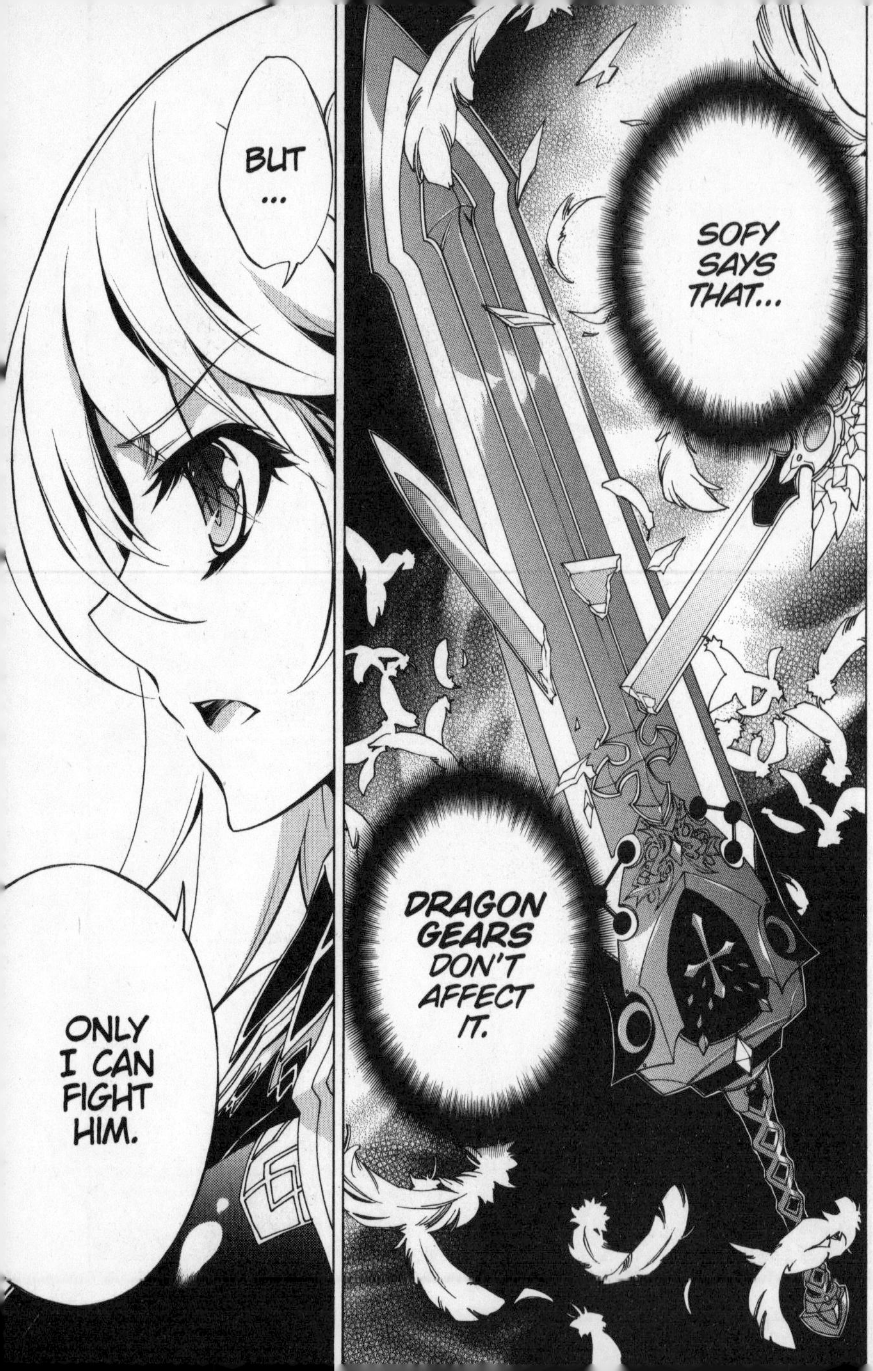
SOFY SAYS THAT...
DRAGON GEARS DON'T AFFECT IT.
BUT ...
ONLY I CAN FIGHT HIM.

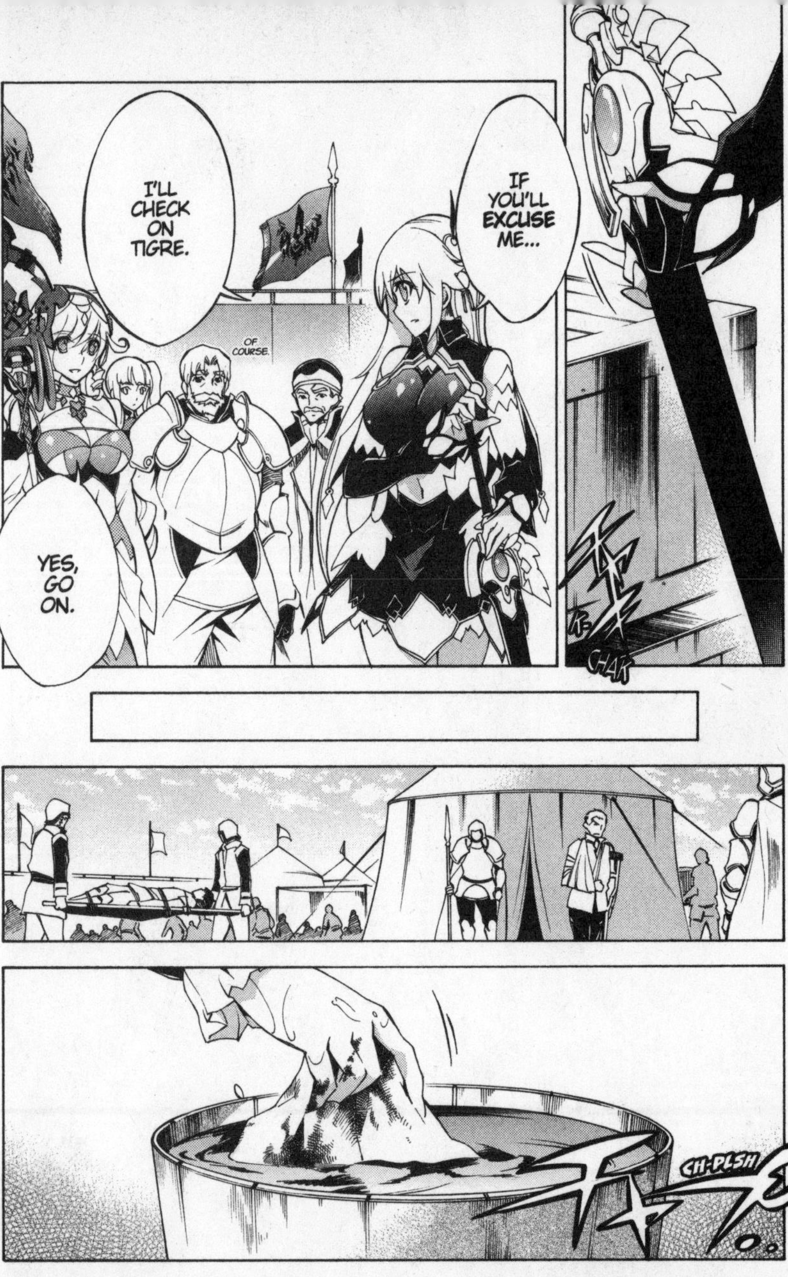
KA-
CHAK
IF YOU'LL EXCUSE ME...
I'LL CHECK ON TIGRE.
OF COURSE.
YES, GO ON.
CH-PLSH

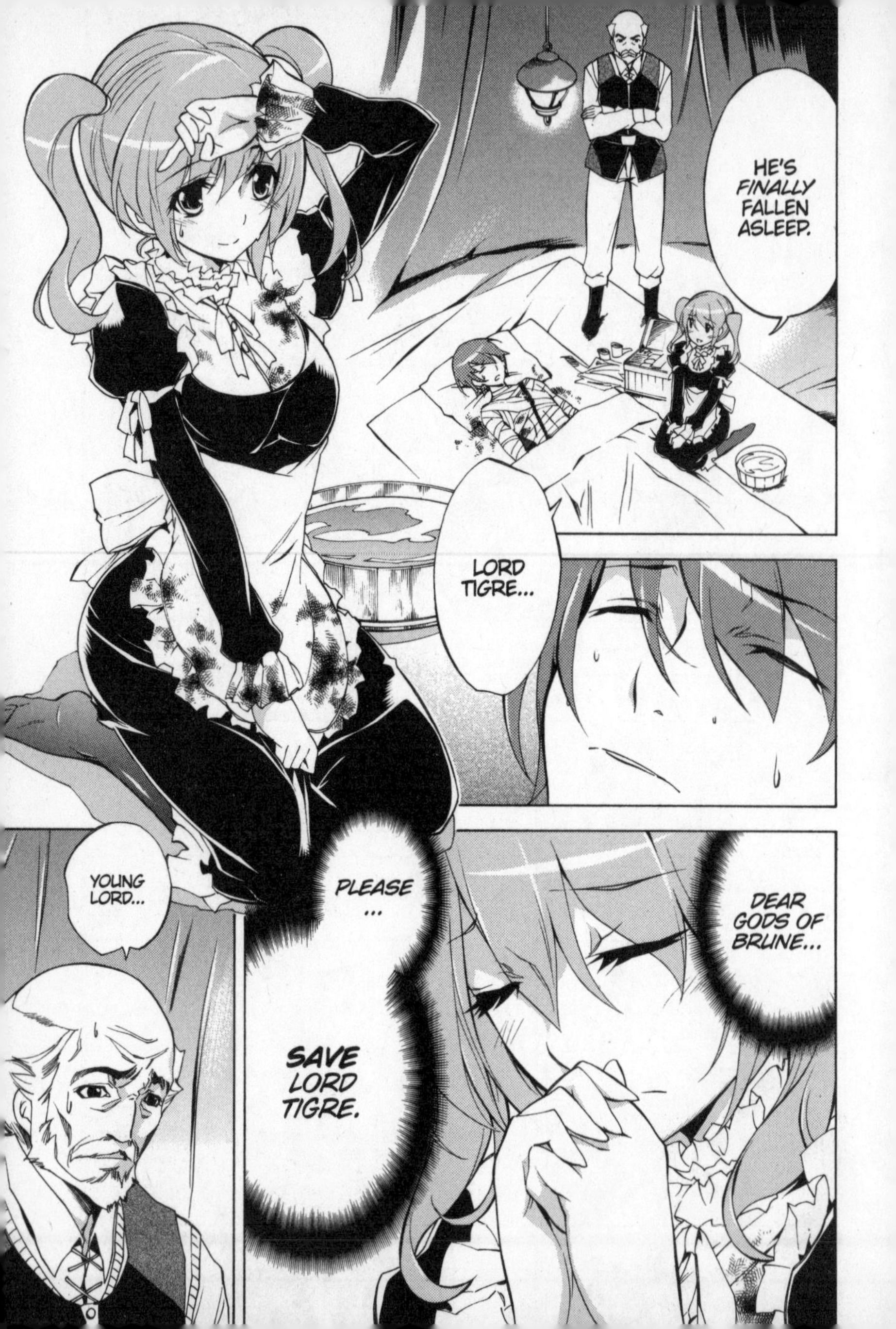
HE'S FINALLY FALLEN ASLEEP.
LORD TIGRE...
DEAR GODS OF BRUNE...
PLEASE ...
SAVE LORD TIGRE.
YOUNG LORD...

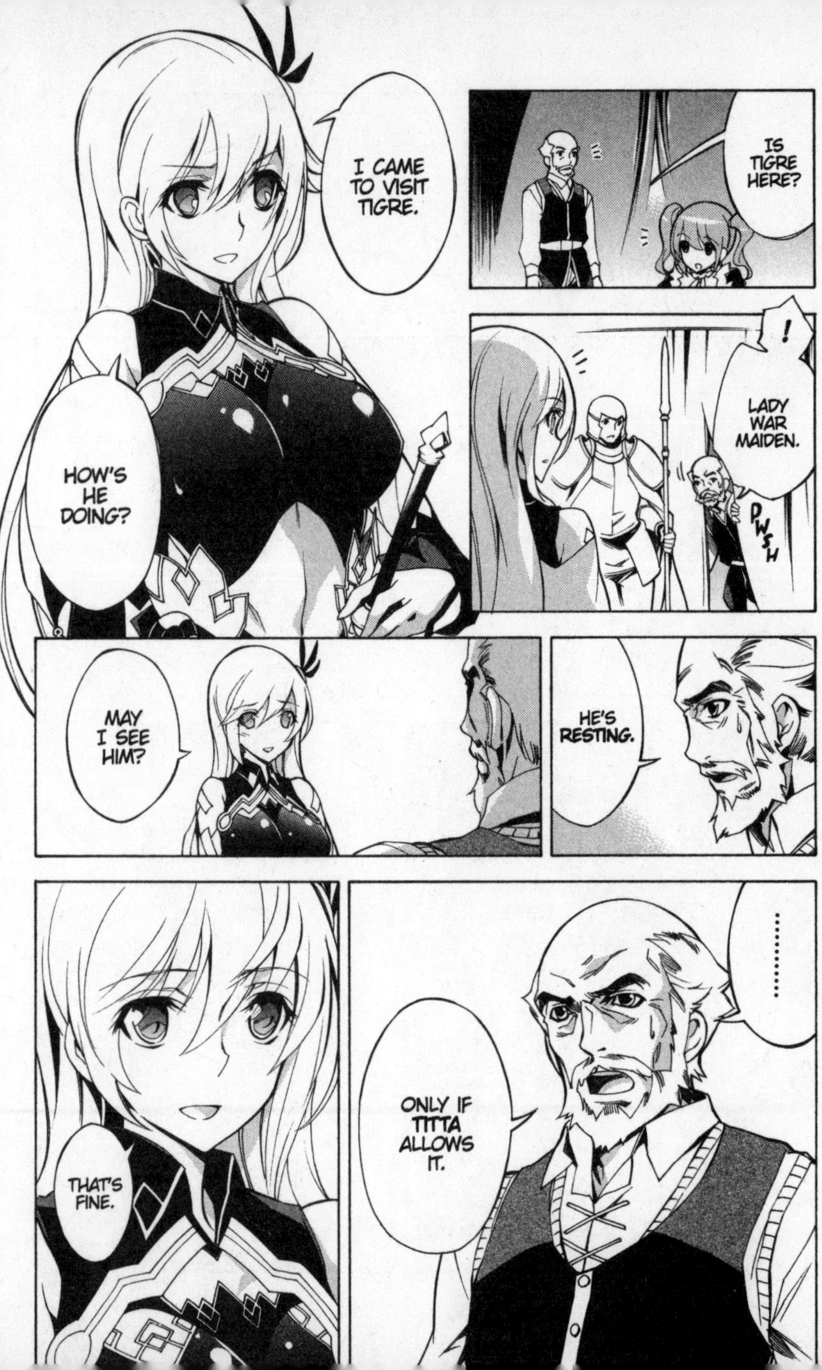
IS TIGRE HERE?
!
LADY WAR MAIDEN.
DWSH
I CAME TO VISIT TIGRE.
HOW'S HE DOING?
HE'S RESTING.
MAY I SEE HIM?
......
ONLY IF TITTA ALLOWS IT.
THAT'S FINE.

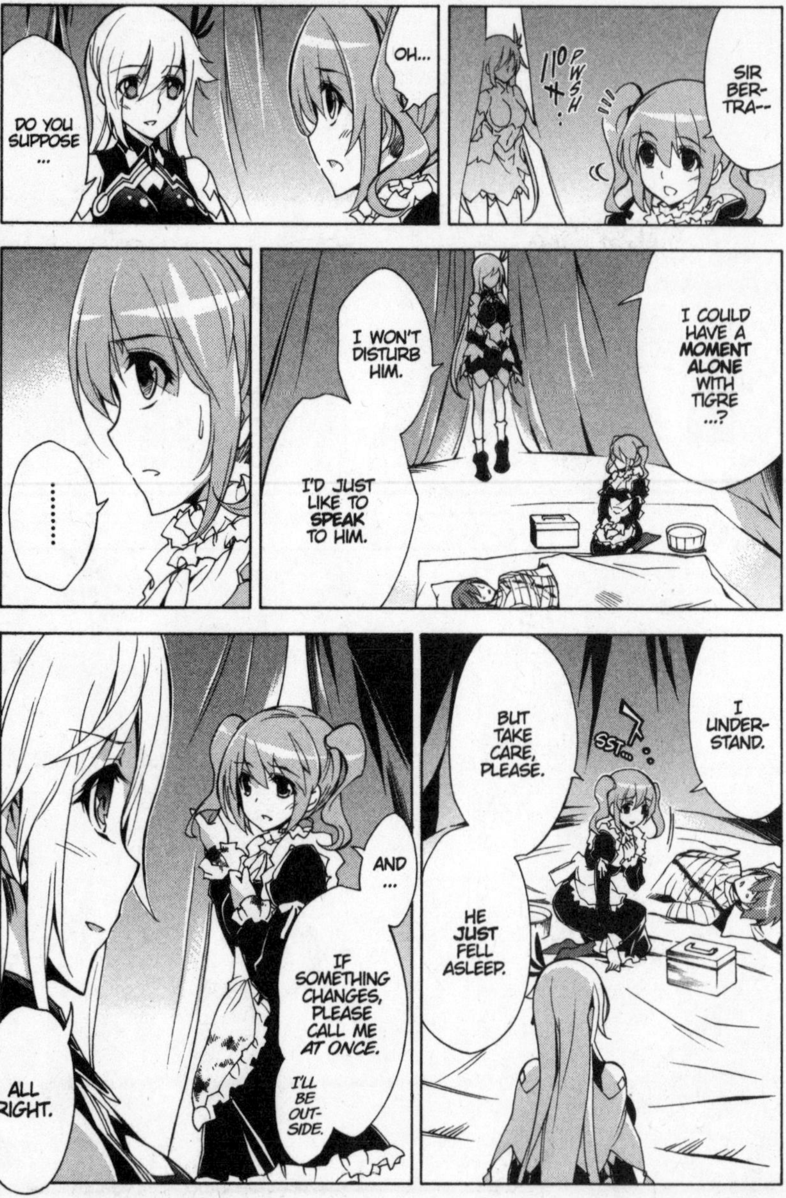
SIR BER-TRA--
PWSH
OH...
DO YOU SUPPOSE ...
I COULD HAVE A MOMENT ALONE WITH TIGRE ...?
I WON'T DISTURB HIM.
I'D JUST LIKE TO SPEAK TO HIM.
....
I UNDER-STAND.
SST...
BUT TAKE CARE, PLEASE.
HE JUST FELL ASLEEP.
AND ...
IF SOMETHING CHANGES, PLEASE CALL ME AT ONCE.
I'LL BE OUT-SIDE.
ALL RIGHT.

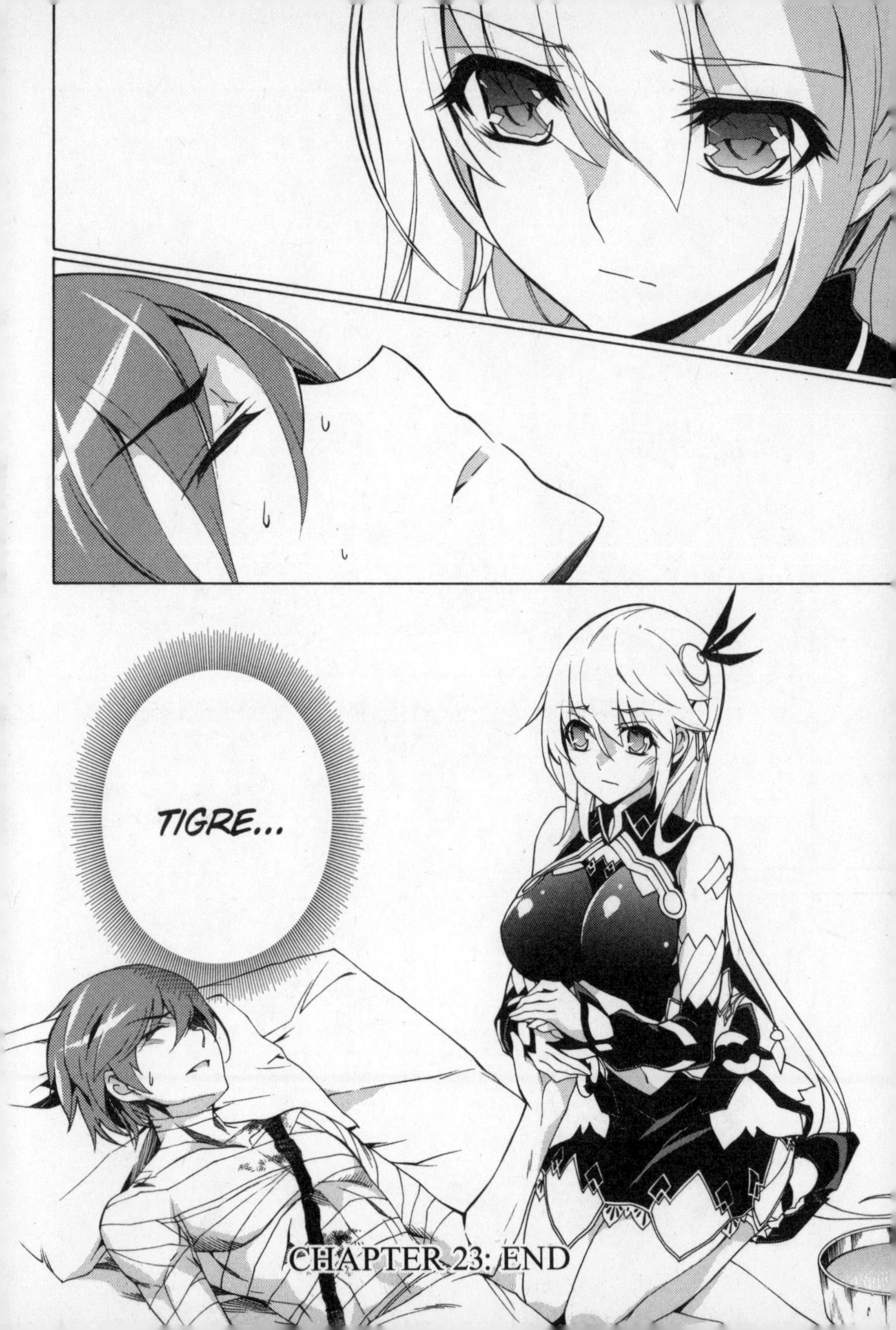
TIGRE...
CHAPTER 23: END

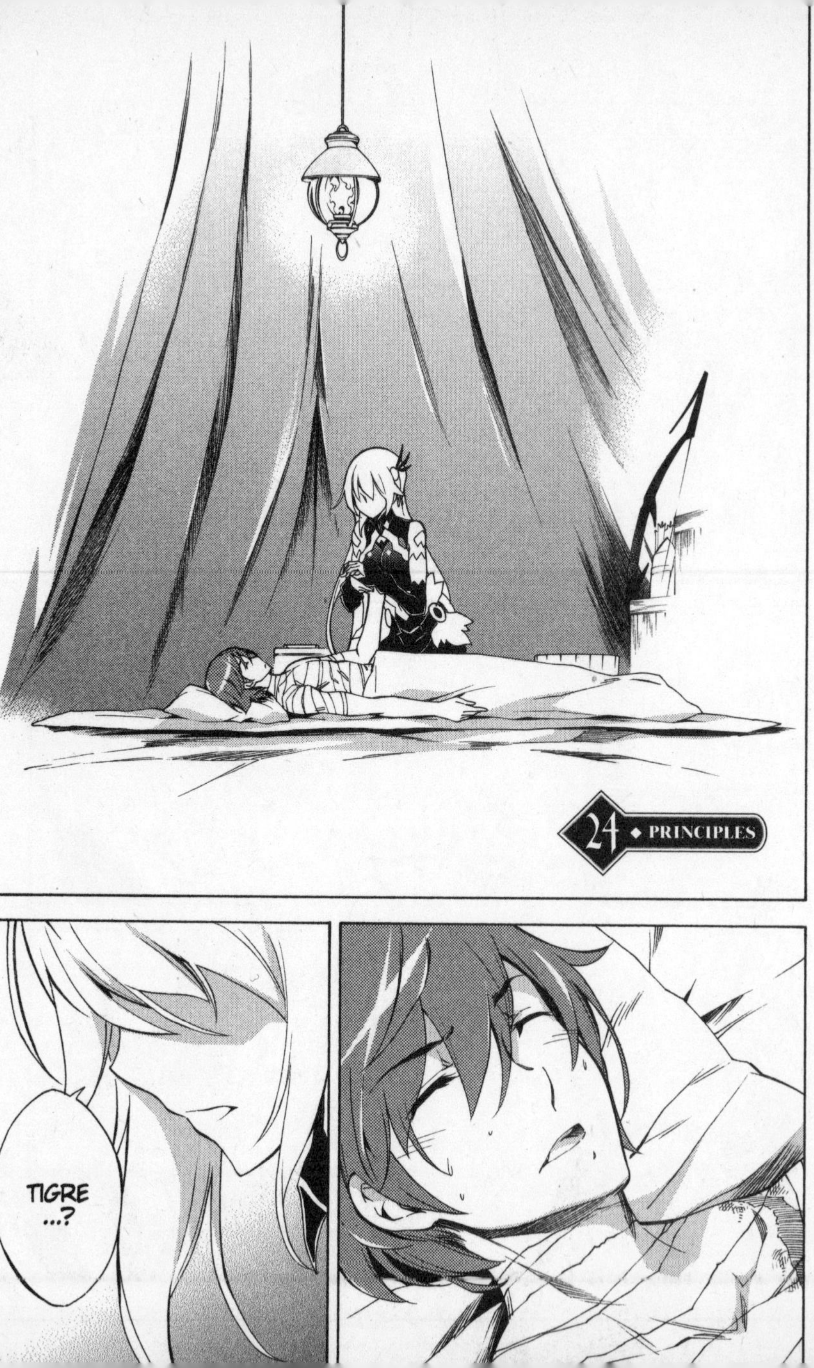
24 ◆ PRINCIPLES
TIGRE ...?

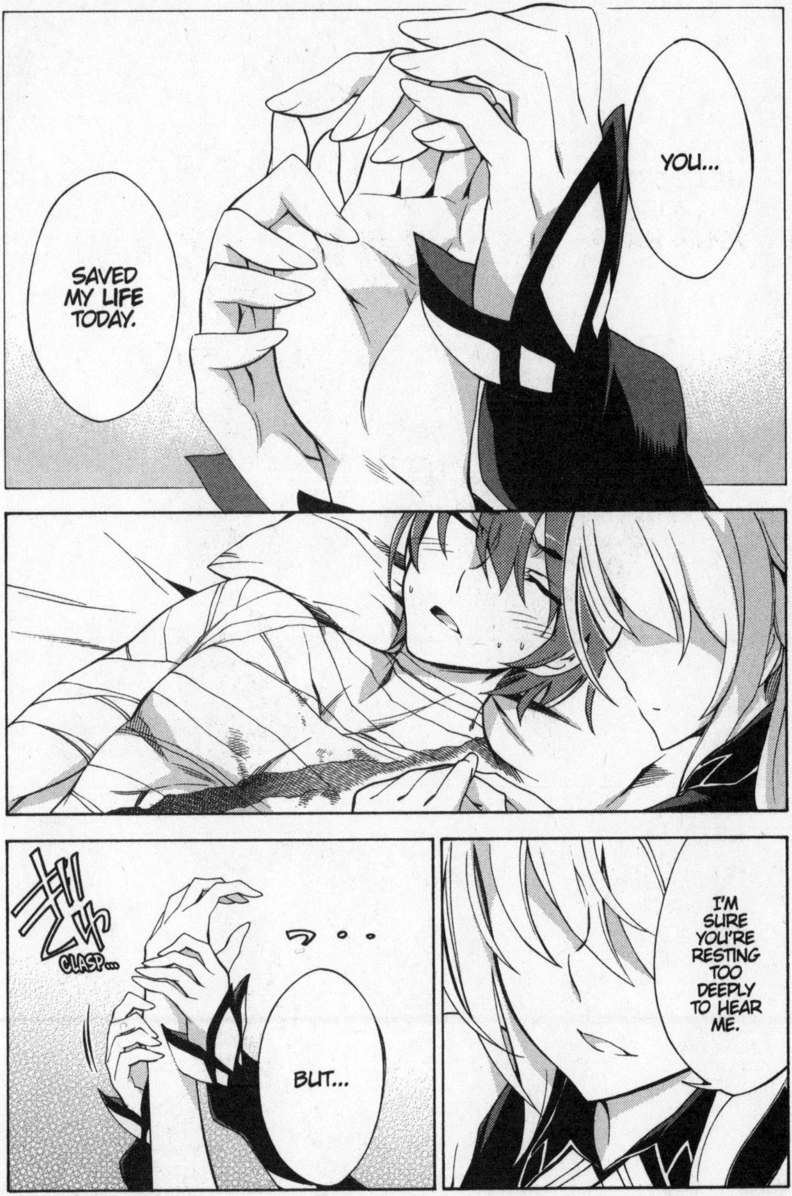
YOU...
SAVED MY LIFE TODAY.
I'M SURE YOU'RE RESTING TOO DEEPLY TO HEAR ME.
BUT...
CLASP...

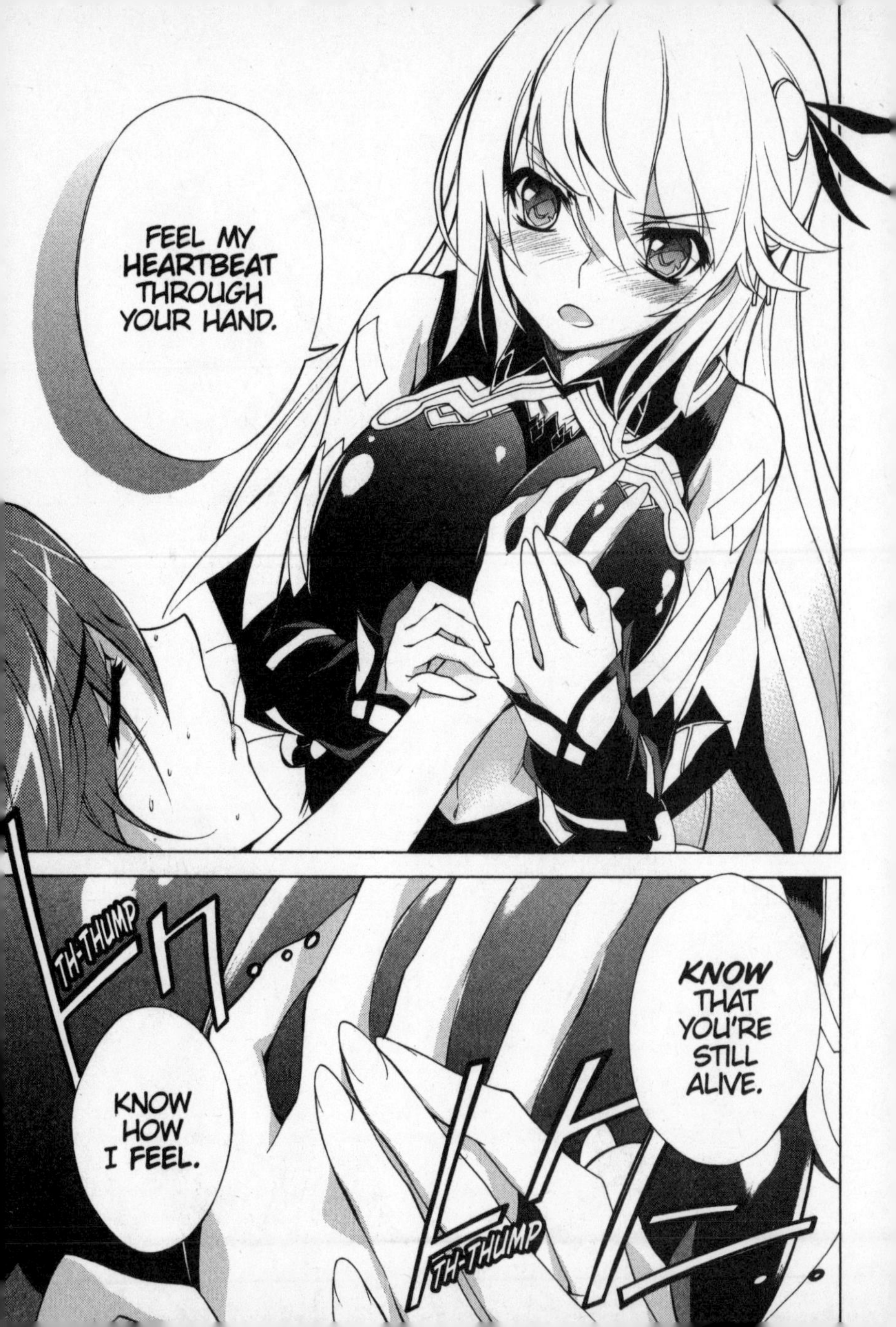
FEEL MY HEARTBEAT THROUGH YOUR HAND.
KNOW THAT YOU'RE STILL ALIVE.
TH-THUMP
KNOW HOW I FEEL.
TH-THUMP

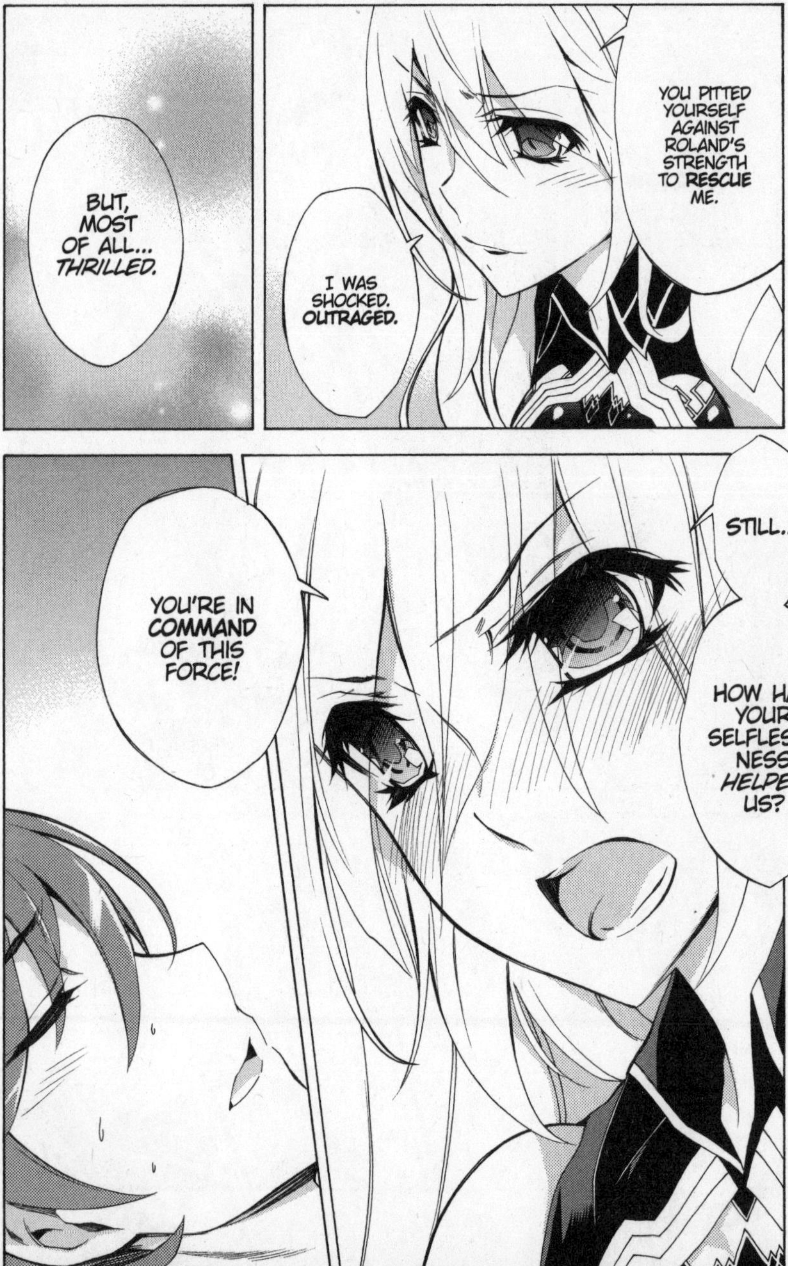
YOU PITTED YOURSELF AGAINST ROLAND'S STRENGTH TO RESCUE ME.
I WAS SHOCKED. OUTRAGED.
BUT, MOST OF ALL... THRILLED.
STILL...
HOW HAS YOUR SELFLESS-NESS HELPED US?
YOU'RE IN COMMAND OF THIS FORCE!

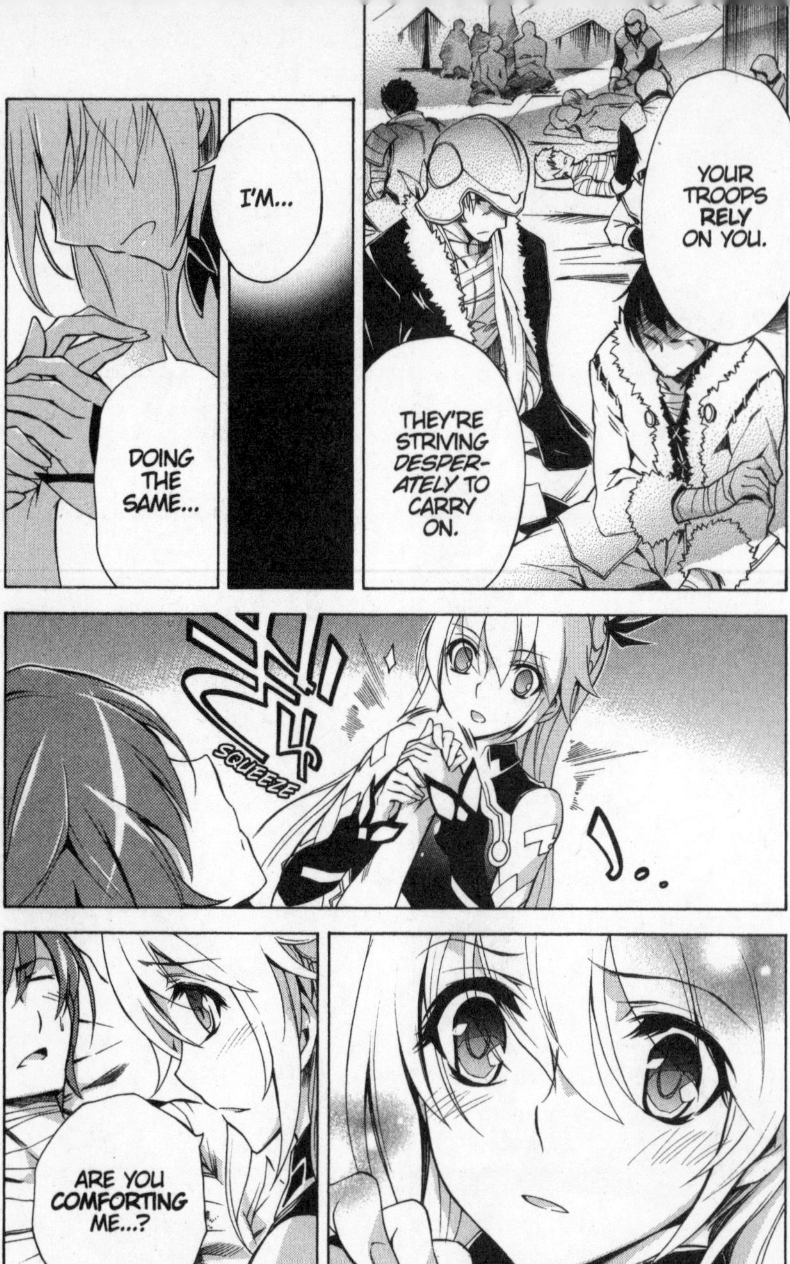
YOUR TROOPS RELY ON YOU.
THEY'RE STRIVING DESPER-ATELY TO CARRY ON.
I'M...
DOING THE SAME...
SQUEEZE
!..
ARE YOU COMFORTING ME...?

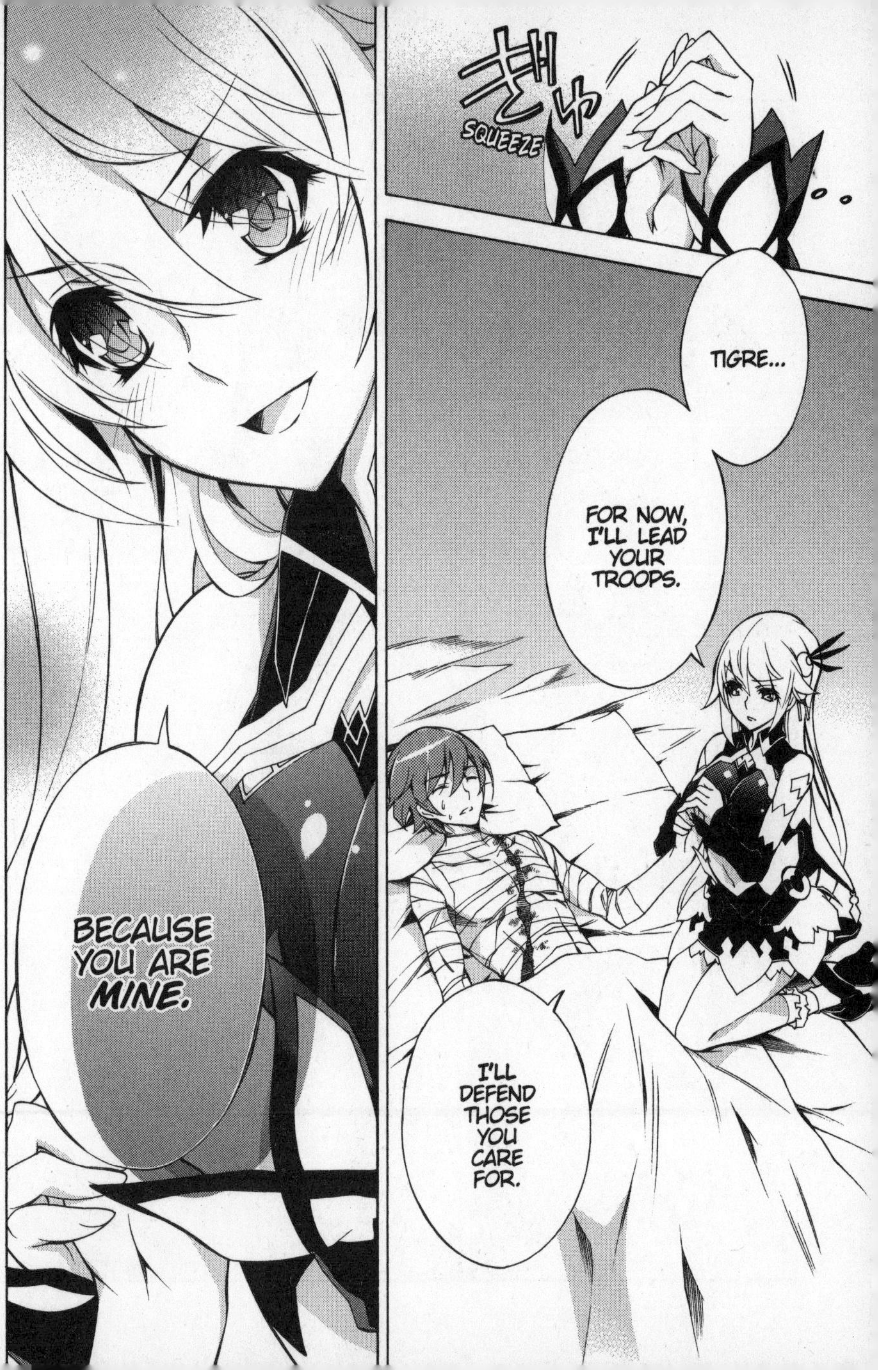
ぎゅ
SQUEEZE
...
TIGRE...
FOR NOW, I'LL LEAD YOUR TROOPS.
I'LL DEFEND THOSE YOU CARE FOR.
BECAUSE YOU ARE MINE.

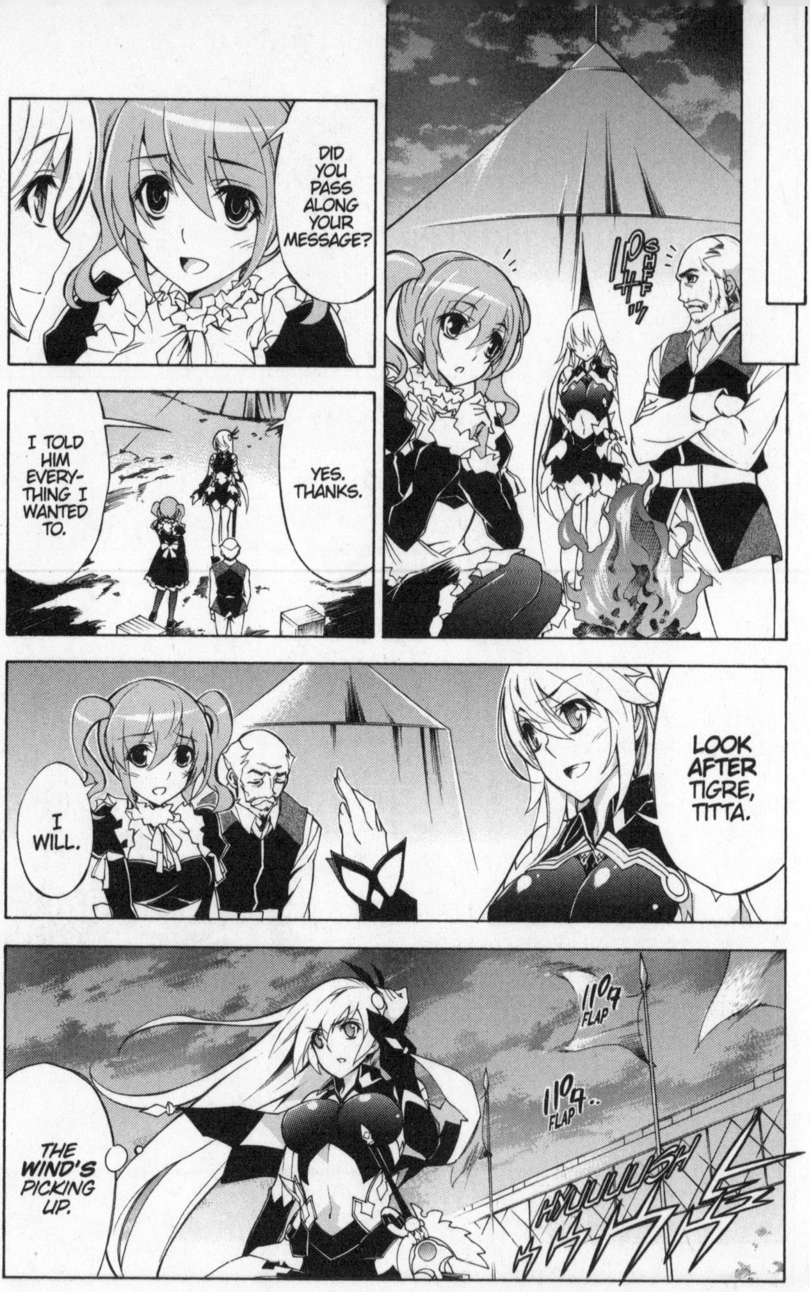
SHFF
DID YOU PASS ALONG YOUR MESSAGE?
YES. THANKS.
I TOLD HIM EVERY-THING I WANTED TO.
LOOK AFTER TIGRE, TITTA.
I WILL.
FLAP
FLAP..
HYUUUUSH
THE WIND'S PICKING UP.

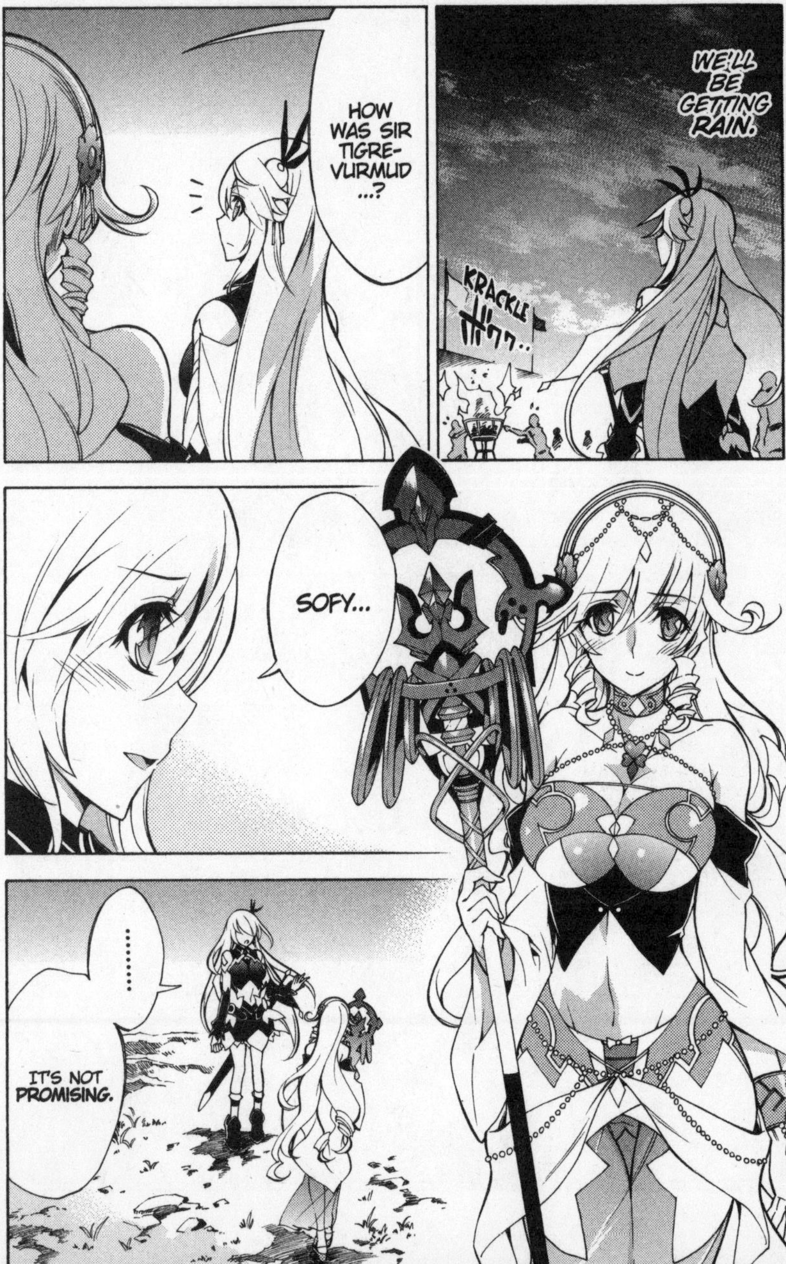
WE'LL BE GETTING RAIN.
KRACKLE
ザワワ..
HOW WAS SIR TIGRE-VURMUD ...?
SOFY...
....
IT'S NOT PROMISING.

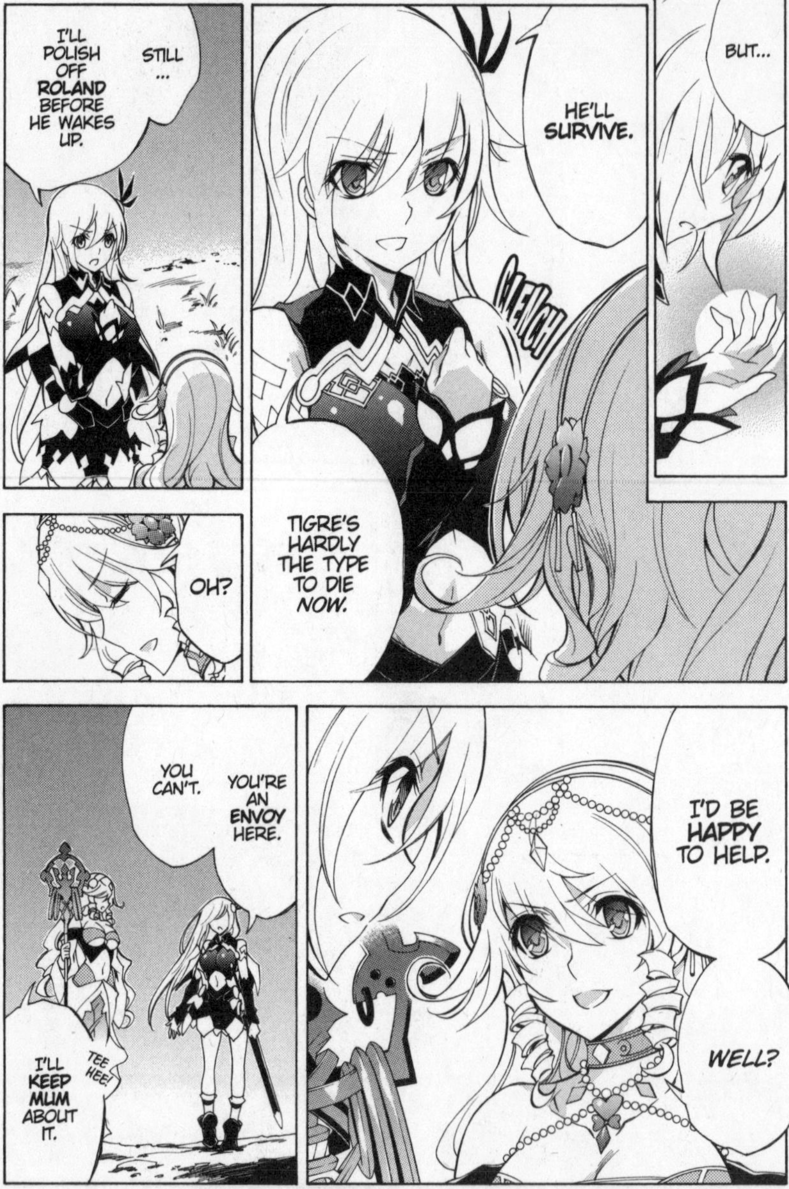
BUT...
HE'LL SURVIVE.
CLENCH
TIGRE'S HARDLY THE TYPE TO DIE NOW.
STILL ...
I'LL POLISH OFF ROLAND BEFORE HE WAKES UP.
OH?
I'D BE HAPPY TO HELP.
WELL?
YOU CAN'T.
YOU'RE AN ENVOY HERE.
TEE HEE!
I'LL KEEP MUM ABOUT IT.

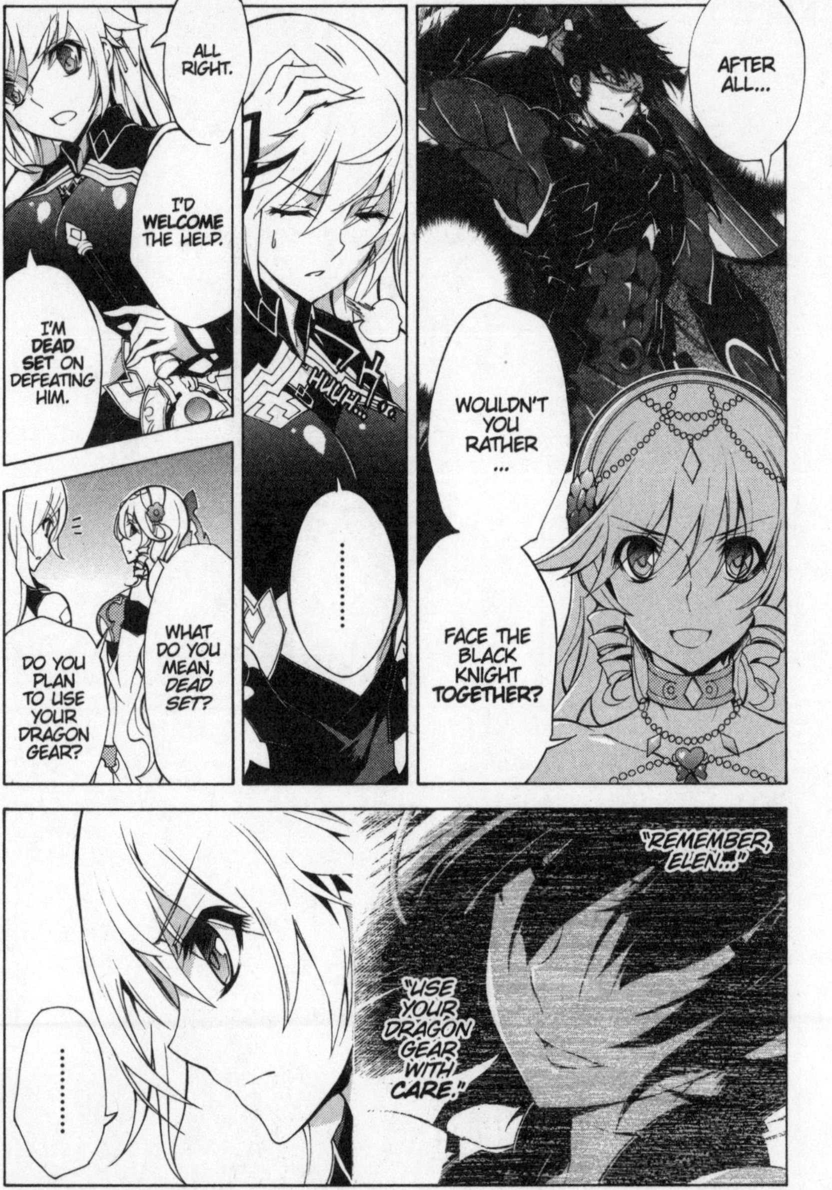
AFTER ALL...
WOULDN'T YOU RATHER ...
FACE THE BLACK KNIGHT TOGETHER?
HUUH...
......
ALL RIGHT.
I'D WELCOME THE HELP.
I'M DEAD SET ON DEFEATING HIM.
WHAT DO YOU MEAN, DEAD SET?
DO YOU PLAN TO USE YOUR DRAGON GEAR?
"REMEMBER, ELEN..."
"USE YOUR DRAGON GEAR WITH CARE."
......

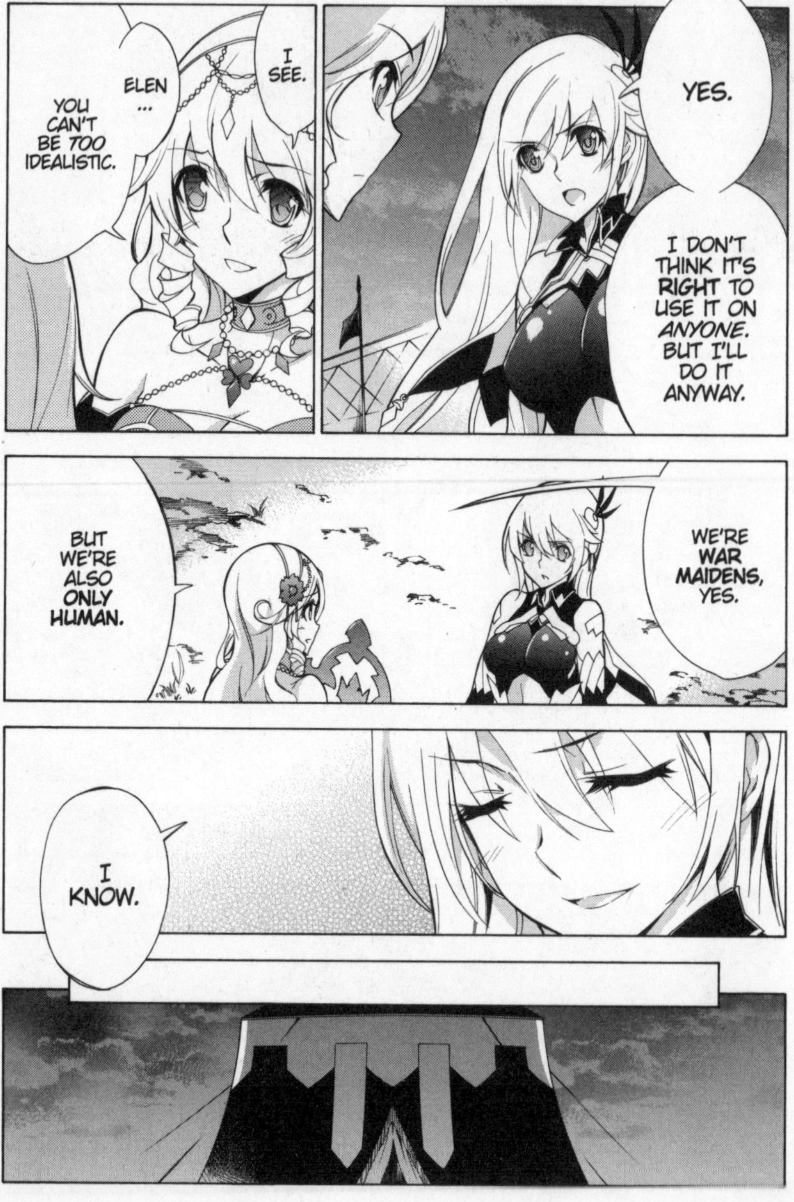
YES.
I DON'T THINK IT'S RIGHT TO USE IT ON *ANYONE*. BUT I'LL DO IT ANYWAY.
I SEE.
ELEN ...
YOU CAN'T BE *TOO* IDEALISTIC.
WE'RE WAR MAIDENS, YES.
BUT WE'RE ALSO ONLY HUMAN.
I KNOW.

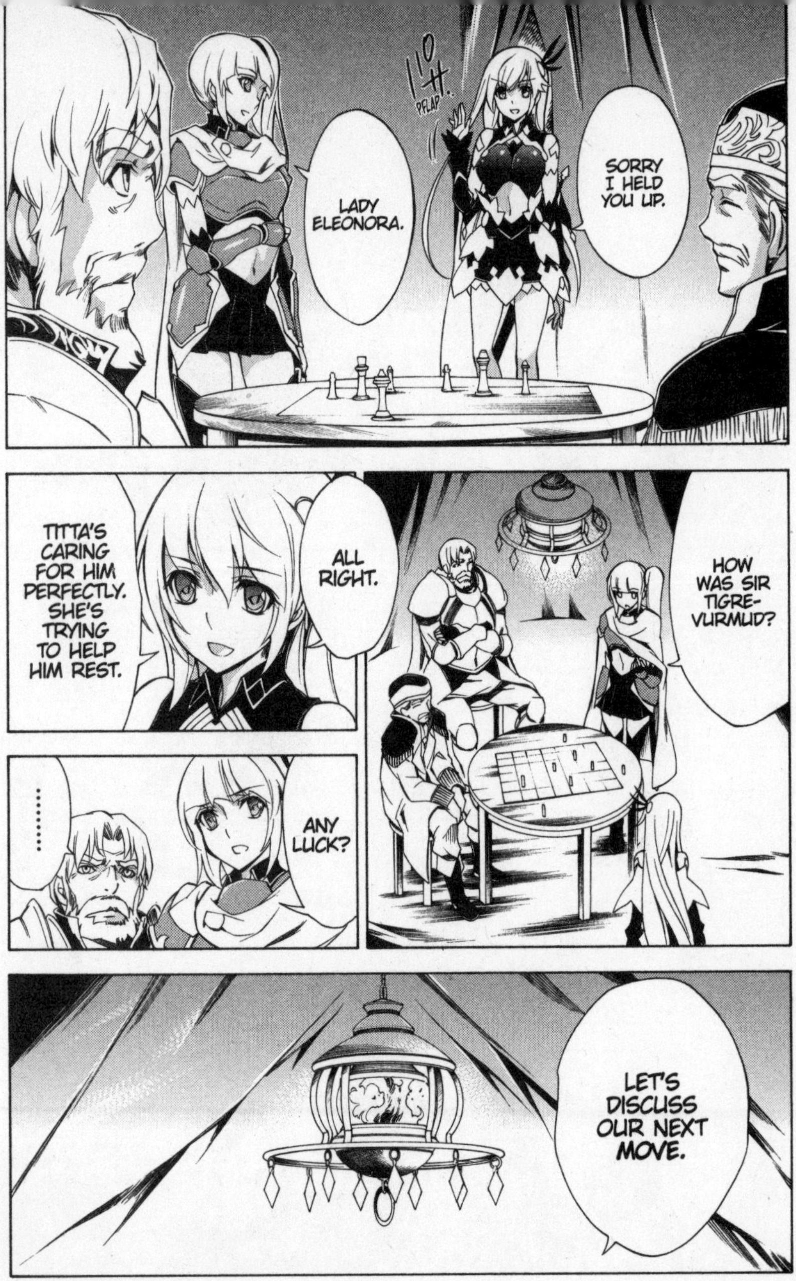
PFLAP
SORRY I HELD YOU UP.
LADY ELEONORA.
HOW WAS SIR TIGRE-VURMUD?
ALL RIGHT.
TITTA'S CARING FOR HIM PERFECTLY. SHE'S TRYING TO HELP HIM REST.
ANY LUCK?
......
LET'S DISCUSS OUR NEXT MOVE.

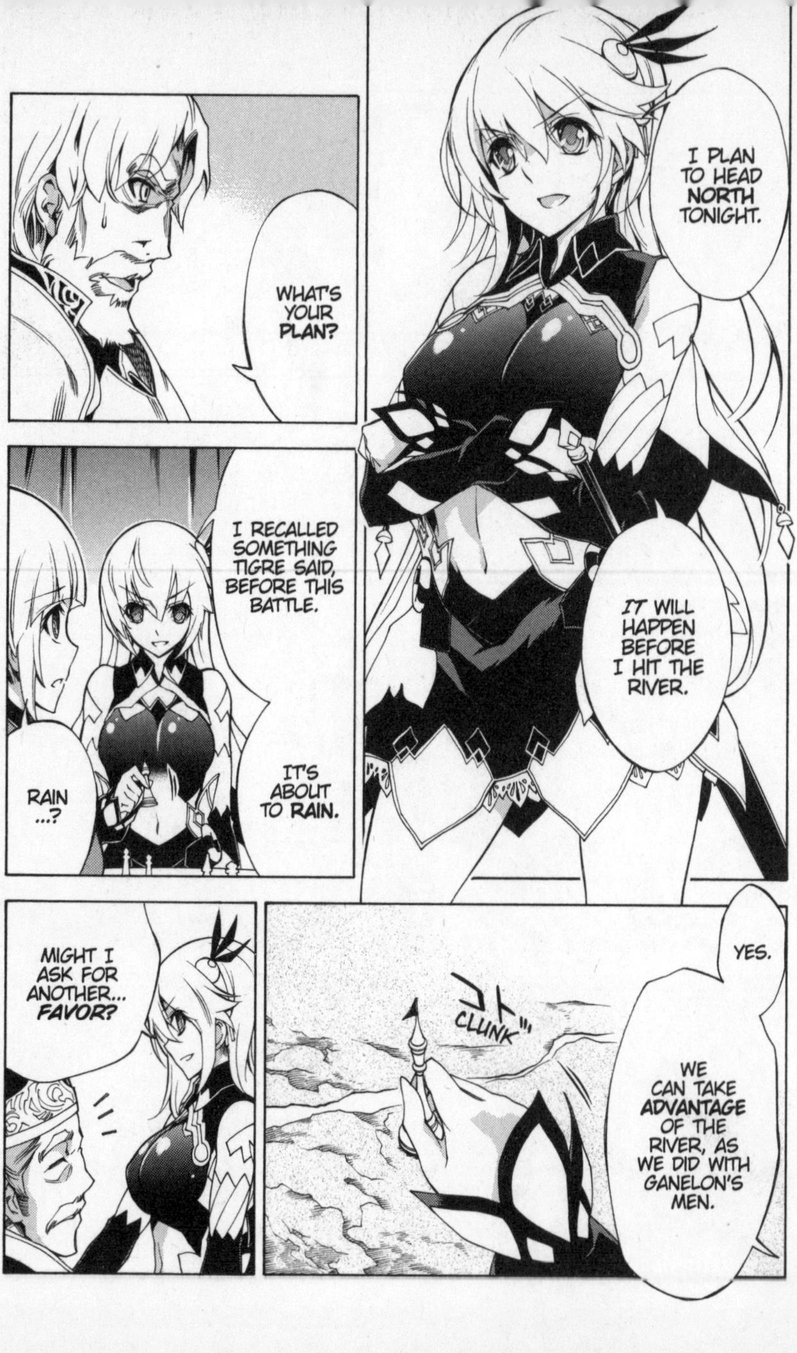
I PLAN TO HEAD NORTH TONIGHT.
WHAT'S YOUR PLAN?
IT WILL HAPPEN BEFORE I HIT THE RIVER.
I RECALLED SOMETHING TIGRE SAID, BEFORE THIS BATTLE.
IT'S ABOUT TO RAIN.
RAIN ...?
YES.
WE CAN TAKE ADVANTAGE OF THE RIVER, AS WE DID WITH GANELON'S MEN.
CLUNK
MIGHT I ASK FOR ANOTHER... FAVOR?

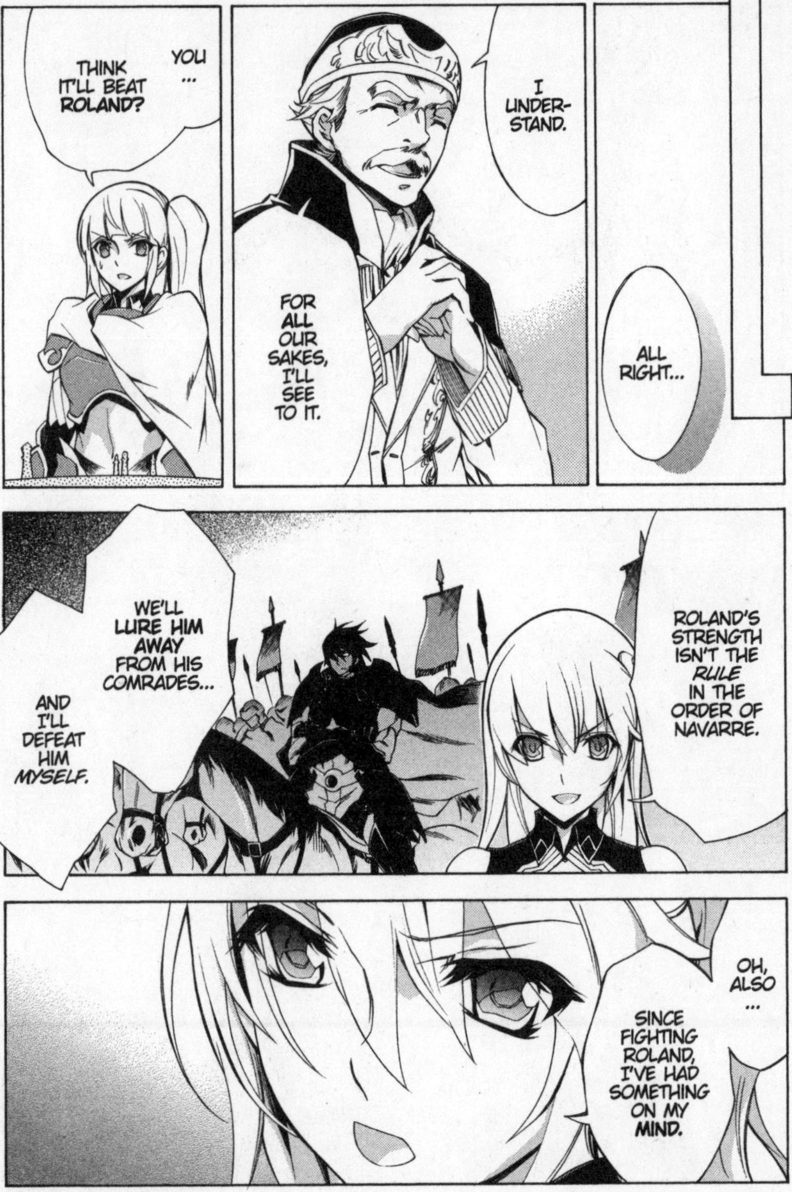
ALL RIGHT...
I UNDER-STAND.
FOR ALL OUR SAKES, I'LL SEE TO IT.
YOU ...
THINK IT'LL BEAT ROLAND?
ROLAND'S STRENGTH ISN'T THE *RULE* IN THE ORDER OF NAVARRE.
WE'LL LURE HIM AWAY FROM HIS COMRADES...
AND I'LL DEFEAT HIM *MYSELF*.
OH, ALSO ...
SINCE FIGHTING ROLAND, I'VE HAD SOMETHING ON MY MIND.

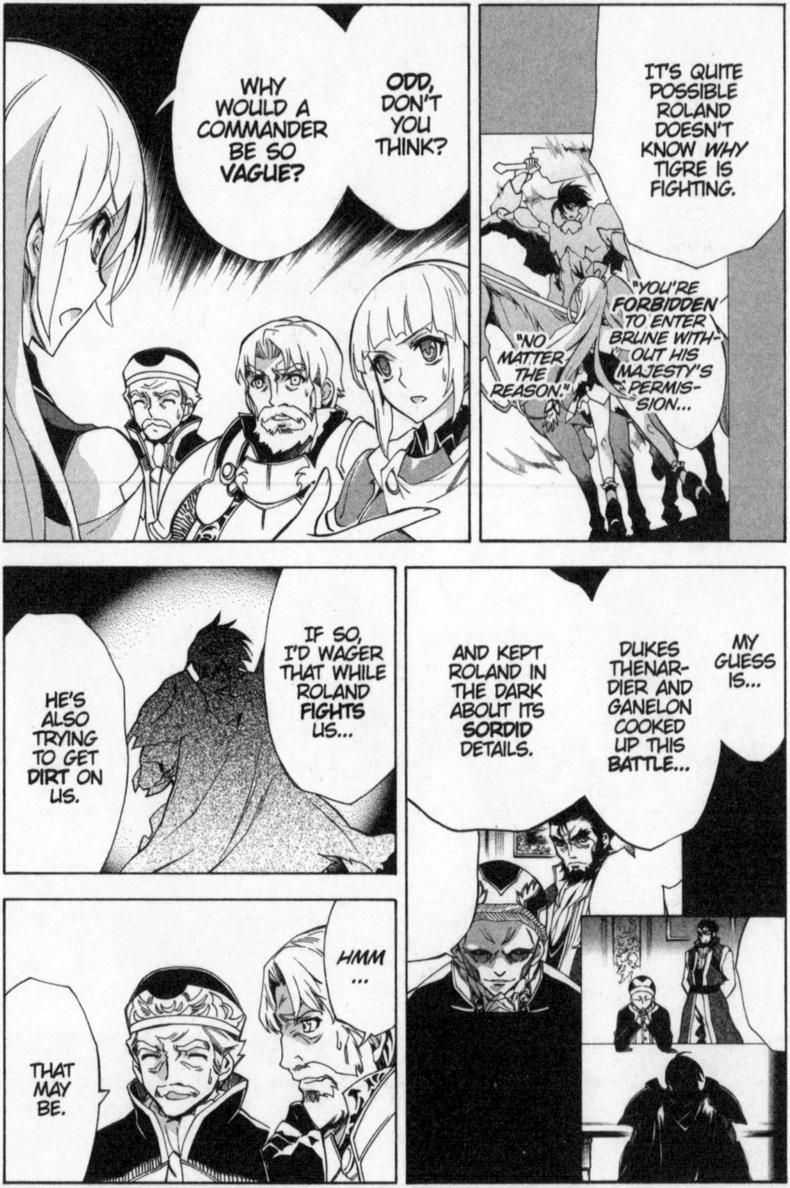
IT'S QUITE POSSIBLE ROLAND DOESN'T KNOW WHY TIGRE IS FIGHTING.
"YOU'RE FORBIDDEN TO ENTER BRUNE WITHOUT HIS MAJESTY'S PERMISSION...
"NO MATTER THE REASON."
ODD, DON'T YOU THINK?
WHY WOULD A COMMANDER BE SO VAGUE?
MY GUESS IS...
DUKES THENARDIER AND GANELON COOKED UP THIS BATTLE...
AND KEPT ROLAND IN THE DARK ABOUT ITS SORDID DETAILS.
IF SO, I'D WAGER THAT WHILE ROLAND FIGHTS US...
HE'S ALSO TRYING TO GET DIRT ON US.
HMM...
THAT MAY BE.

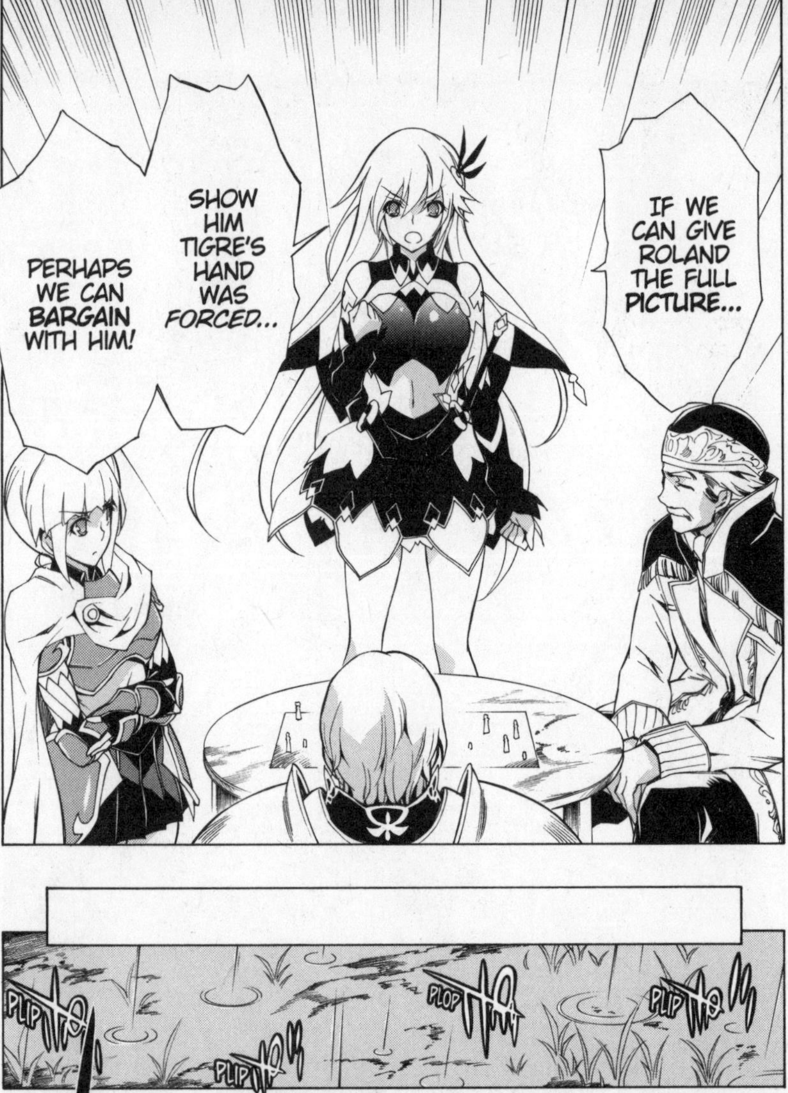
IF WE CAN GIVE ROLAND THE FULL PICTURE...
SHOW HIM TIGRE'S HAND WAS FORCED...
PERHAPS WE CAN BARGAIN WITH HIM!

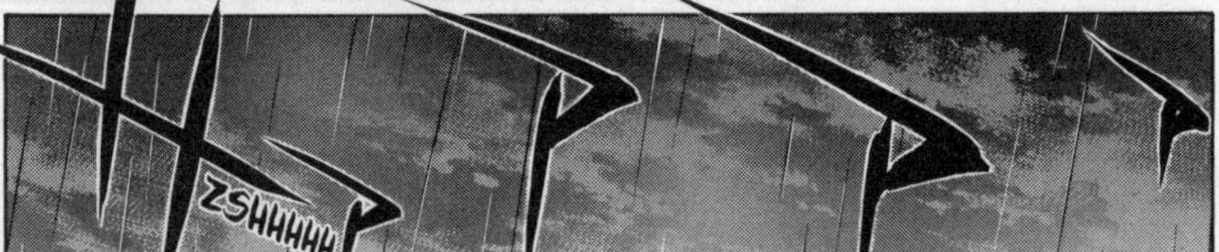
PLIP
PLOP
PLIP
PLIP

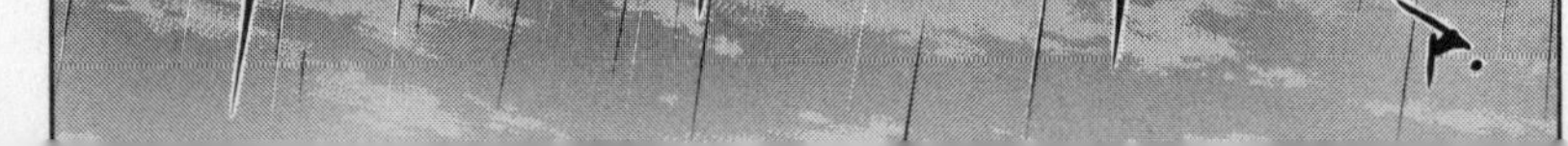
ZSHHHHH

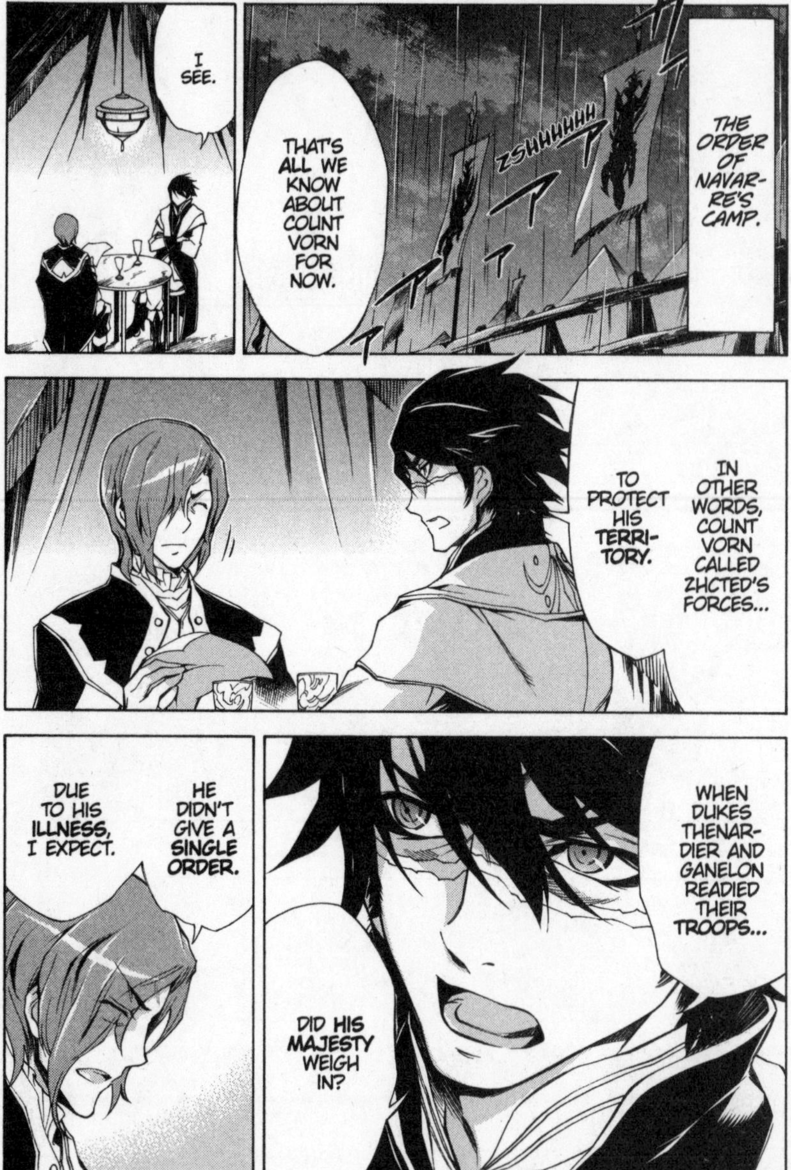

THE ORDER OF NAVARRE'S CAMP.
ZSHHHHHH
THAT'S ALL WE KNOW ABOUT COUNT VORN FOR NOW.
I SEE.
IN OTHER WORDS, COUNT VORN CALLED ZHCTED'S FORCES...
TO PROTECT HIS TERRITORY.
WHEN DUKES THENARDIER AND GANELON READIED THEIR TROOPS...
DID HIS MAJESTY WEIGH IN?
HE DIDN'T GIVE A SINGLE ORDER.
DUE TO HIS ILLNESS, I EXPECT.

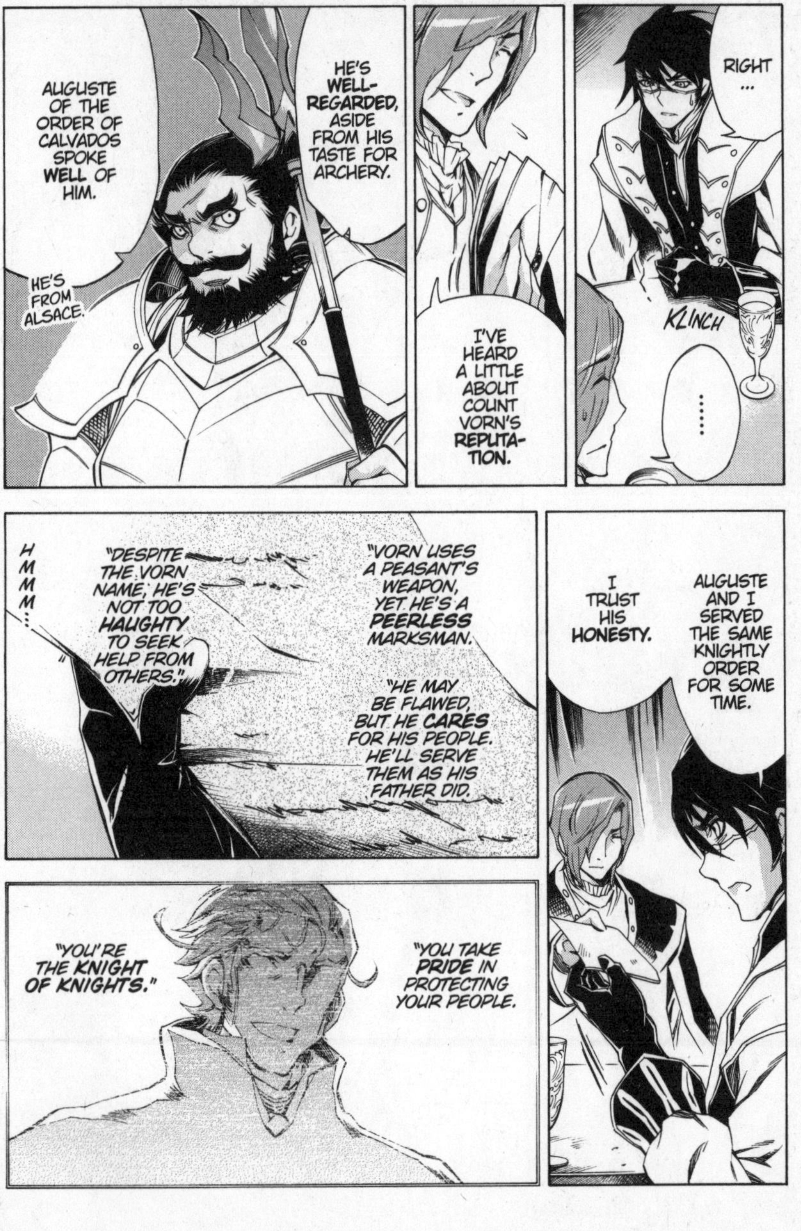
RIGHT ...
KLINCH
......
I'VE HEARD A LITTLE ABOUT COUNT VORN'S REPUTATION.
HE'S WELL-REGARDED, ASIDE FROM HIS TASTE FOR ARCHERY.
AUGUSTE OF THE ORDER OF CALVADOS SPOKE WELL OF HIM.
HE'S FROM ALSACE.
AUGUSTE AND I SERVED THE SAME KNIGHTLY ORDER FOR SOME TIME.
I TRUST HIS HONESTY.
"VORN USES A PEASANT'S WEAPON, YET HE'S A PEERLESS MARKSMAN.
"HE MAY BE FLAWED, BUT HE CARES FOR HIS PEOPLE. HE'LL SERVE THEM AS HIS FATHER DID.
"DESPITE THE VORN NAME, HE'S NOT TOO HAUGHTY TO SEEK HELP FROM OTHERS."
HMMM...
"YOU TAKE PRIDE IN PROTECTING YOUR PEOPLE.
"YOU'RE THE KNIGHT OF KNIGHTS."

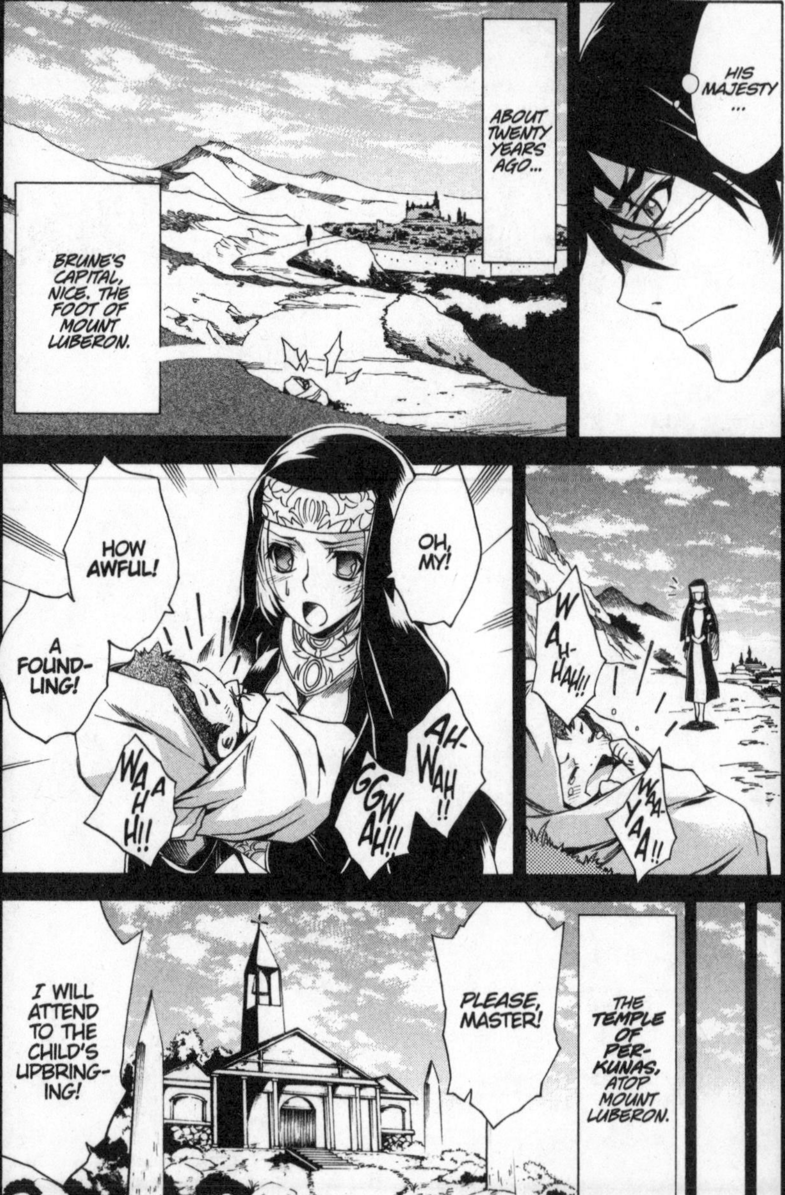

HIS MAJESTY ...
ABOUT TWENTY YEARS AGO...
BRUNE'S CAPITAL, NICE. THE FOOT OF MOUNT LUBERON.
WAH-HAH!!
WAA-YAA!!
OH, MY!
HOW AWFUL!
A FOUNDLING!
AH-WAH!!
GGWAH!!
WAAHH!!
THE TEMPLE OF PERKUNAS, ATOP MOUNT LUBERON.
PLEASE, MASTER!
I WILL ATTEND TO THE CHILD'S UPBRINGING!

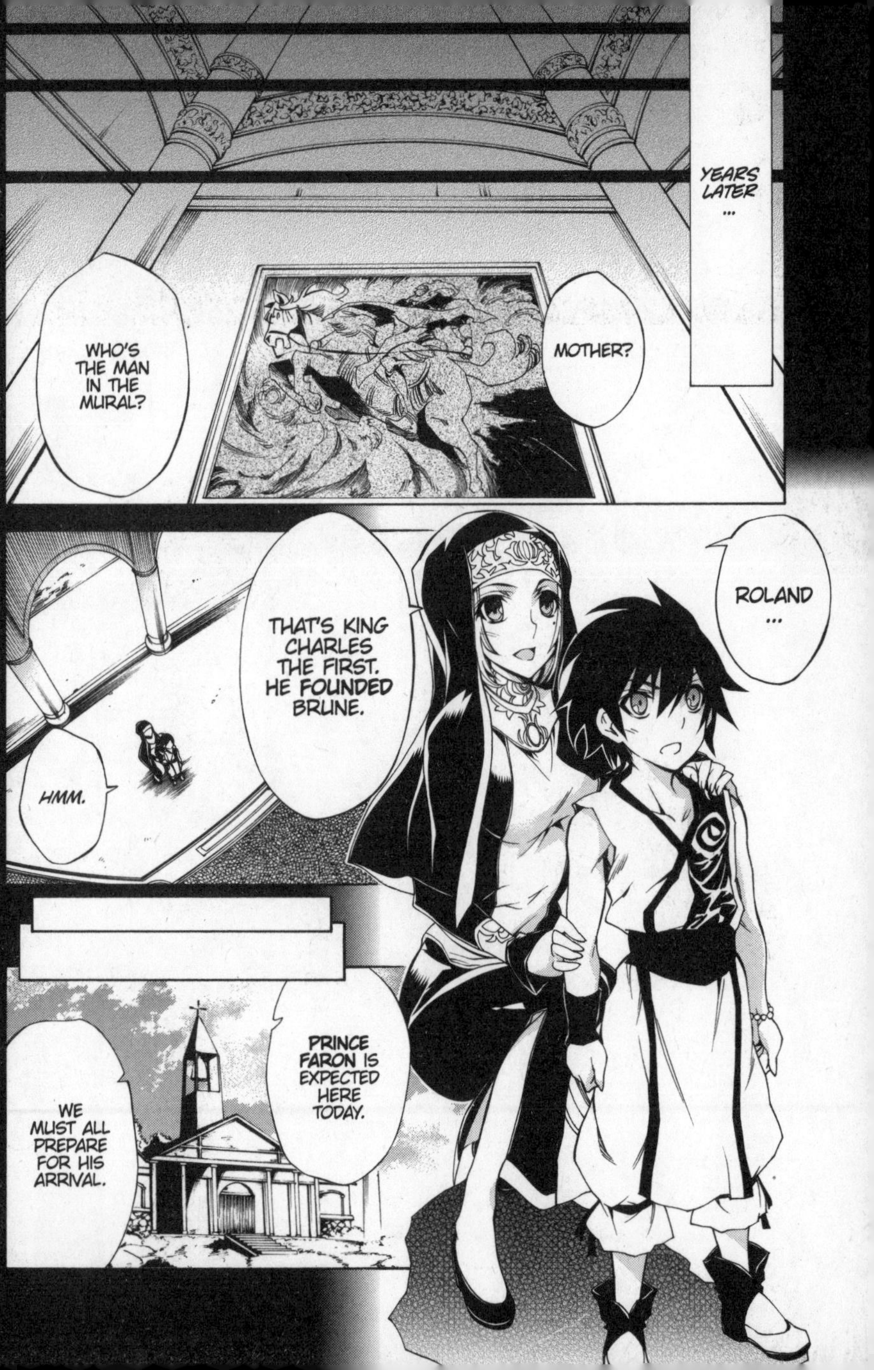
YEARS LATER ...
MOTHER?
WHO'S THE MAN IN THE MURAL?
ROLAND ...
THAT'S KING CHARLES THE FIRST. HE FOUNDED BRUNE.
HMM.
PRINCE FARON IS EXPECTED HERE TODAY.
WE MUST ALL PREPARE FOR HIS ARRIVAL.

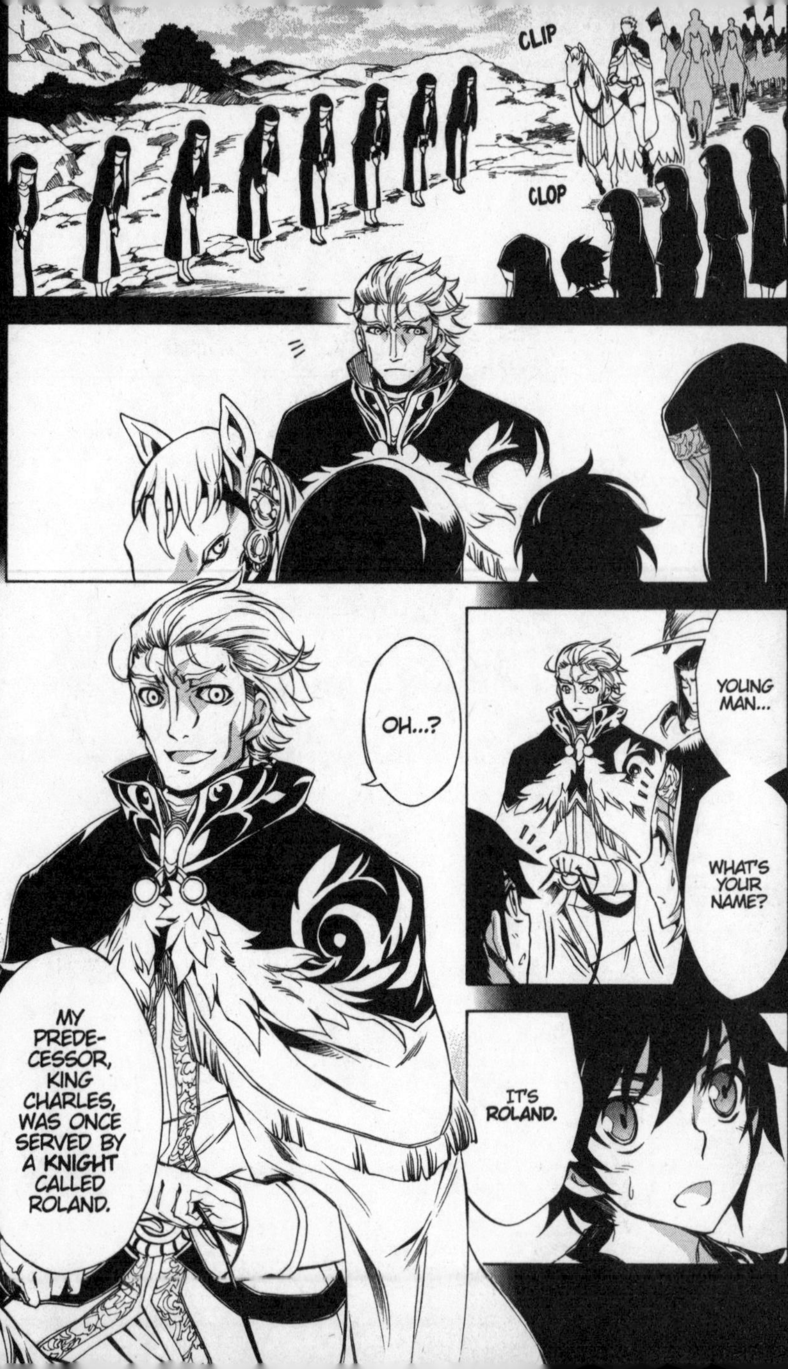
CLIP
CLOP
YOUNG MAN...
WHAT'S YOUR NAME?
IT'S ROLAND.
OH...?
MY PREDE-CESSOR, KING CHARLES, WAS ONCE SERVED BY A KNIGHT CALLED ROLAND.

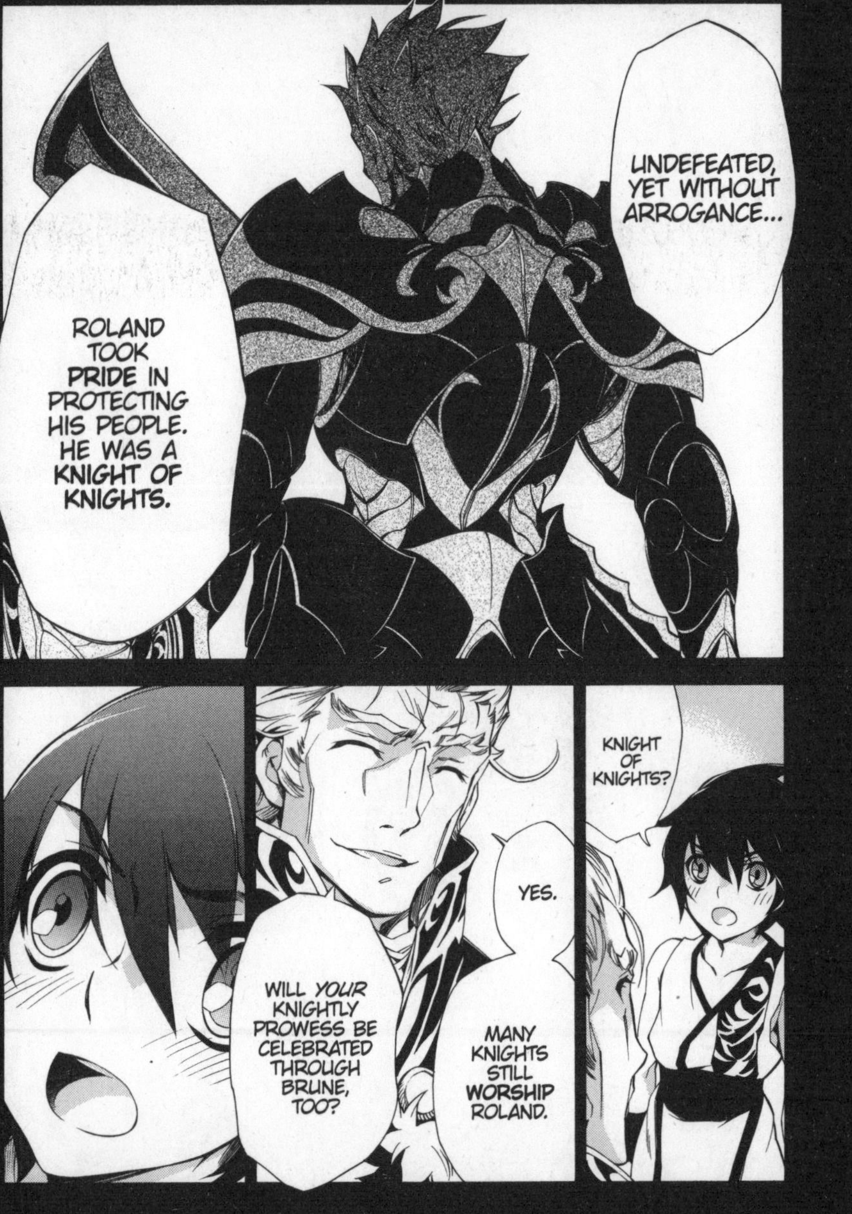
UNDEFEATED, YET WITHOUT ARROGANCE...
ROLAND TOOK PRIDE IN PROTECTING HIS PEOPLE. HE WAS A KNIGHT OF KNIGHTS.
KNIGHT OF KNIGHTS?
YES.
MANY KNIGHTS STILL WORSHIP ROLAND.
WILL *YOUR* KNIGHTLY PROWESS BE CELEBRATED THROUGH BRUNE, TOO?

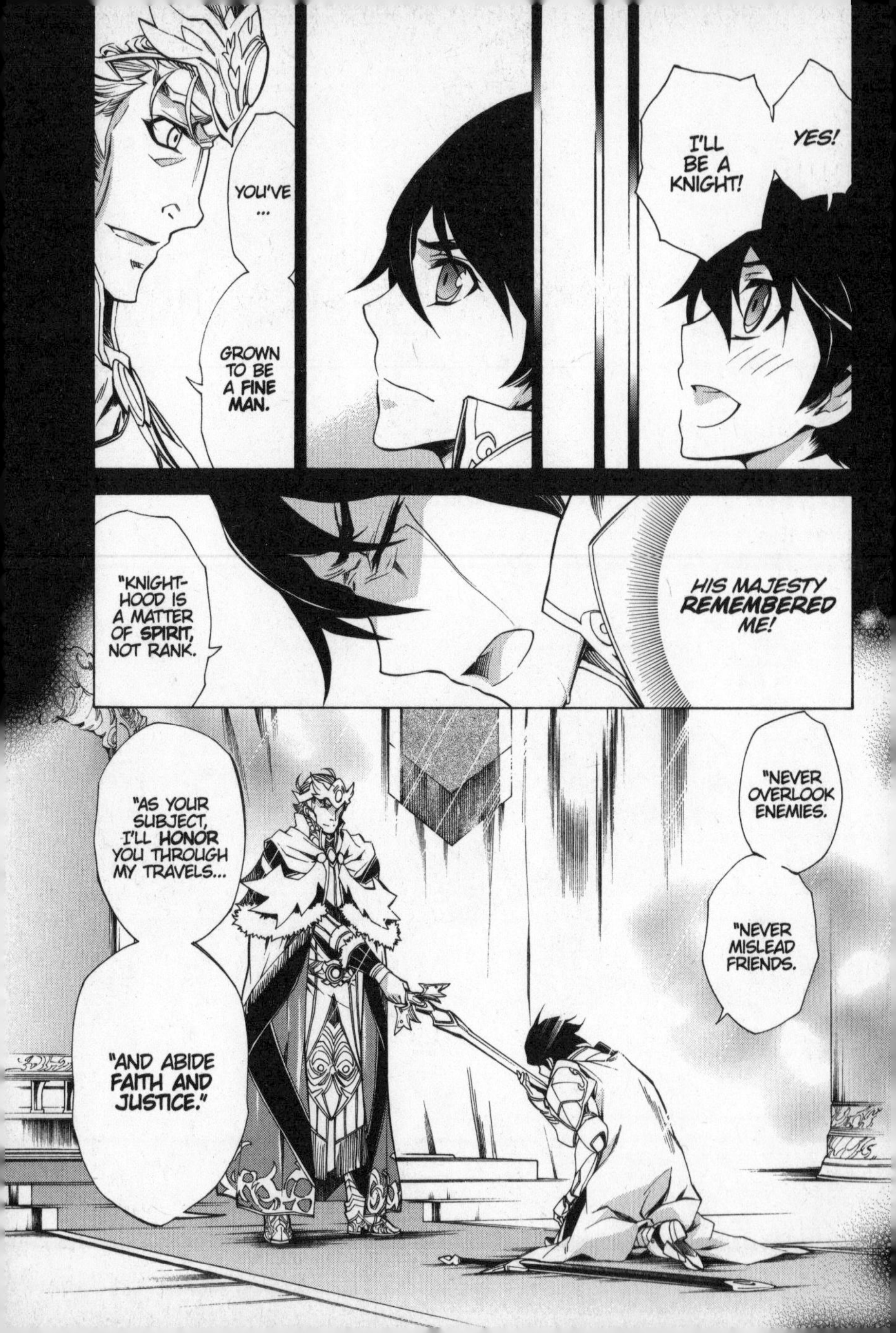
YES!
I'LL BE A KNIGHT!
YOU'VE ...
GROWN TO BE A FINE MAN.
HIS MAJESTY REMEMBERED ME!
"KNIGHTHOOD IS A MATTER OF SPIRIT, NOT RANK.
"NEVER OVERLOOK ENEMIES.
"NEVER MISLEAD FRIENDS.
"AS YOUR SUBJECT, I'LL HONOR YOU THROUGH MY TRAVELS...
"AND ABIDE FAITH AND JUSTICE."

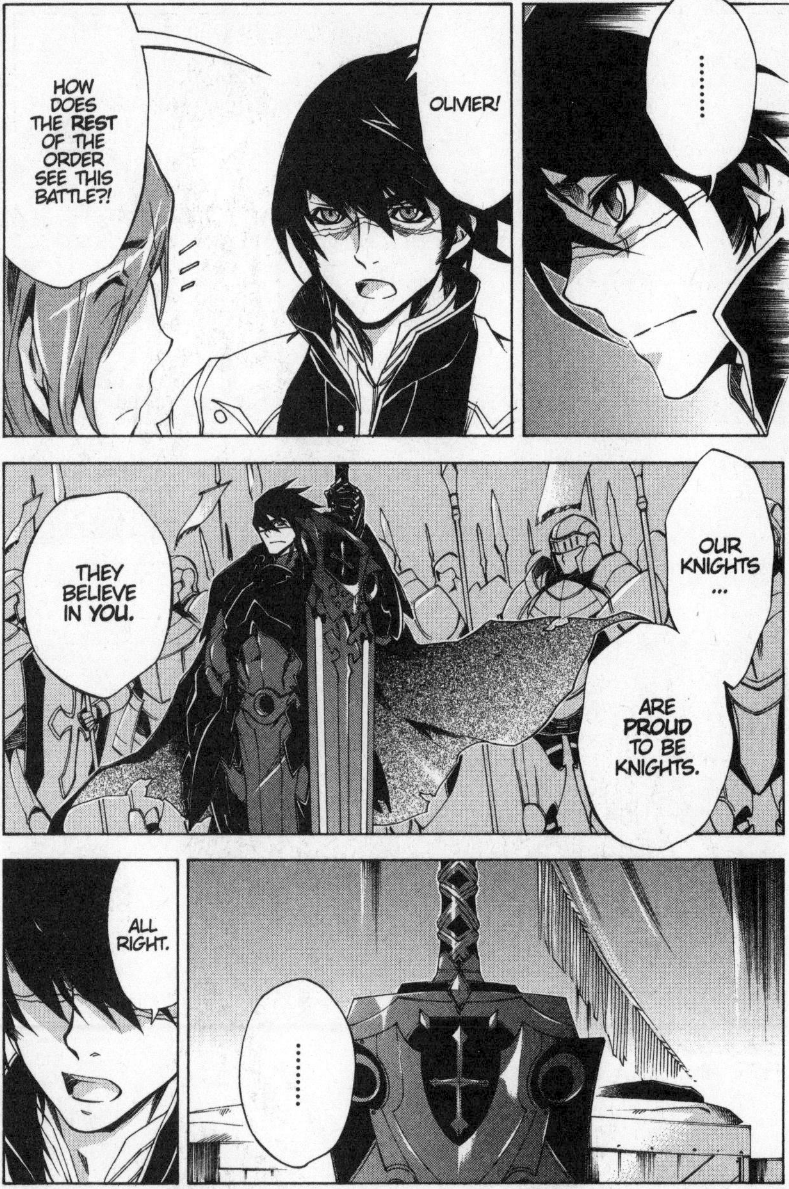
......
OLIVIER!
HOW DOES THE REST OF THE ORDER SEE THIS BATTLE?!
OUR KNIGHTS ...
ARE PROUD TO BE KNIGHTS.
THEY BELIEVE IN YOU.
......
ALL RIGHT.

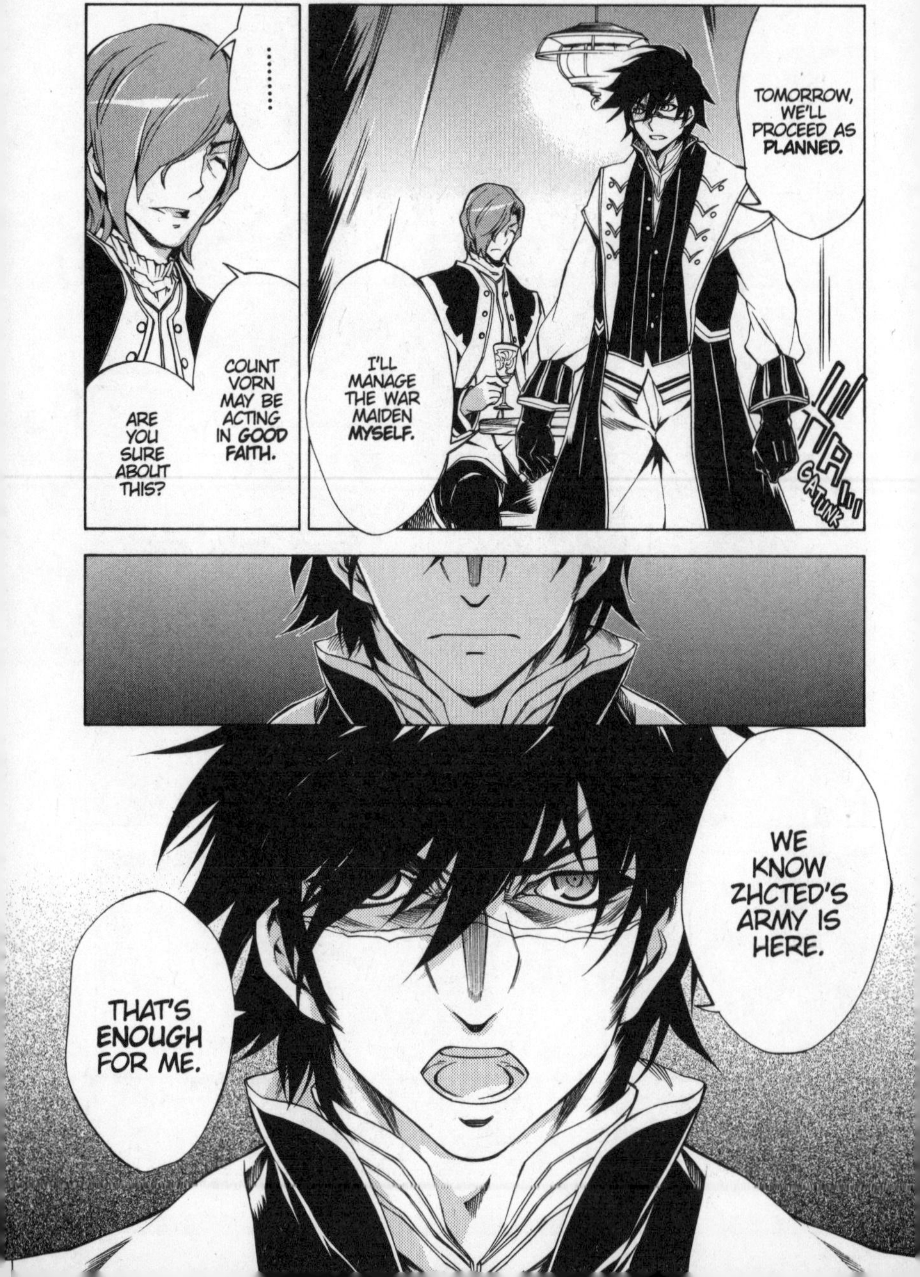
TOMORROW, WE'LL PROCEED AS PLANNED.
GATUNK
I'LL MANAGE THE WAR MAIDEN MYSELF.
......
COUNT VORN MAY BE ACTING IN GOOD FAITH.
ARE YOU SURE ABOUT THIS?
WE KNOW ZHCTED'S ARMY IS HERE.
THAT'S ENOUGH FOR ME.

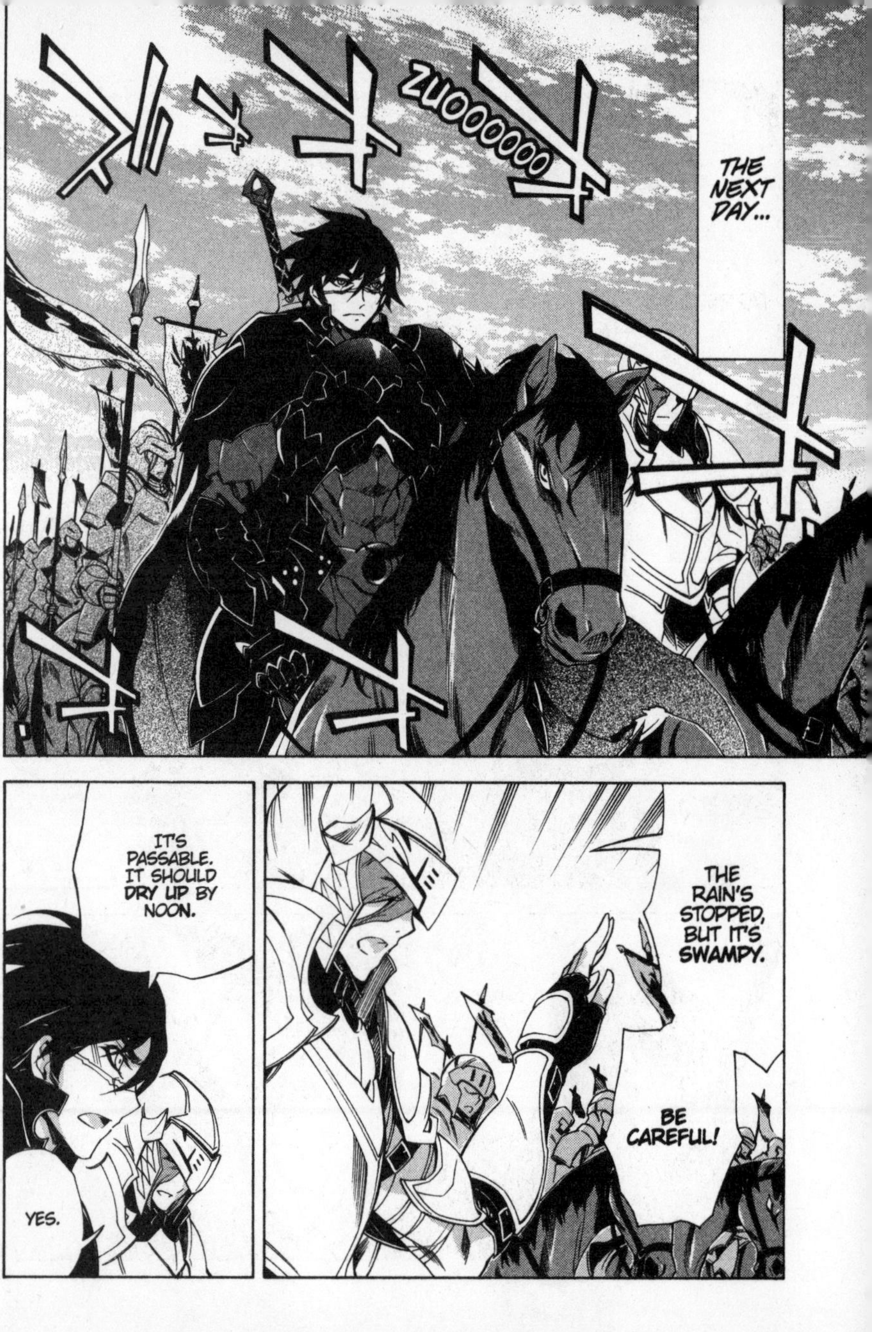
THE NEXT DAY...
ZUOOOOOO
THE RAIN'S STOPPED, BUT IT'S SWAMPY.
BE CAREFUL!
IT'S PASSABLE. IT SHOULD DRY UP BY NOON.
YES.

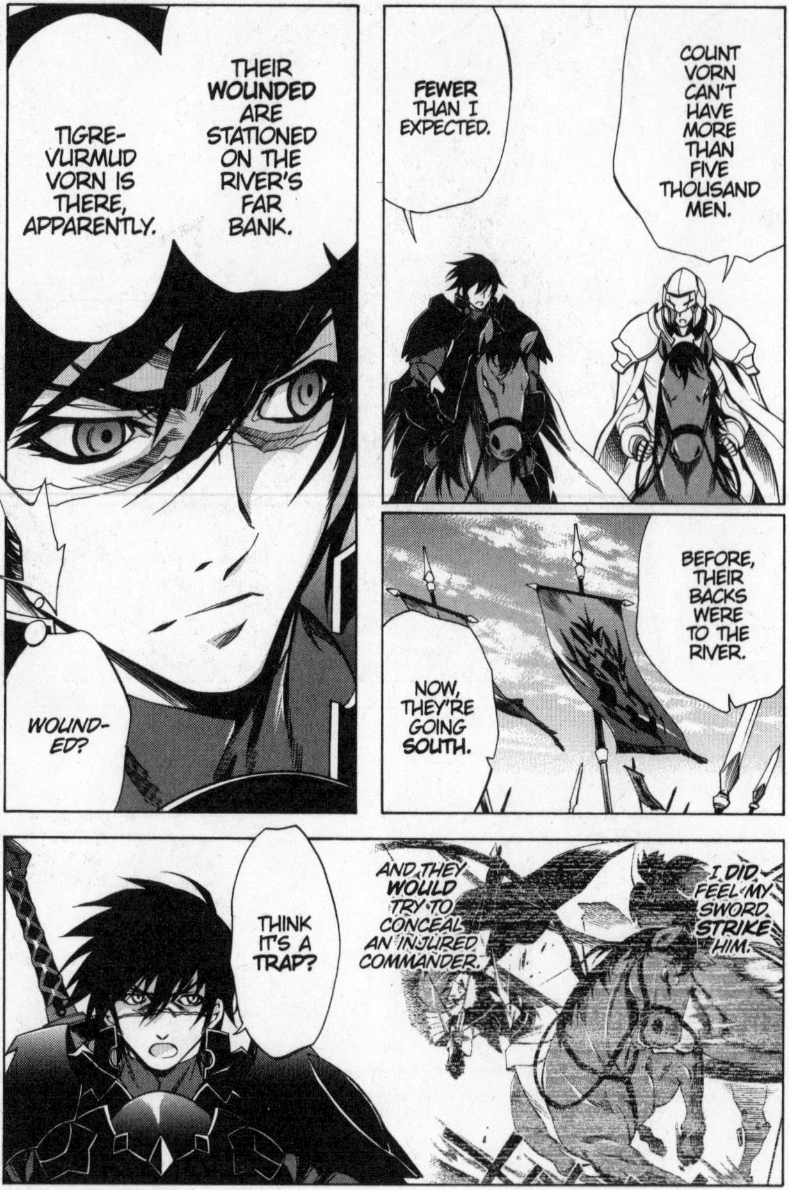
COUNT VORN CAN'T HAVE MORE THAN FIVE THOUSAND MEN.
FEWER THAN I EXPECTED.
BEFORE, THEIR BACKS WERE TO THE RIVER.
NOW, THEY'RE GOING SOUTH.
THEIR WOUNDED ARE STATIONED ON THE RIVER'S FAR BANK.
TIGRE-VURMUD VORN IS THERE, APPARENTLY.
WOUND-ED?
I DID FEEL MY SWORD STRIKE HIM.
AND THEY WOULD TRY TO CONCEAL AN INJURED COMMANDER.
THINK IT'S A TRAP?

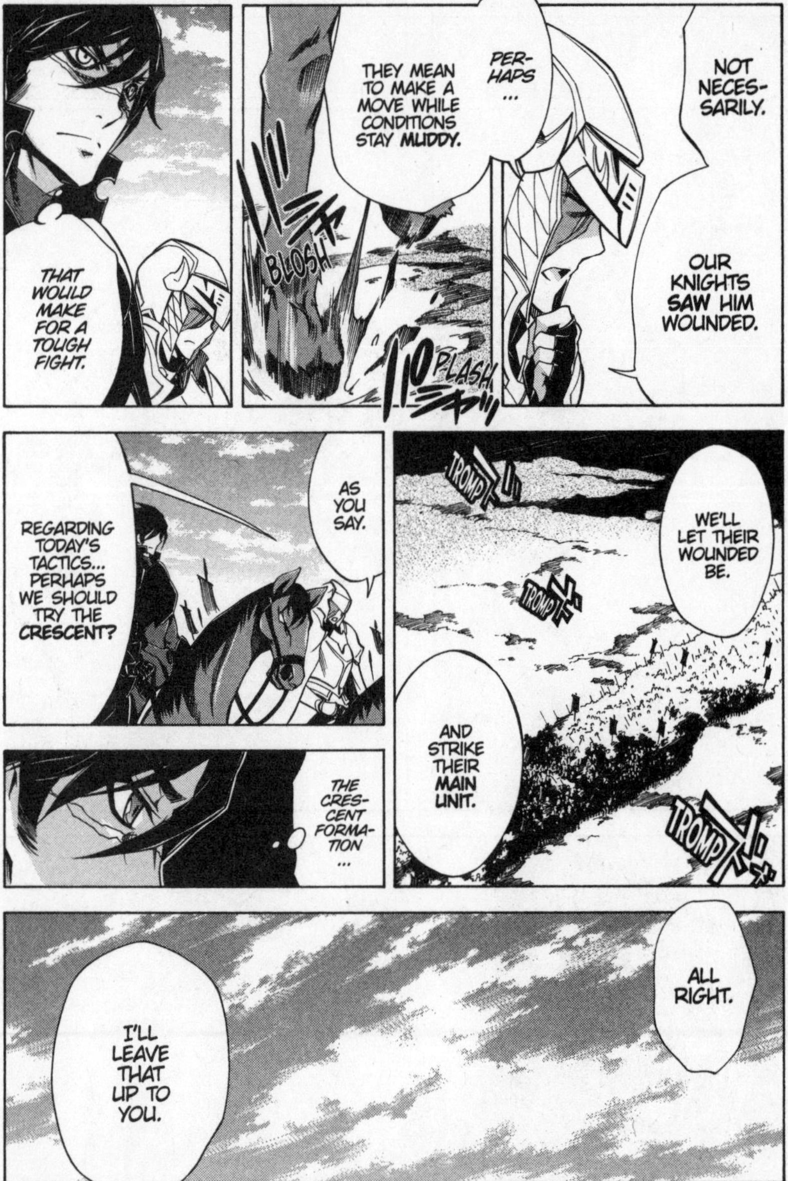
NOT NECES-SARILY.
OUR KNIGHTS SAW HIM WOUNDED.
PER-HAPS ...
THEY MEAN TO MAKE A MOVE WHILE CONDITIONS STAY MUDDY.
BLOSH
PLASH
THAT WOULD MAKE FOR A TOUGH FIGHT.
WE'LL LET THEIR WOUNDED BE.
TROMP
TROMP
AND STRIKE THEIR MAIN UNIT.
TROMP
AS YOU SAY.
REGARDING TODAY'S TACTICS... PERHAPS WE SHOULD TRY THE CRESCENT?
THE CRES-CENT FORMA-TION ...
ALL RIGHT.
I'LL LEAVE THAT UP TO YOU.

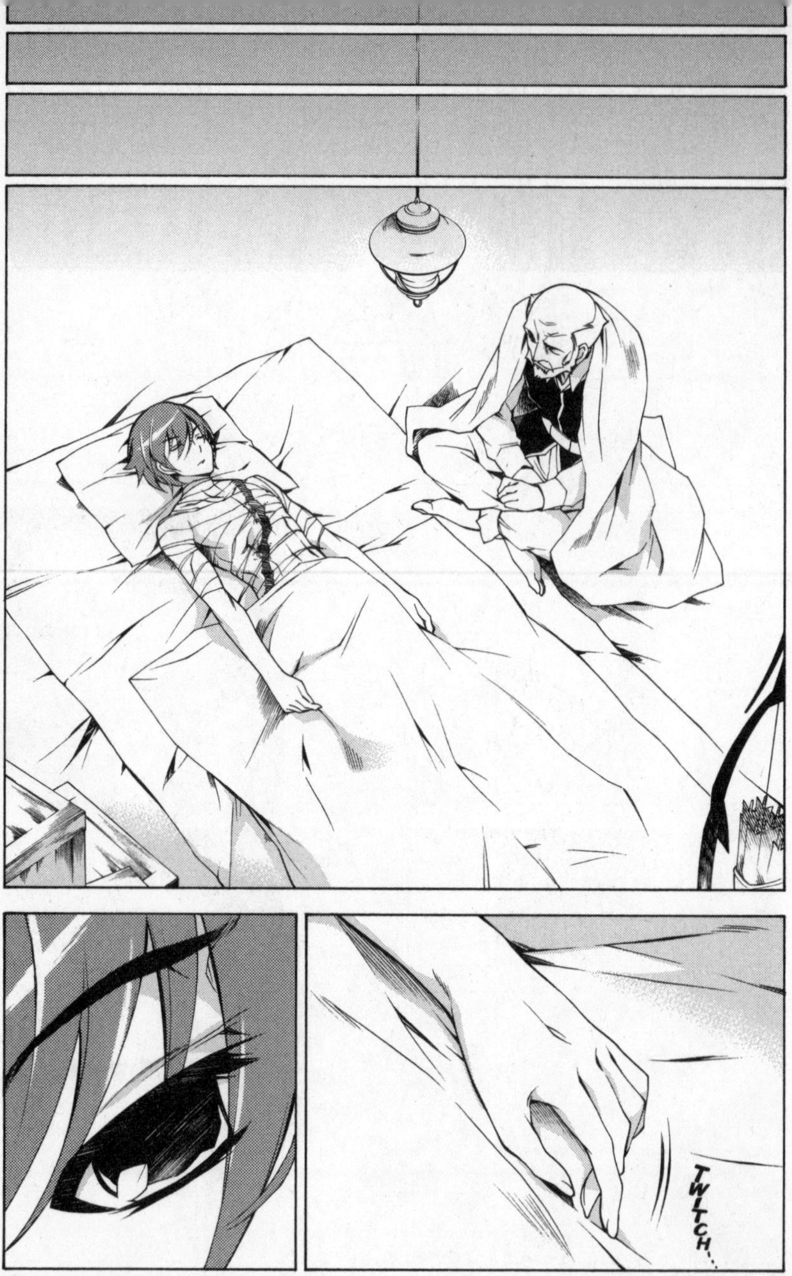
TWITCH...

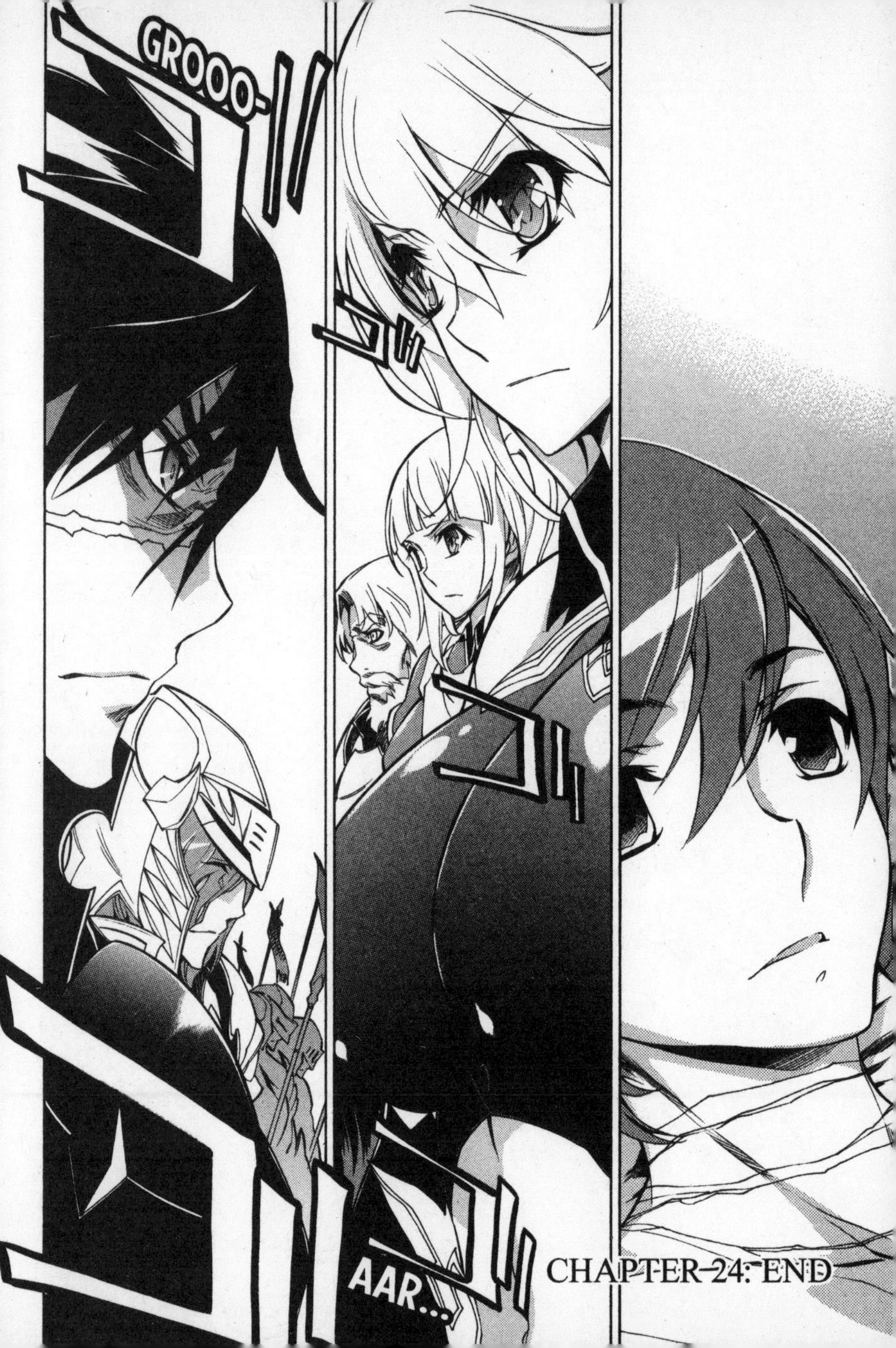
GROOO-
AAR...
CHAPTER 24: END

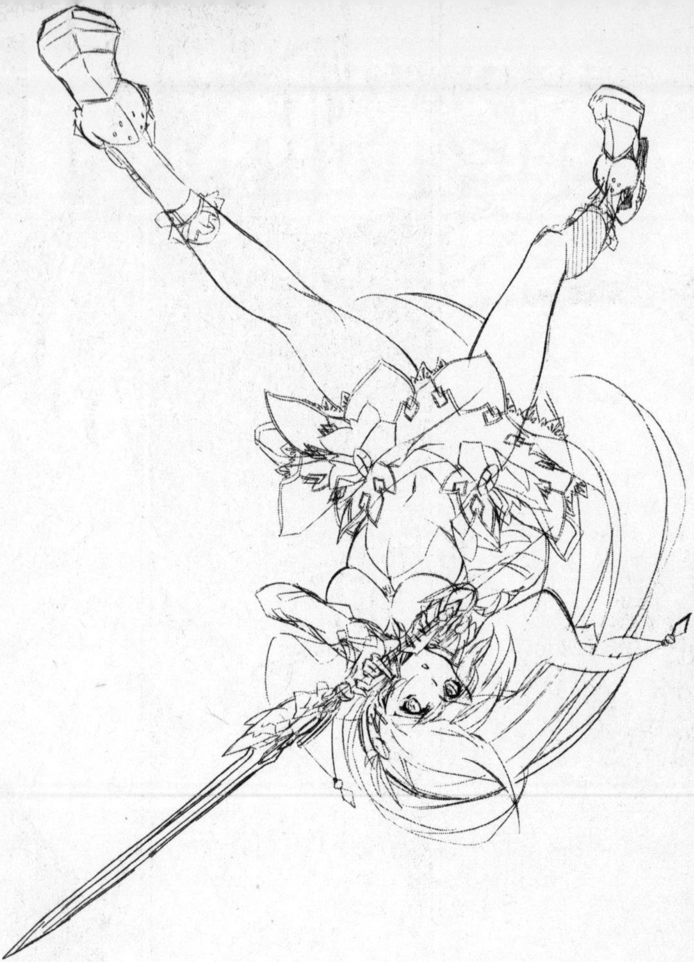

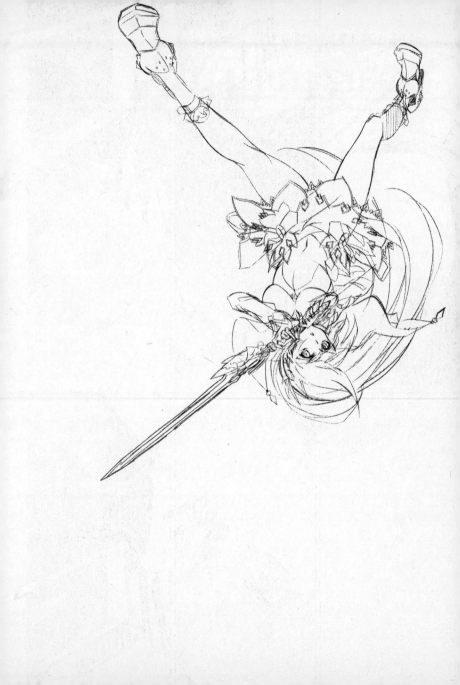

Lord Marksman and Vanadis

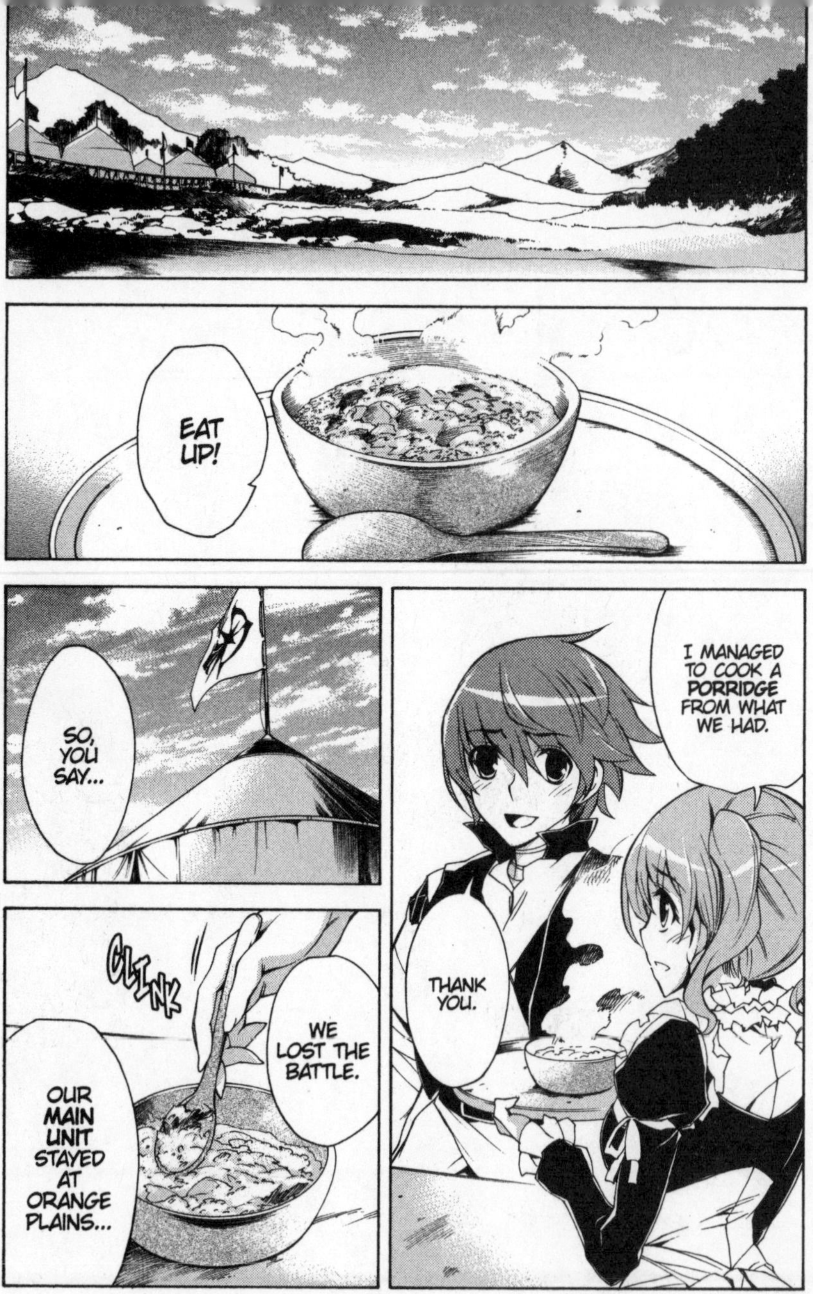
EAT UP!
I MANAGED TO COOK A PORRIDGE FROM WHAT WE HAD.
THANK YOU.
SO, YOU SAY...
CLINK
WE LOST THE BATTLE.
OUR MAIN UNIT STAYED AT ORANGE PLAINS...

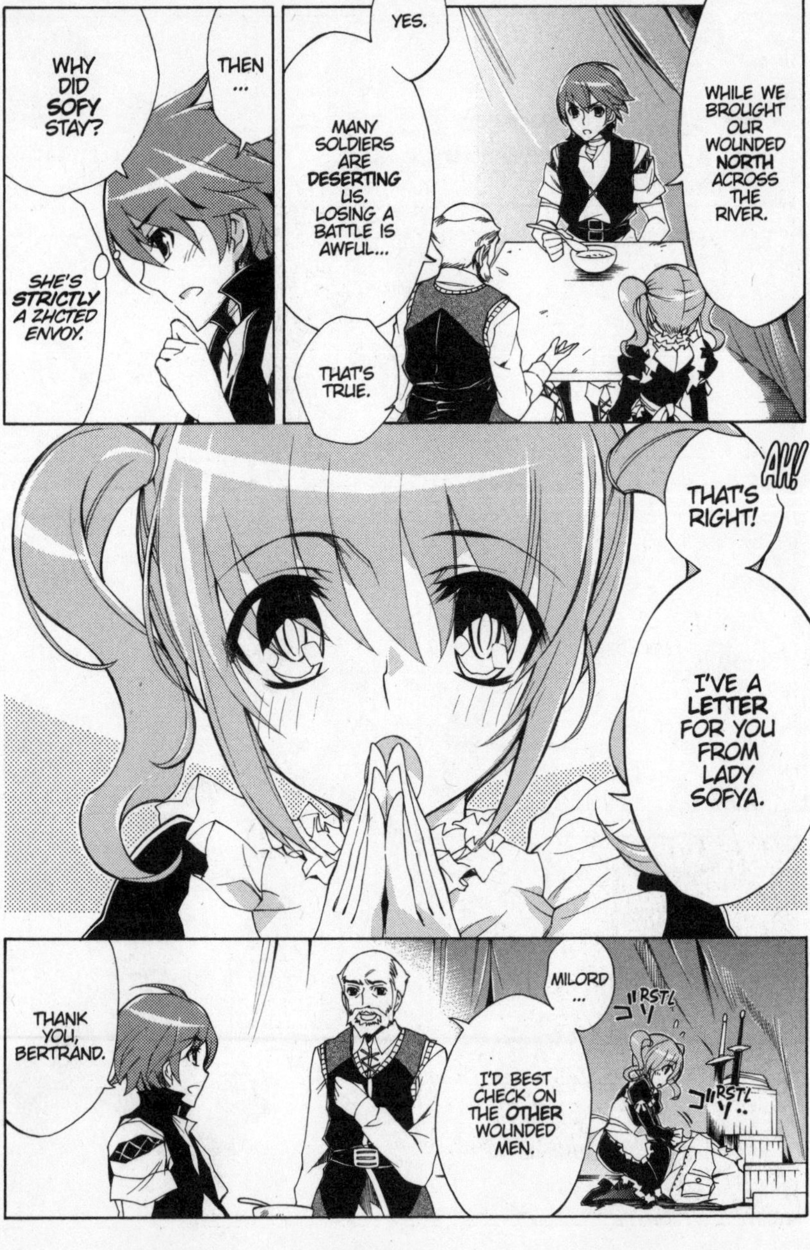

WHILE WE BROUGHT OUR WOUNDED NORTH ACROSS THE RIVER.
YES.
MANY SOLDIERS ARE DESERTING US. LOSING A BATTLE IS AWFUL...
THAT'S TRUE.
THEN ...
WHY DID SOFY STAY?
SHE'S STRICTLY A ZHCTED ENVOY.
AH!
THAT'S RIGHT!
I'VE A LETTER FOR YOU FROM LADY SOFYA.
RSTL
RSTL
MILORD ...
I'D BEST CHECK ON THE OTHER WOUNDED MEN.
THANK YOU, BERTRAND.

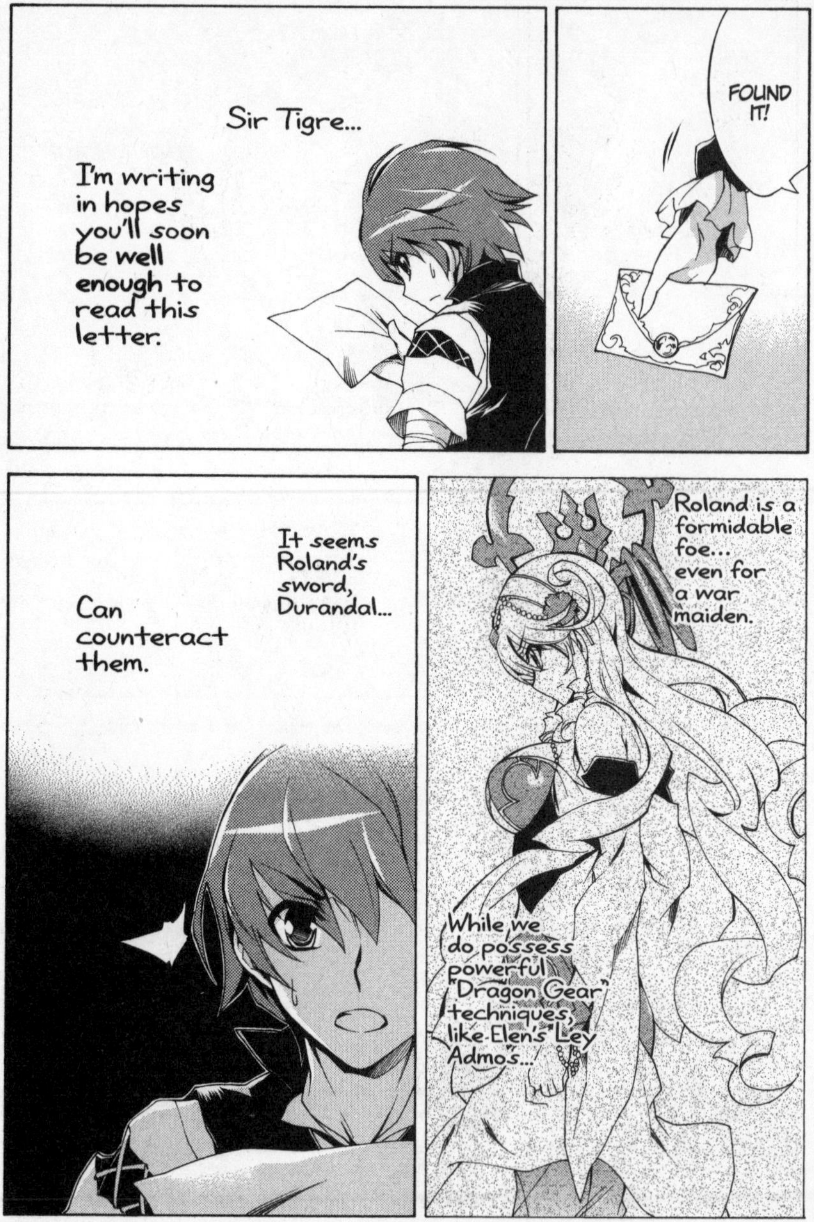
FOUND IT!
Sir Tigre...
I'm writing in hopes you'll soon be well enough to read this letter.
Roland is a formidable foe... even for a war maiden.
While we do possess powerful "Dragon Gear" techniques, like Elen's Ley Admos...
It seems Roland's sword, Durandal...
Can counteract them.

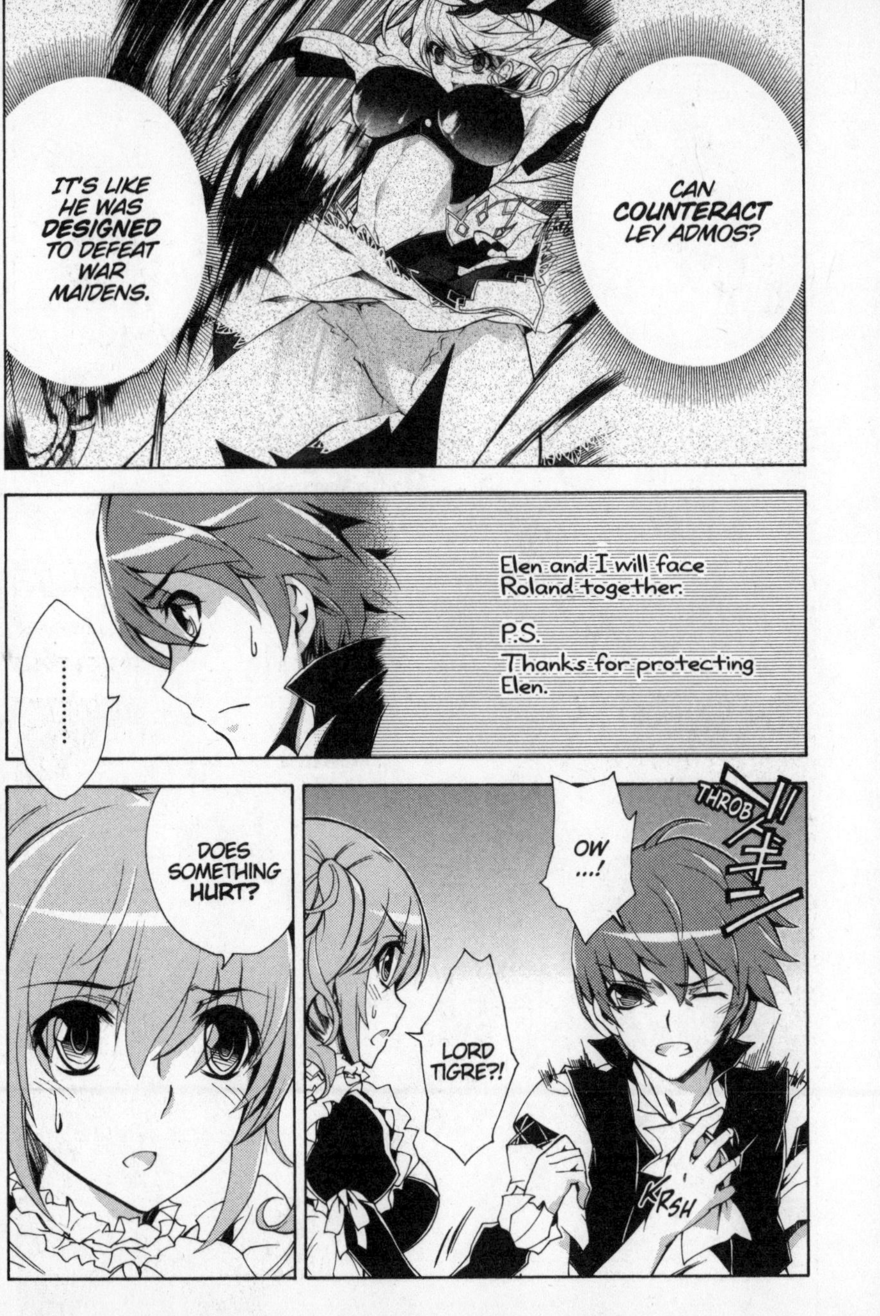
CAN COUNTERACT LEY ADMOS?
IT'S LIKE HE WAS DESIGNED TO DEFEAT WAR MAIDENS.
Elen and I will face Roland together.
P.S.
Thanks for protecting Elen.
......
THROB
OW ...!
LORD TIGRE?!
KRSH
DOES SOMETHING HURT?

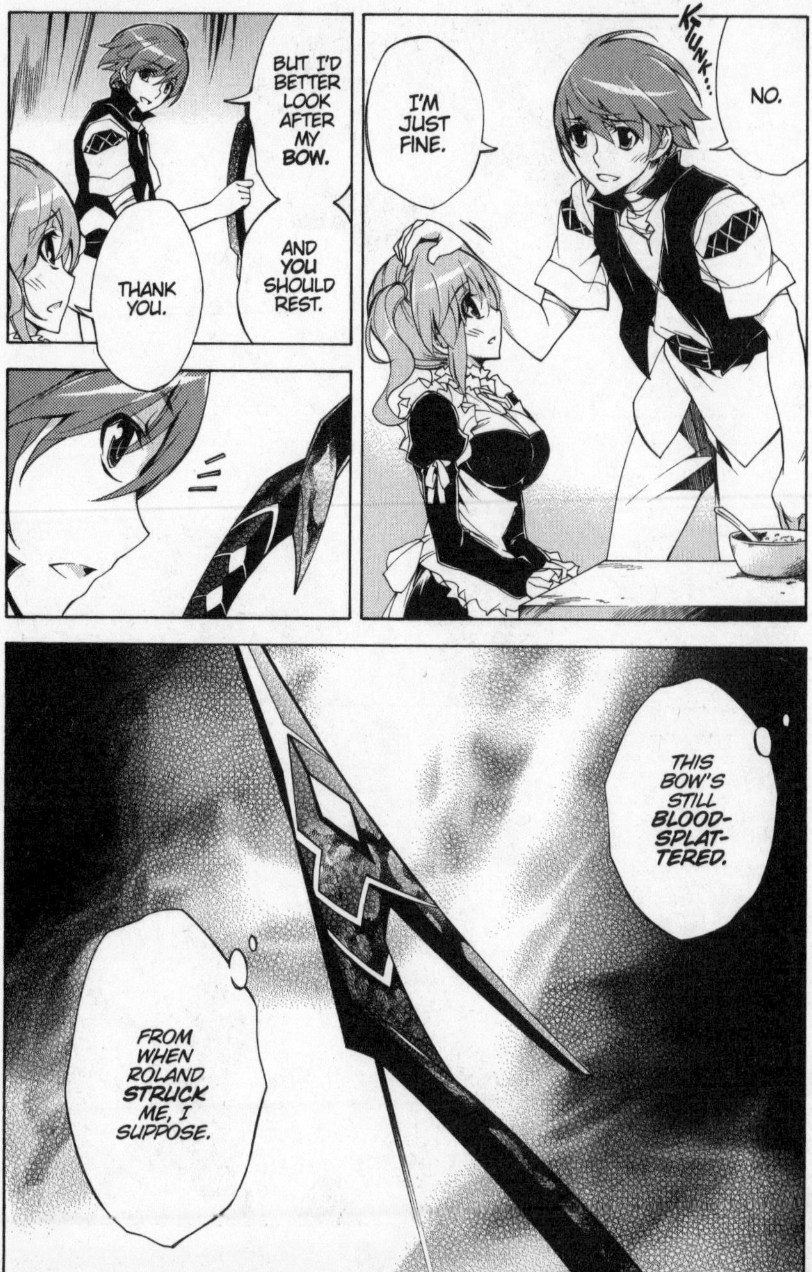
KTUNK...
NO.
I'M JUST FINE.
AND YOU SHOULD REST.
BUT I'D BETTER LOOK AFTER MY BOW.
THANK YOU.
THIS BOW'S STILL BLOOD-SPLAT-TERED.
FROM WHEN ROLAND STRUCK ME, I SUPPOSE.

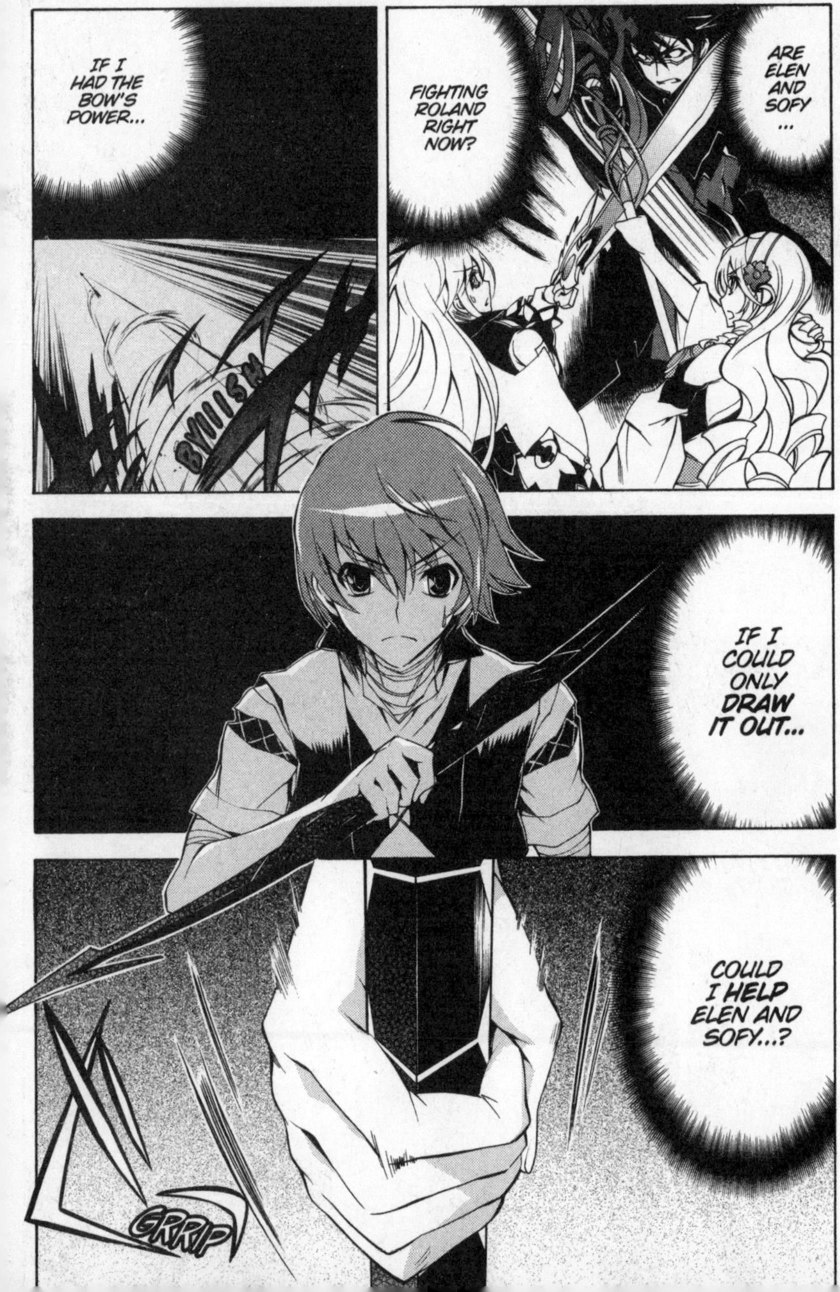
ARE ELEN AND SOFY ...
FIGHTING ROLAND RIGHT NOW?
IF I HAD THE BOW'S POWER...
BYIIISH
IF I COULD ONLY DRAW IT OUT...
COULD I HELP ELEN AND SOFY...?
GRRIP

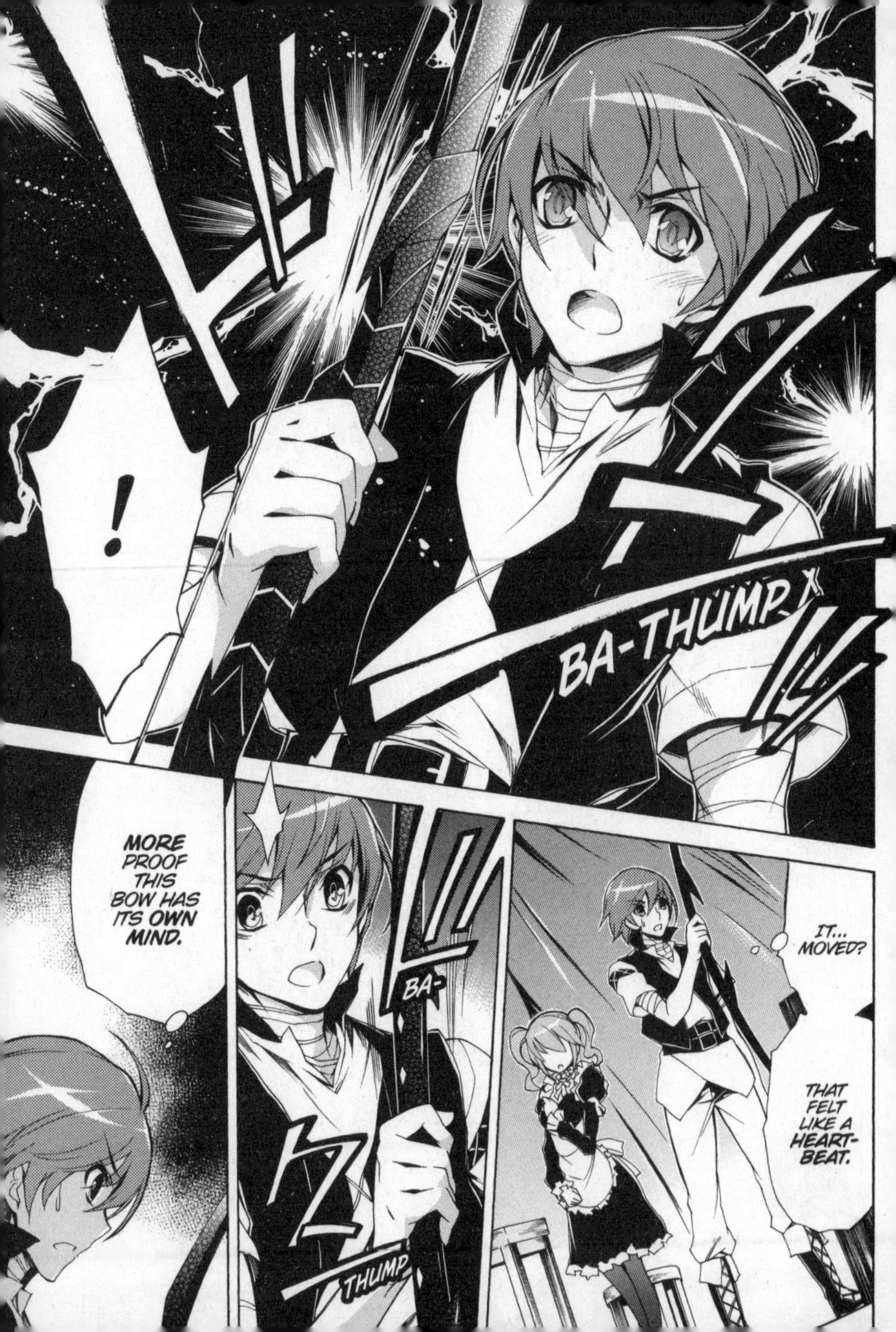
!
BA-THUMP
IT... MOVED?
THAT FELT LIKE A HEART-BEAT.
BA-
THUMP
MORE PROOF THIS BOW HAS ITS OWN MIND.

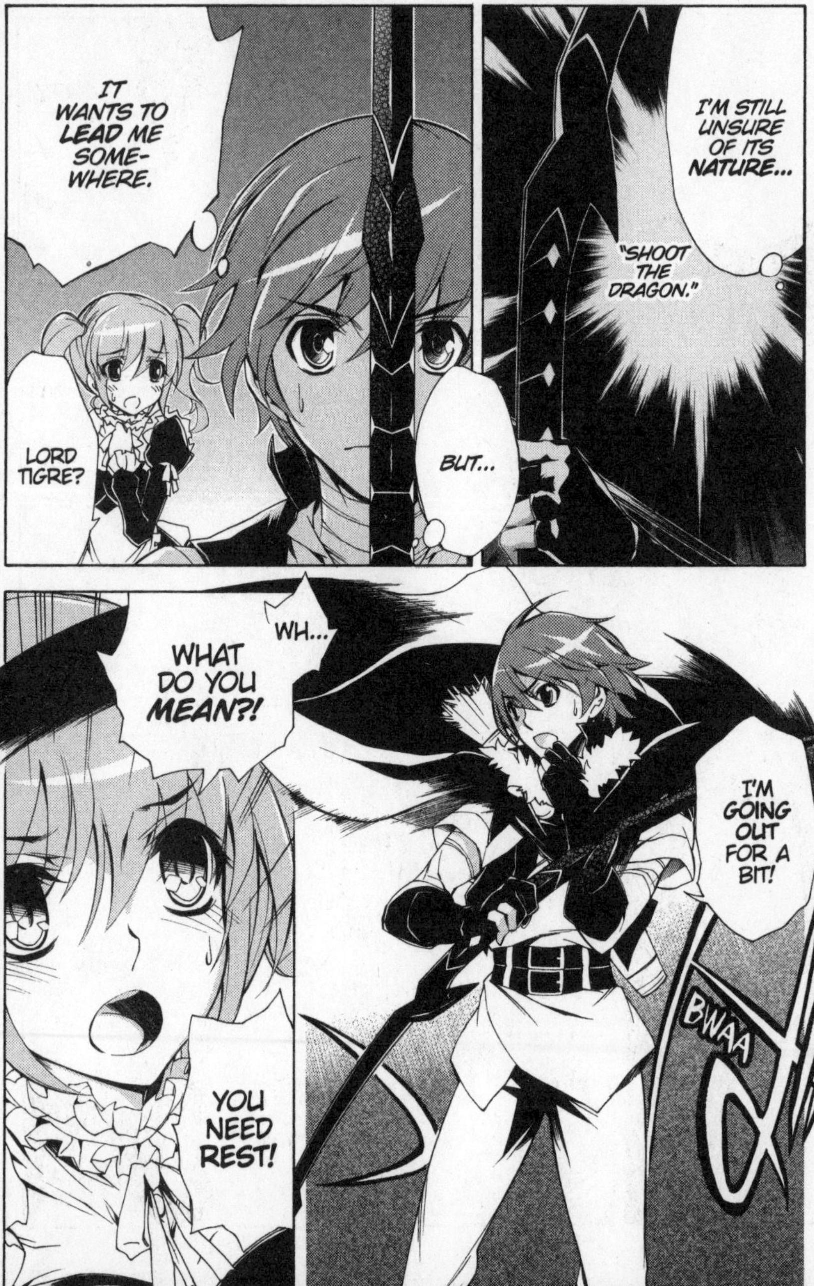
I'M STILL UNSURE OF ITS NATURE...
"SHOOT THE DRAGON."
BUT...
IT WANTS TO LEAD ME SOME-WHERE.
LORD TIGRE?
WH...
WHAT DO YOU MEAN?!
I'M GOING OUT FOR A BIT!
BWAA
YOU NEED REST!

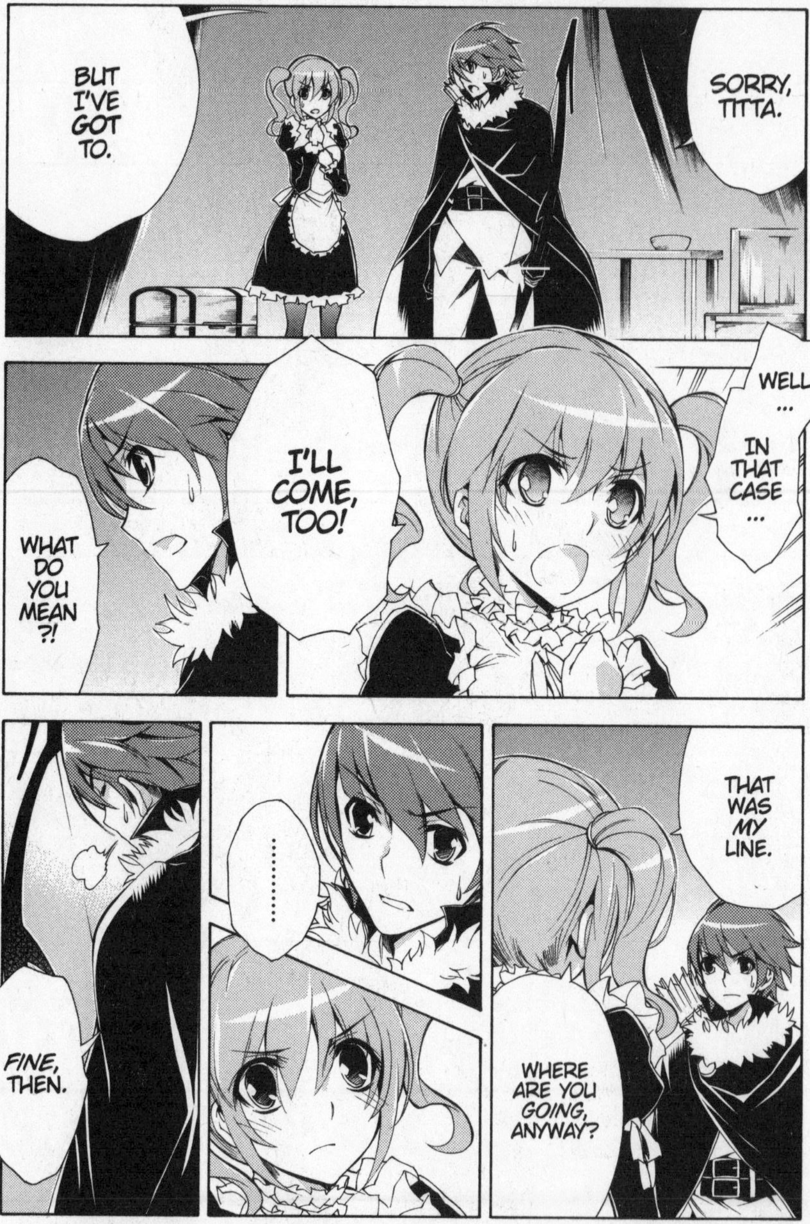
SORRY, TITTA.
BUT I'VE GOT TO.
WELL ... IN THAT CASE ...
I'LL COME, TOO!
WHAT DO YOU MEAN ?!
THAT WAS MY LINE.
WHERE ARE YOU GOING, ANYWAY?
......
FINE, THEN.

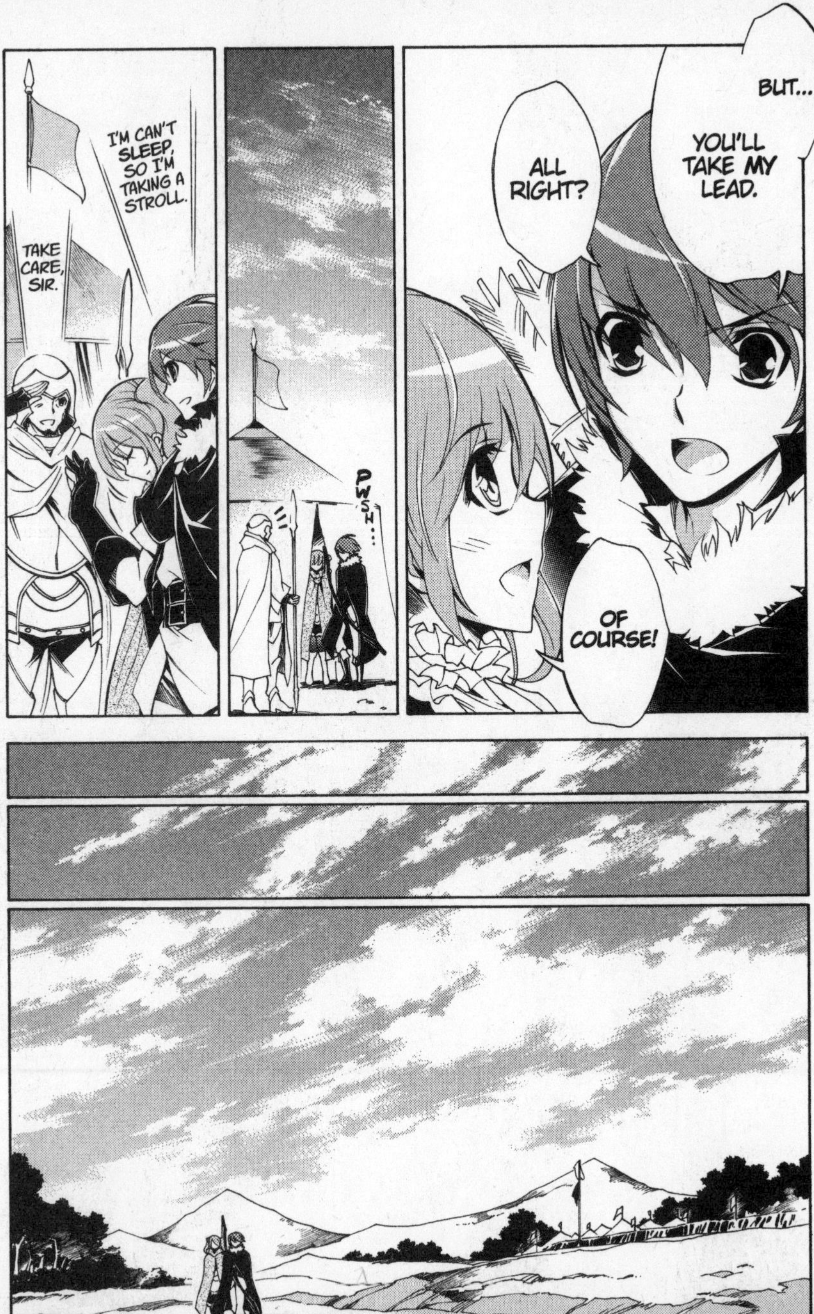
BUT...
YOU'LL TAKE MY LEAD.
ALL RIGHT?
OF COURSE!
PWSH...
I'M CAN'T SLEEP, SO I'M TAKING A STROLL.
TAKE CARE, SIR.

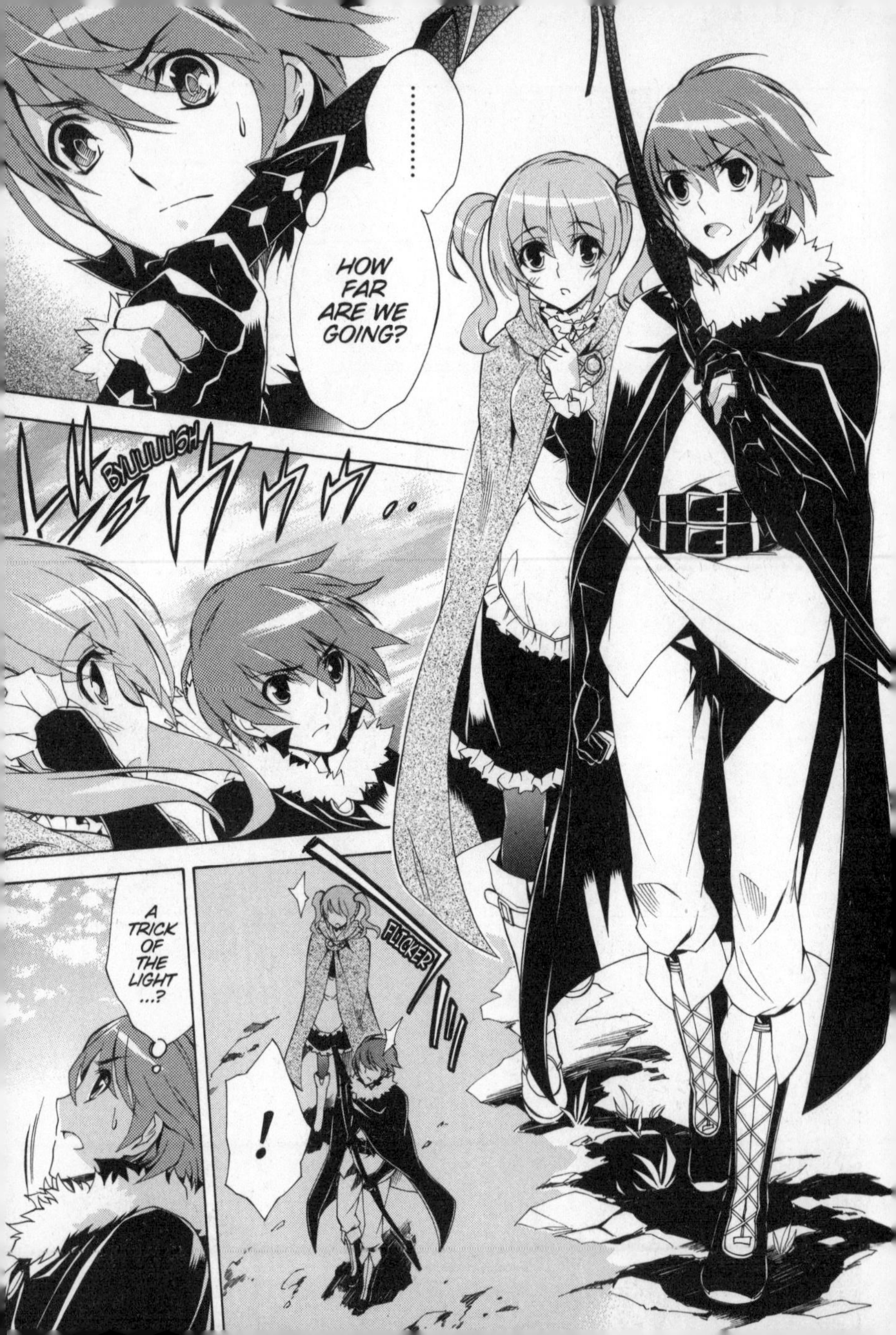
HOW FAR ARE WE GOING?
......
BYUUUUSH
FLICKER
!
A TRICK OF THE LIGHT ...?

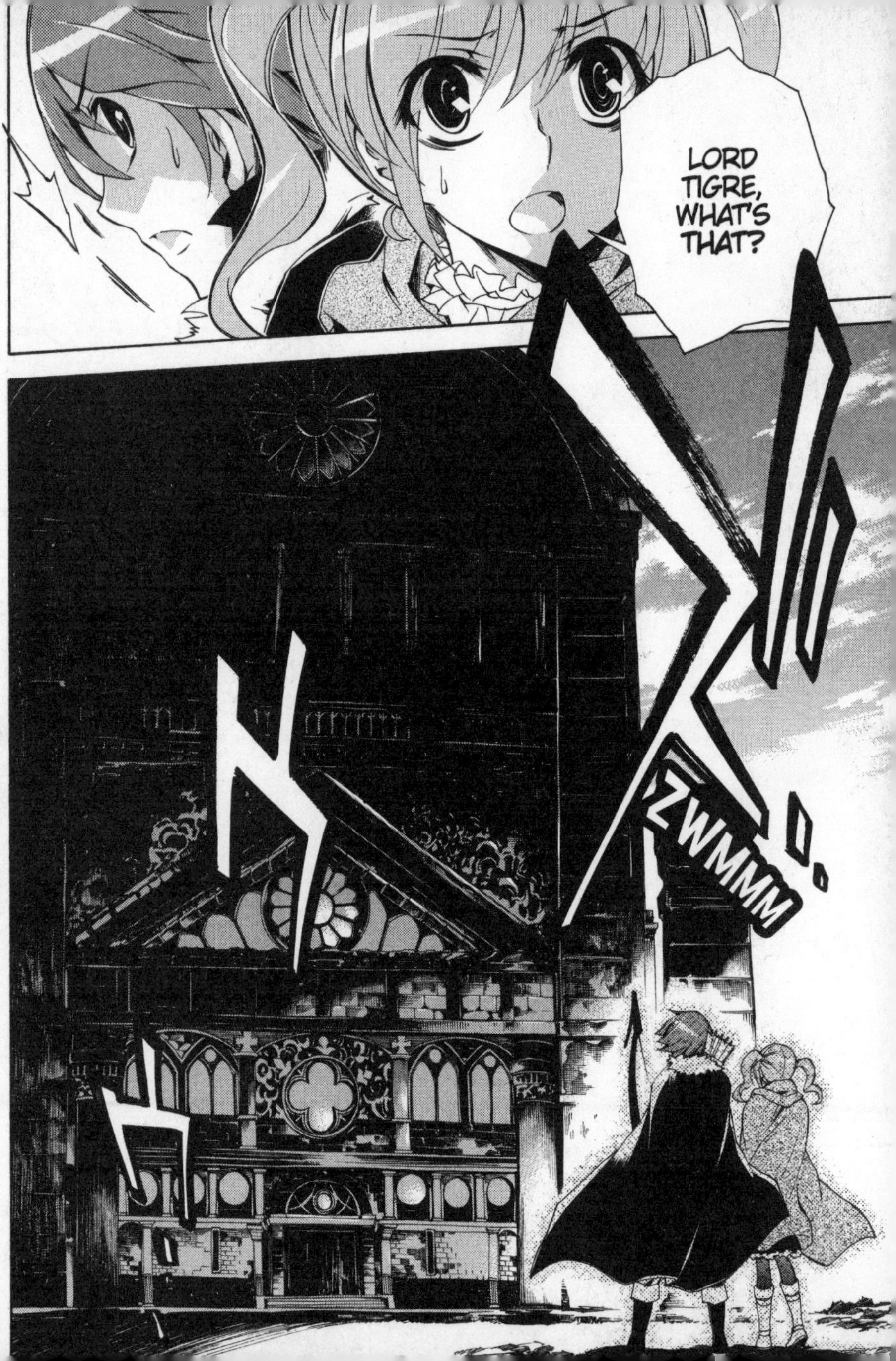
LORD TIGRE, WHAT'S THAT?
ZWMMM

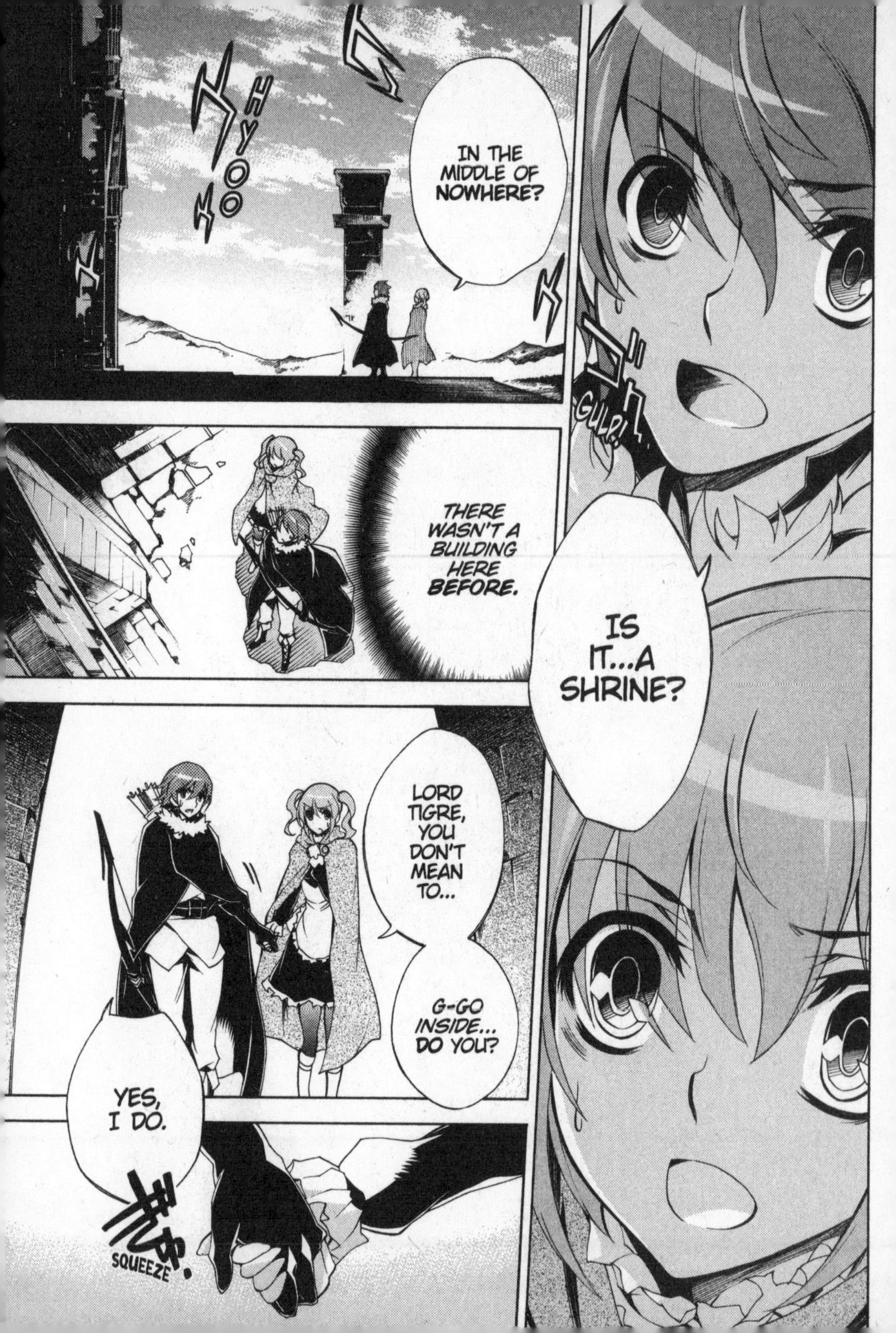
HYOOH
IN THE MIDDLE OF NOWHERE?
GULP!
IS IT...A SHRINE?
THERE WASN'T A BUILDING HERE BEFORE.
LORD TIGRE, YOU DON'T MEAN TO...
G-GO INSIDE... DO YOU?
YES, I DO.
SQUEEZE

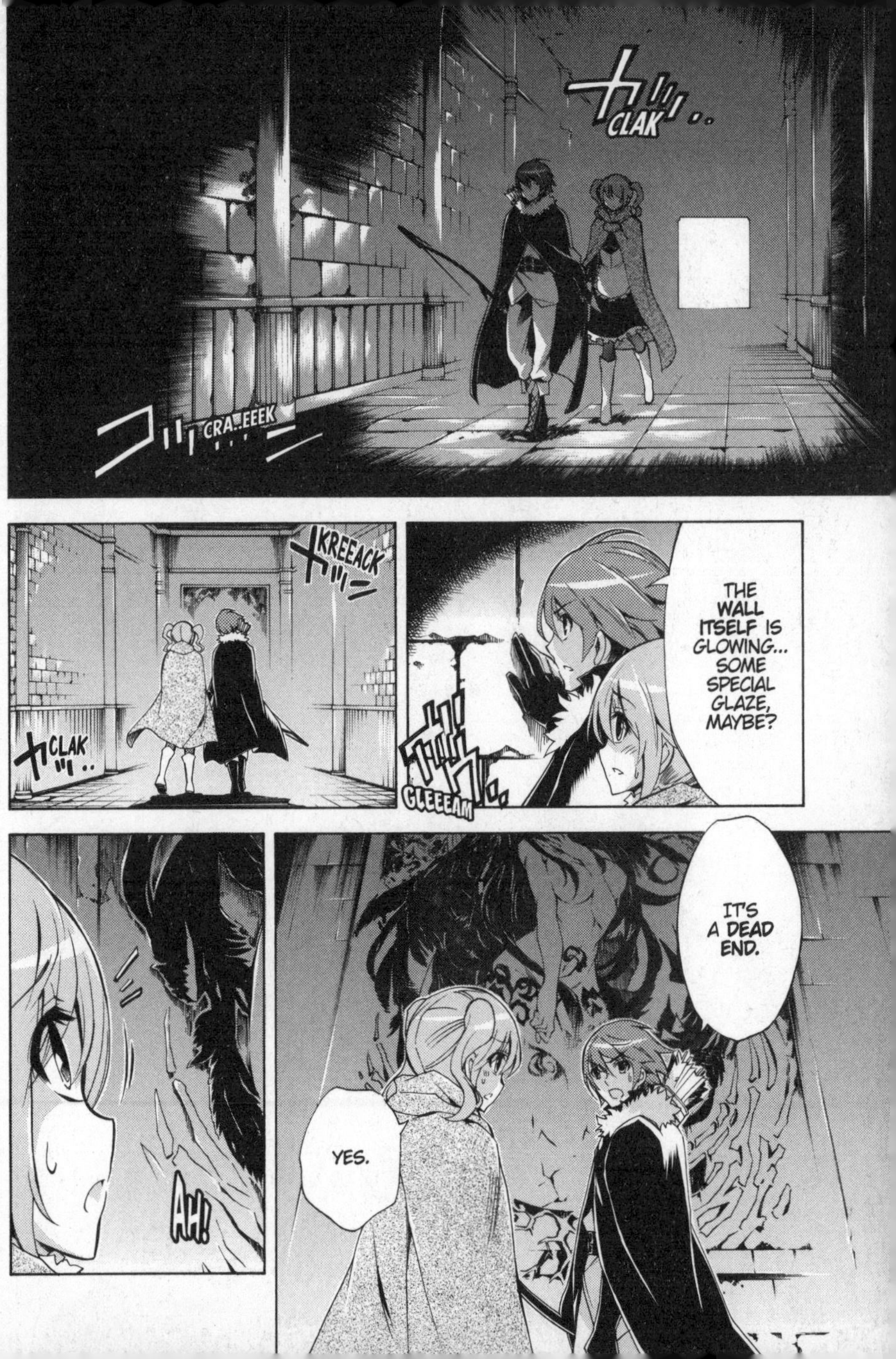
CLAK
CRA..EEEK
THE WALL ITSELF IS GLOWING... SOME SPECIAL GLAZE, MAYBE?
GLEEEAM
KREEACK
CLAK
IT'S A DEAD END.
YES.
AH!

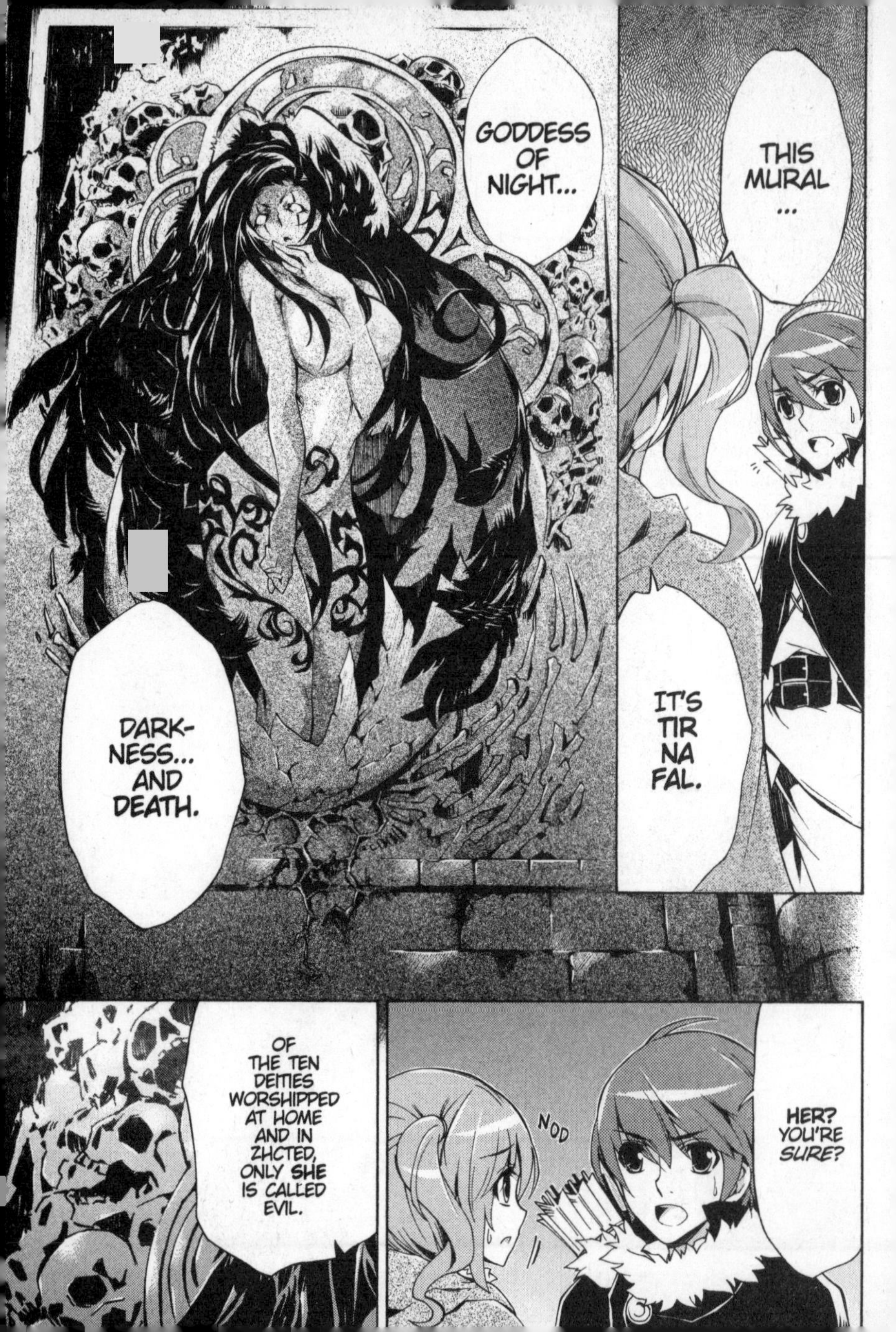
THIS MURAL ...
IT'S TIR NA FAL.
GODDESS OF NIGHT...
DARK-NESS... AND DEATH.
HER? YOU'RE SURE?
NOD
OF THE TEN DEITIES WORSHIPPED AT HOME AND IN ZHCTED, ONLY SHE IS CALLED EVIL.

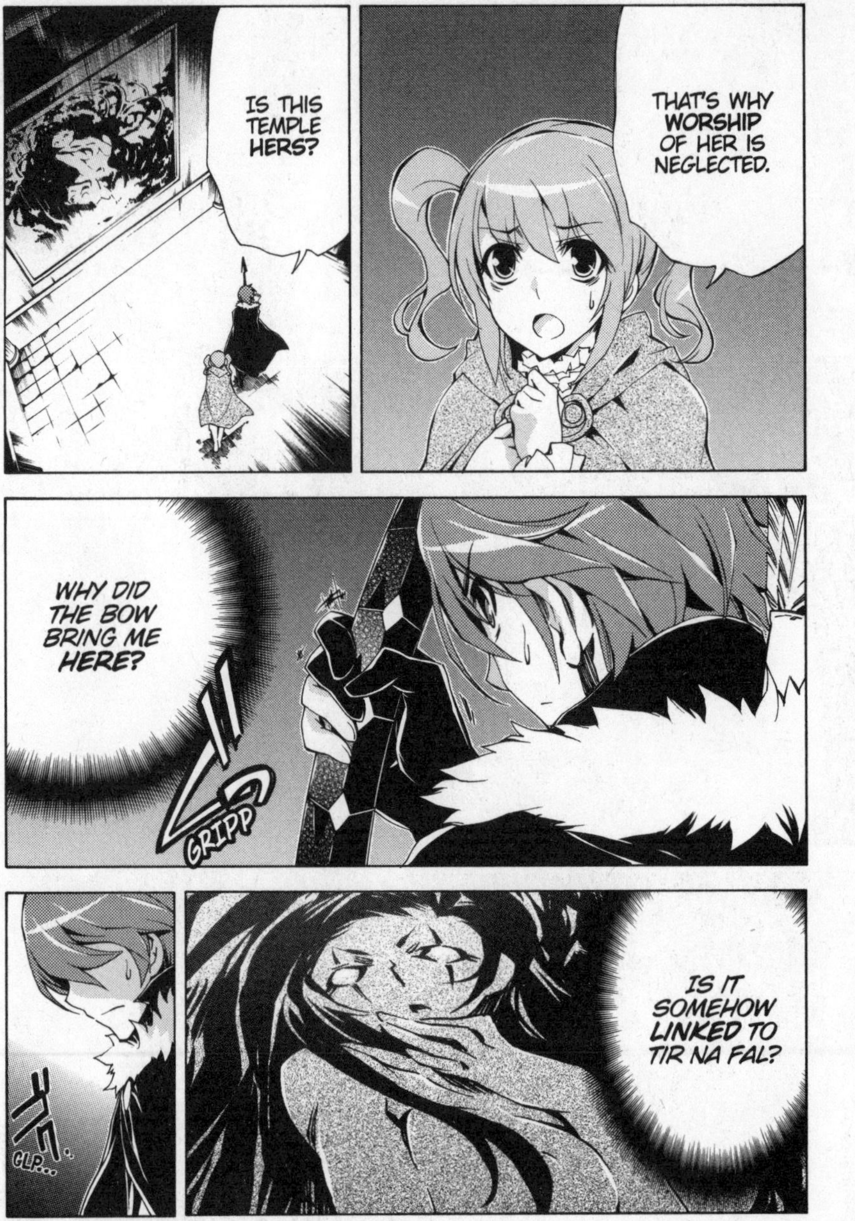
THAT'S WHY WORSHIP OF HER IS NEGLECTED.
IS THIS TEMPLE HERS?
WHY DID THE BOW BRING ME HERE?
GRIPP
IS IT SOMEHOW LINKED TO TIR NA FAL?
GLP...

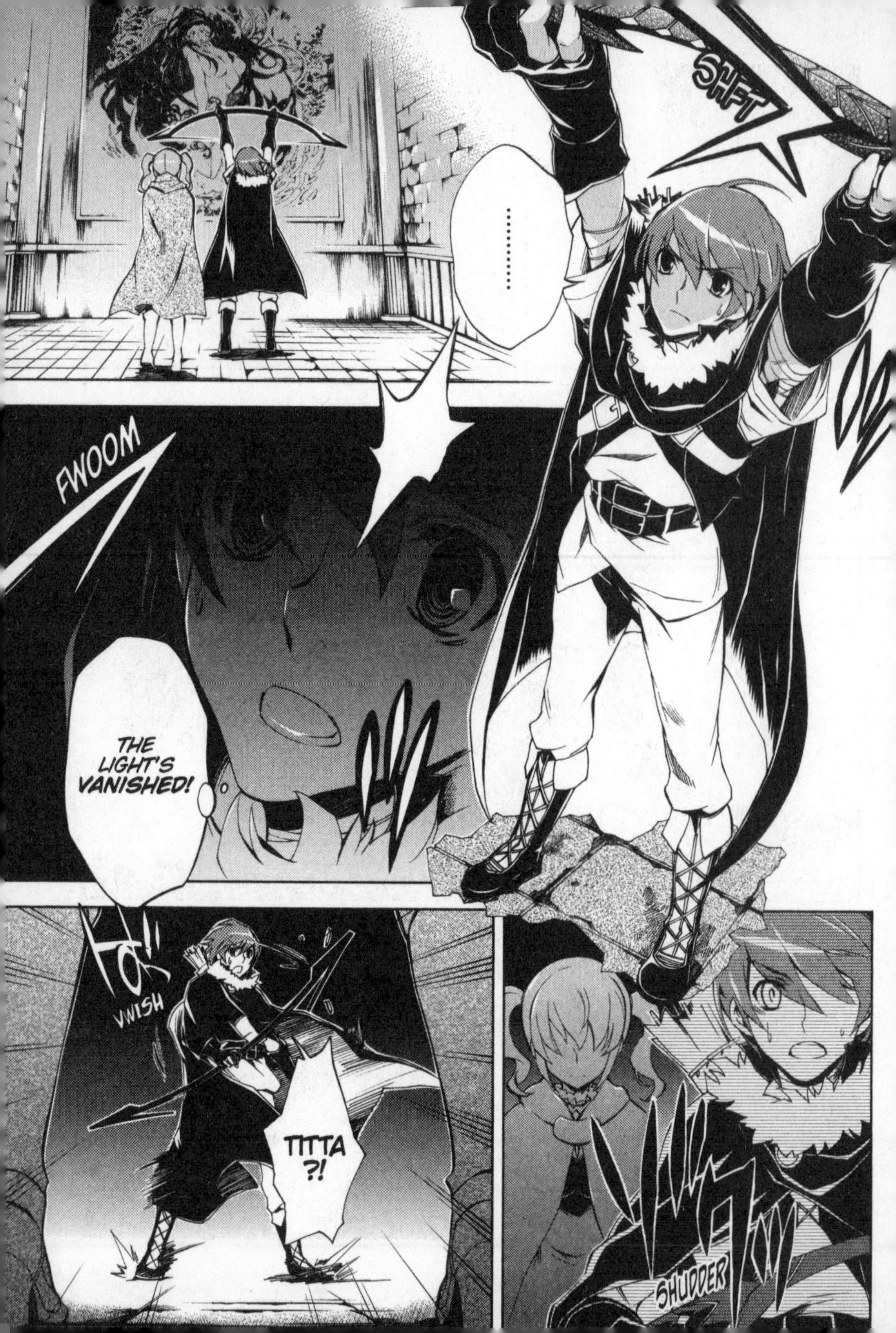
SHFT
……
FWOOM
THE LIGHT'S VANISHED!
SHUDDER
VWISH
TITTA ?!

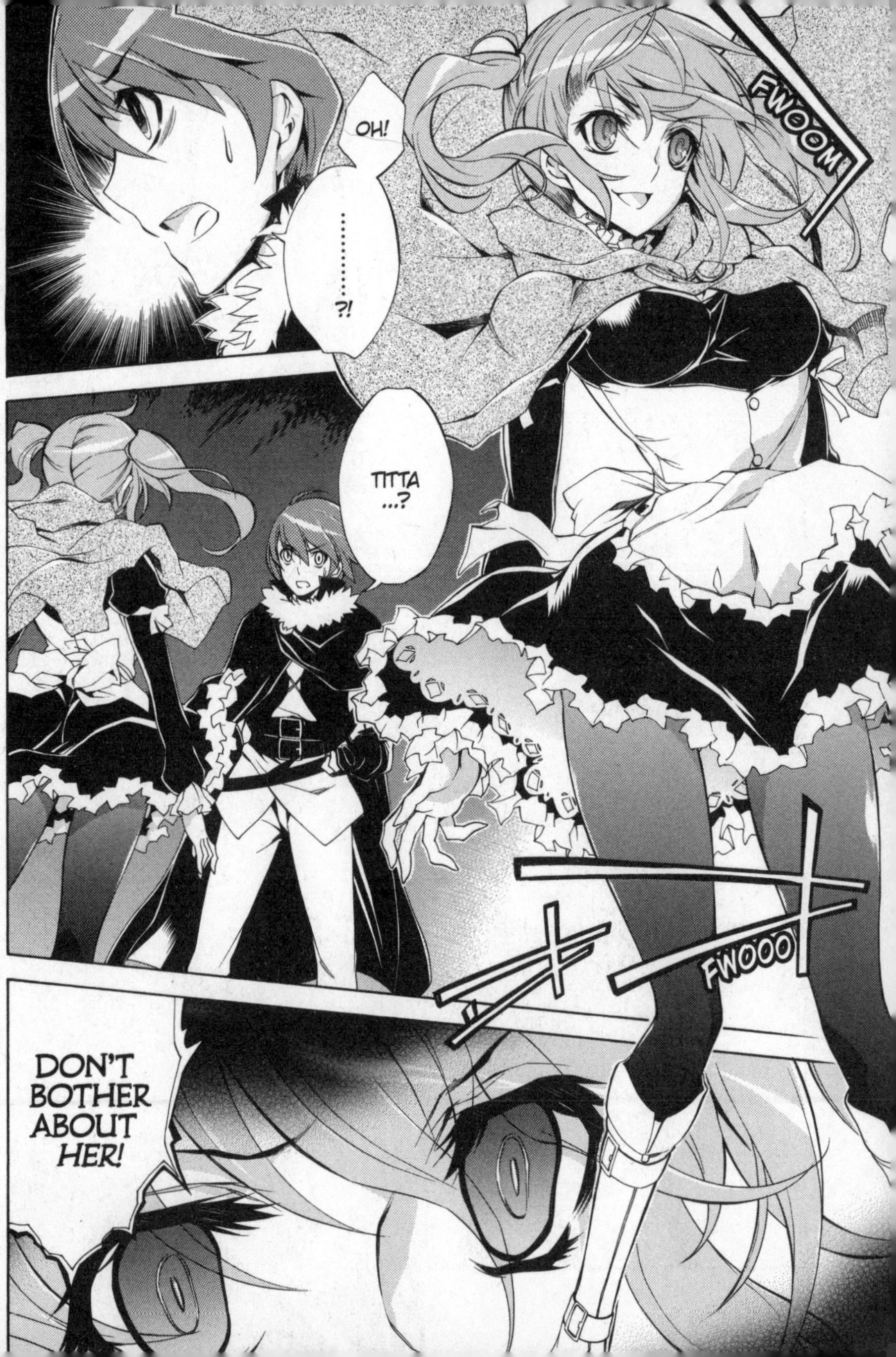
FWOOM
OH!
.........?!
TITTA ...?
FWOOO
DON'T BOTHER ABOUT HER!

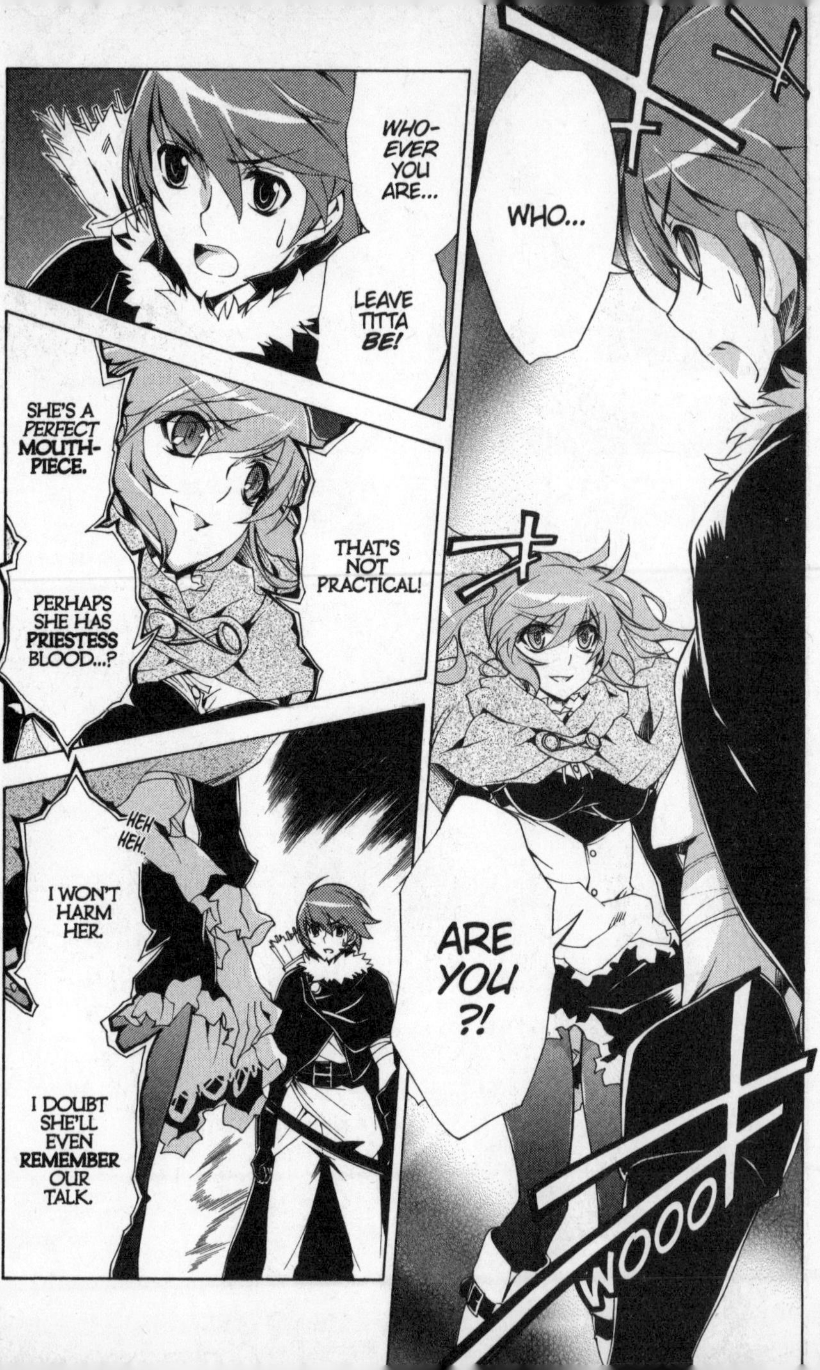
WHO...
ARE YOU?!
WOOO
WHO-EVER YOU ARE...
LEAVE TITTA BE!
SHE'S A PERFECT MOUTH-PIECE.
THAT'S NOT PRACTICAL!
PERHAPS SHE HAS PRIESTESS BLOOD...?
HEH HEH..
I WON'T HARM HER.
I DOUBT SHE'LL EVEN REMEMBER OUR TALK.

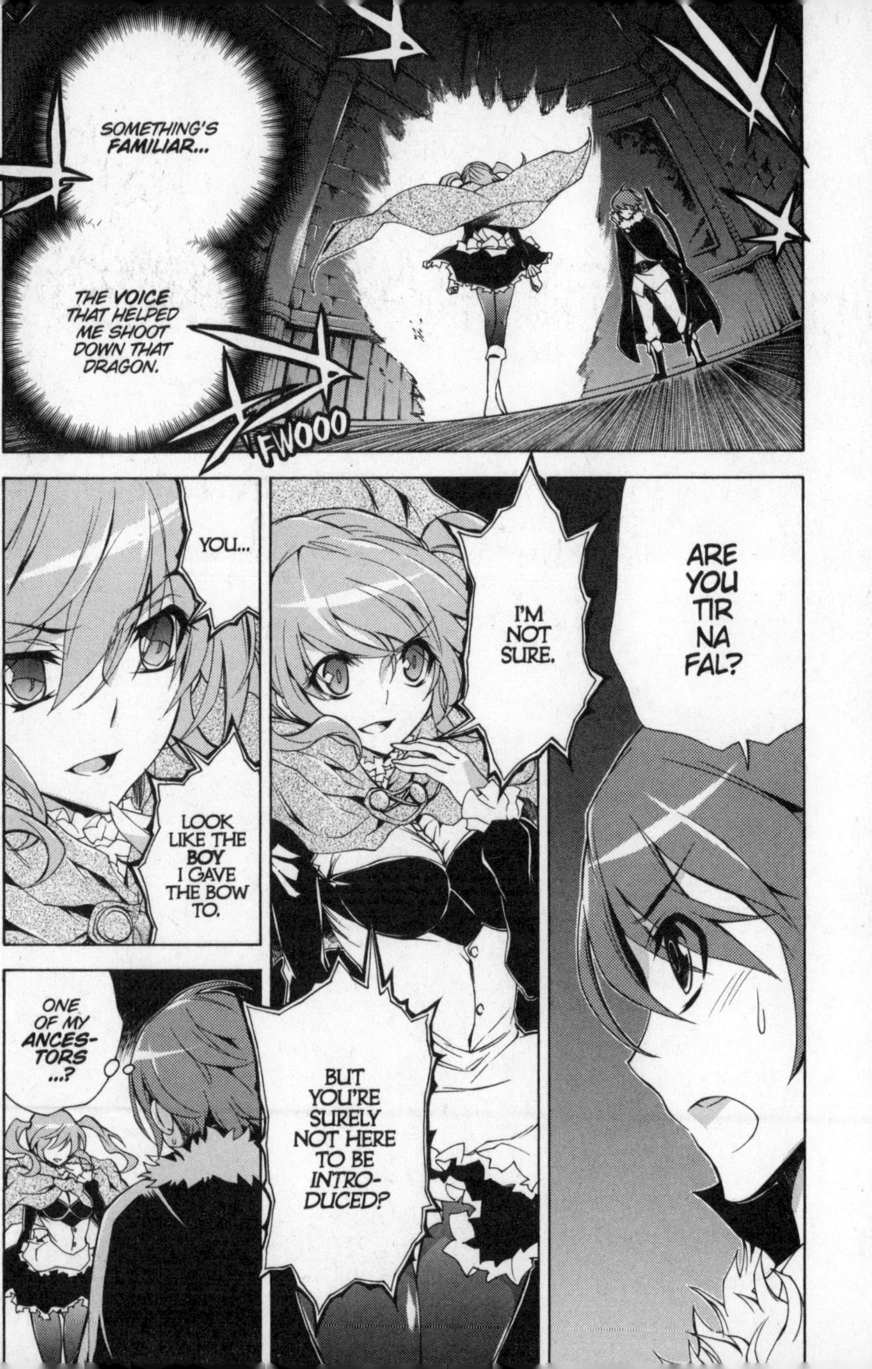
SOMETHING'S FAMILIAR...
THE VOICE THAT HELPED ME SHOOT DOWN THAT DRAGON.
FWOOO
ARE YOU TIR NA FAL?
I'M NOT SURE.
YOU...
LOOK LIKE THE BOY I GAVE THE BOW TO.
ONE OF MY ANCES-TORS ...?
BUT YOU'RE SURELY NOT HERE TO BE INTRO-DUCED?

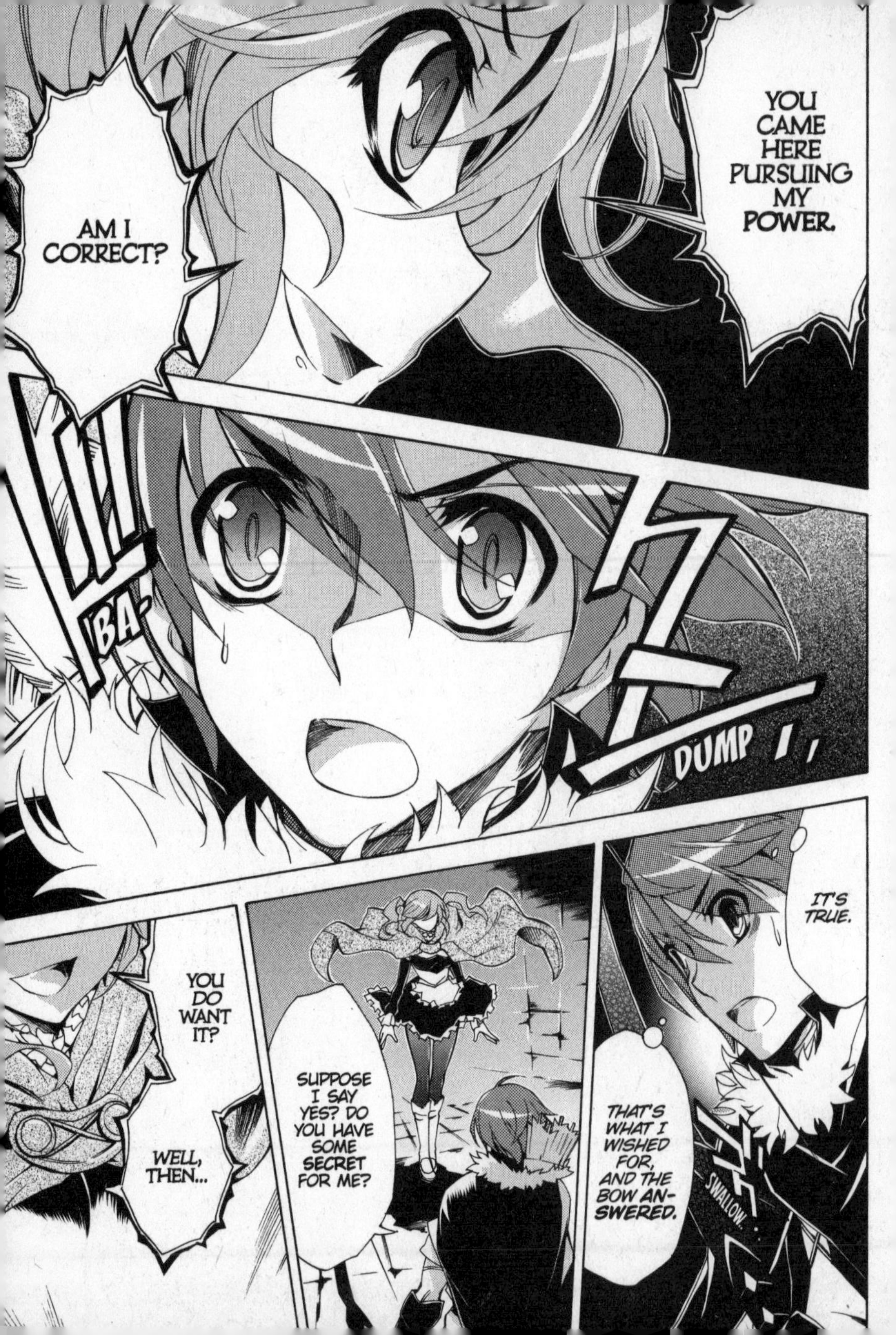
YOU CAME HERE PURSUING MY POWER.
AM I CORRECT?
BA-DUMP
IT'S TRUE.
SWALLOW.
THAT'S WHAT I WISHED FOR, AND THE BOW AN-SWERED.
SUPPOSE I SAY YES? DO YOU HAVE SOME SECRET FOR ME?
YOU DO WANT IT?
WELL, THEN...

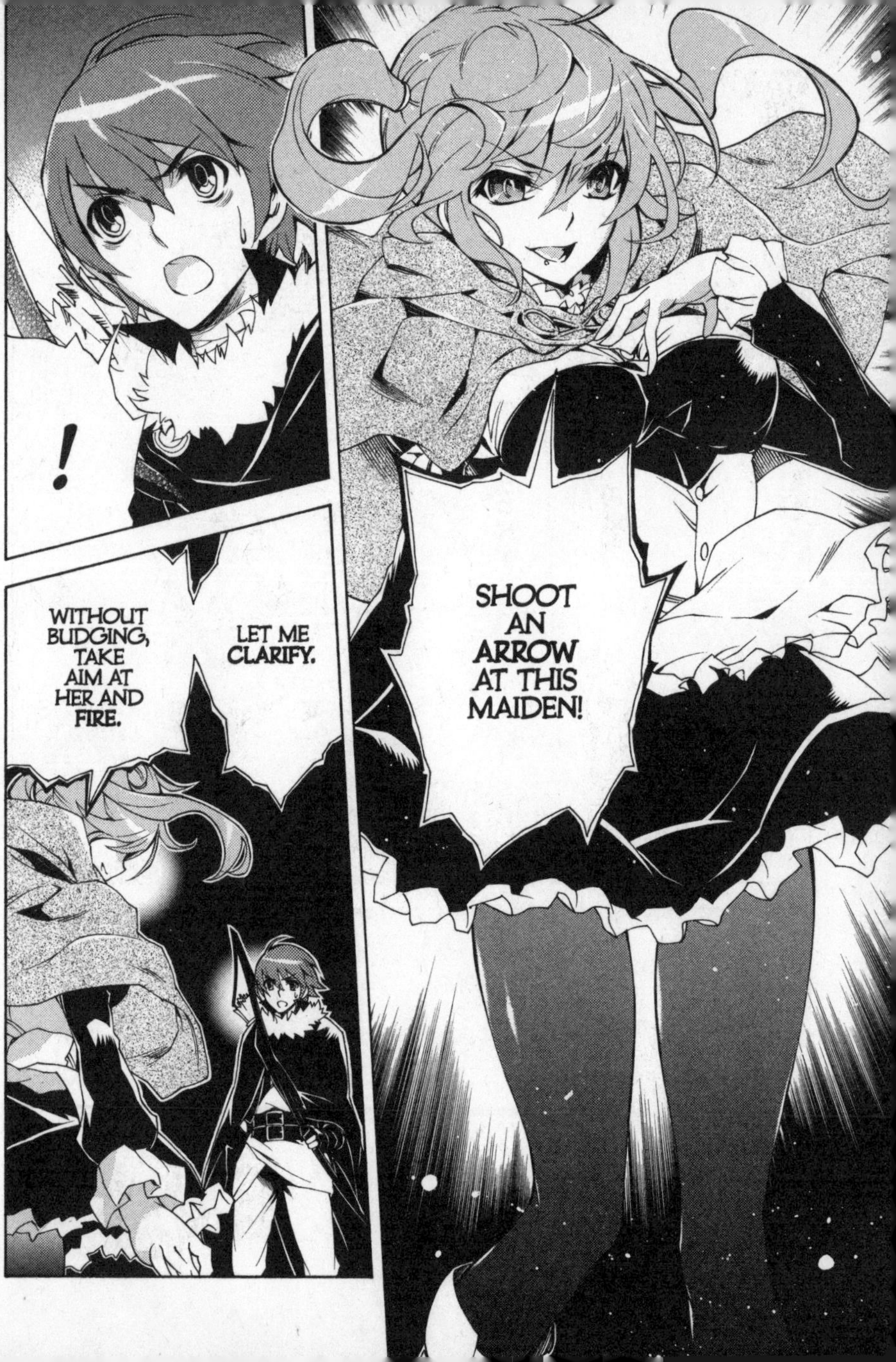
SHOOT AN ARROW AT THIS MAIDEN!
!
LET ME CLARIFY.
WITHOUT BUDGING, TAKE AIM AT HER AND FIRE.

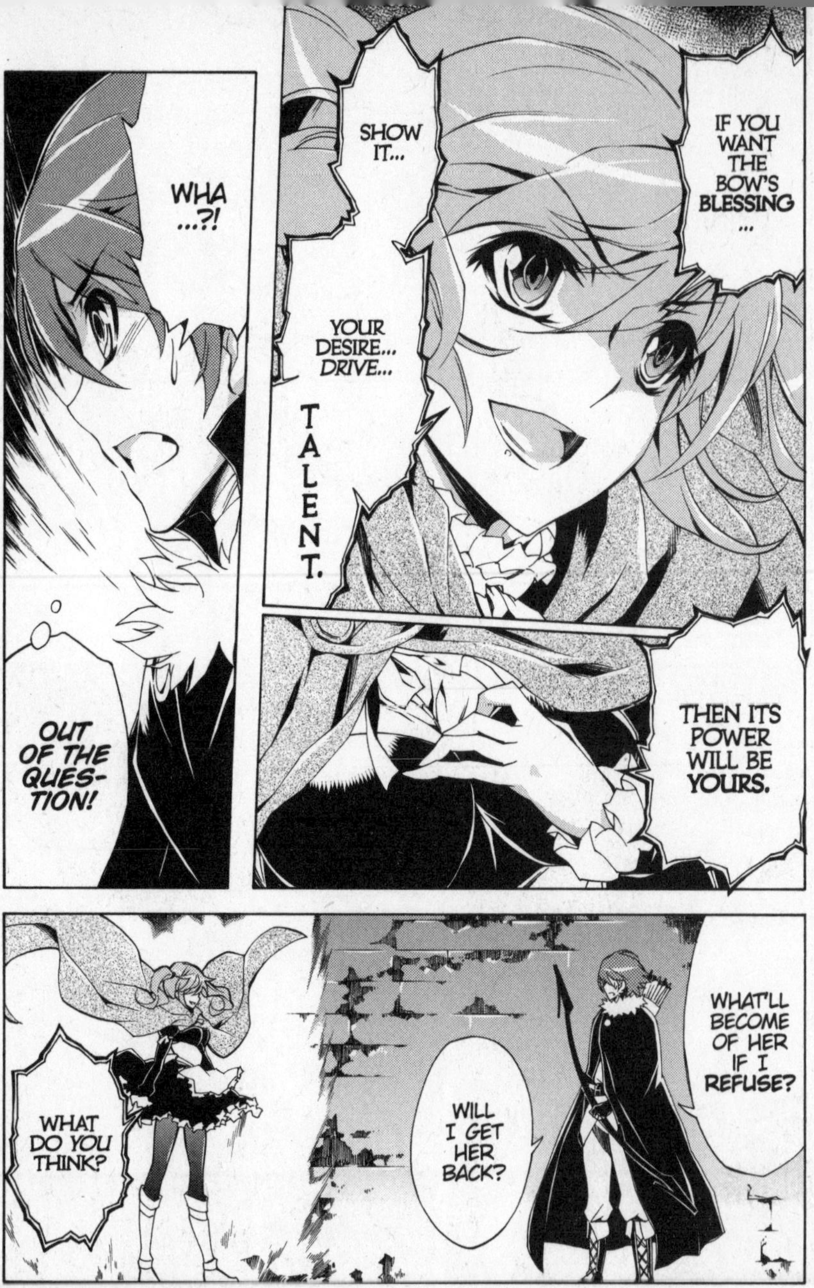
IF YOU WANT THE BOW'S BLESSING ...
SHOW IT...
YOUR DESIRE... DRIVE...
TALENT.
THEN ITS POWER WILL BE YOURS.
WHA ...?!
OUT OF THE QUES-TION!
WHAT'LL BECOME OF HER IF I REFUSE?
WILL I GET HER BACK?
WHAT DO YOU THINK?

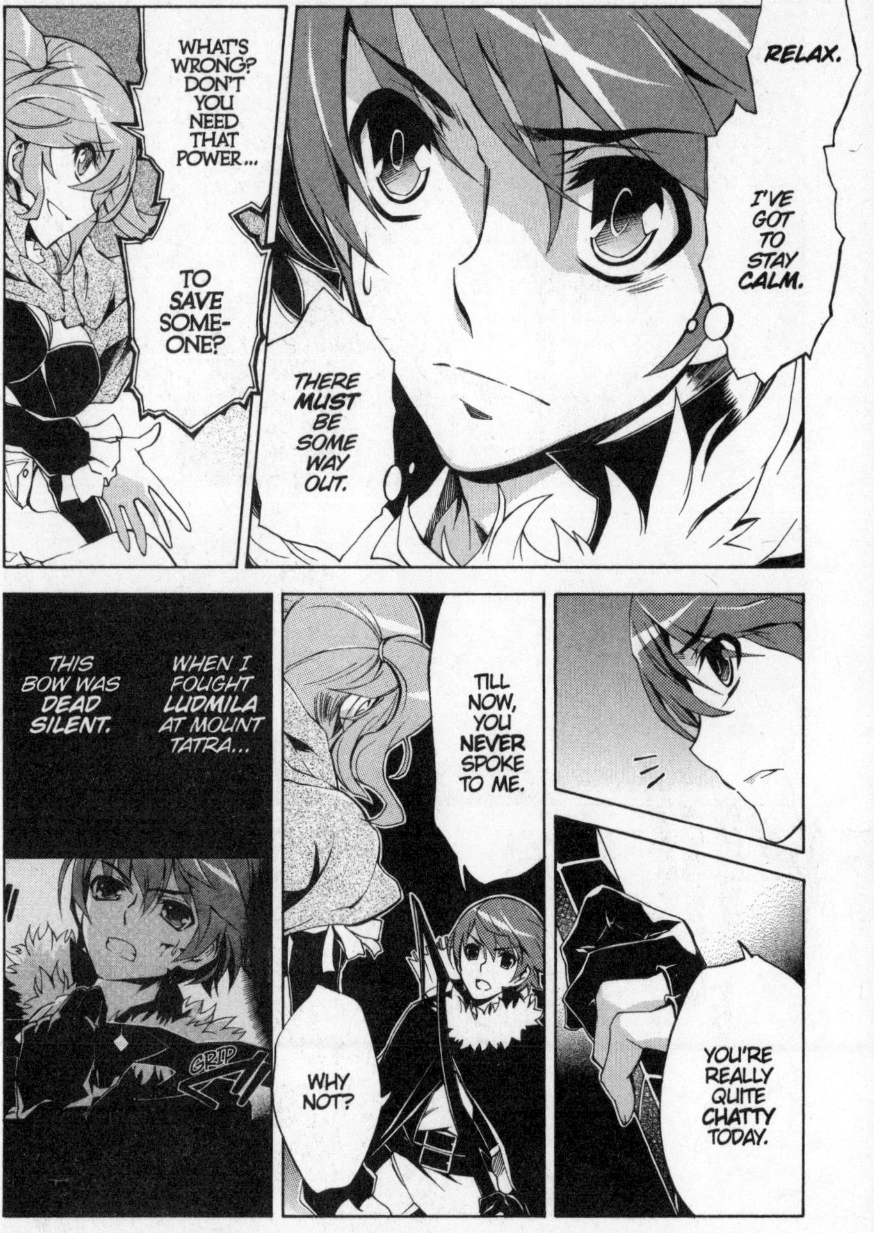
RELAX.
I'VE GOT TO STAY CALM.
THERE MUST BE SOME WAY OUT.
WHAT'S WRONG? DON'T YOU NEED THAT POWER...
TO SAVE SOME-ONE?
YOU'RE REALLY QUITE CHATTY TODAY.
TILL NOW, YOU NEVER SPOKE TO ME.
WHY NOT?
WHEN I FOUGHT LUDMILA AT MOUNT TATRA...
THIS BOW WAS DEAD SILENT.
GRIP

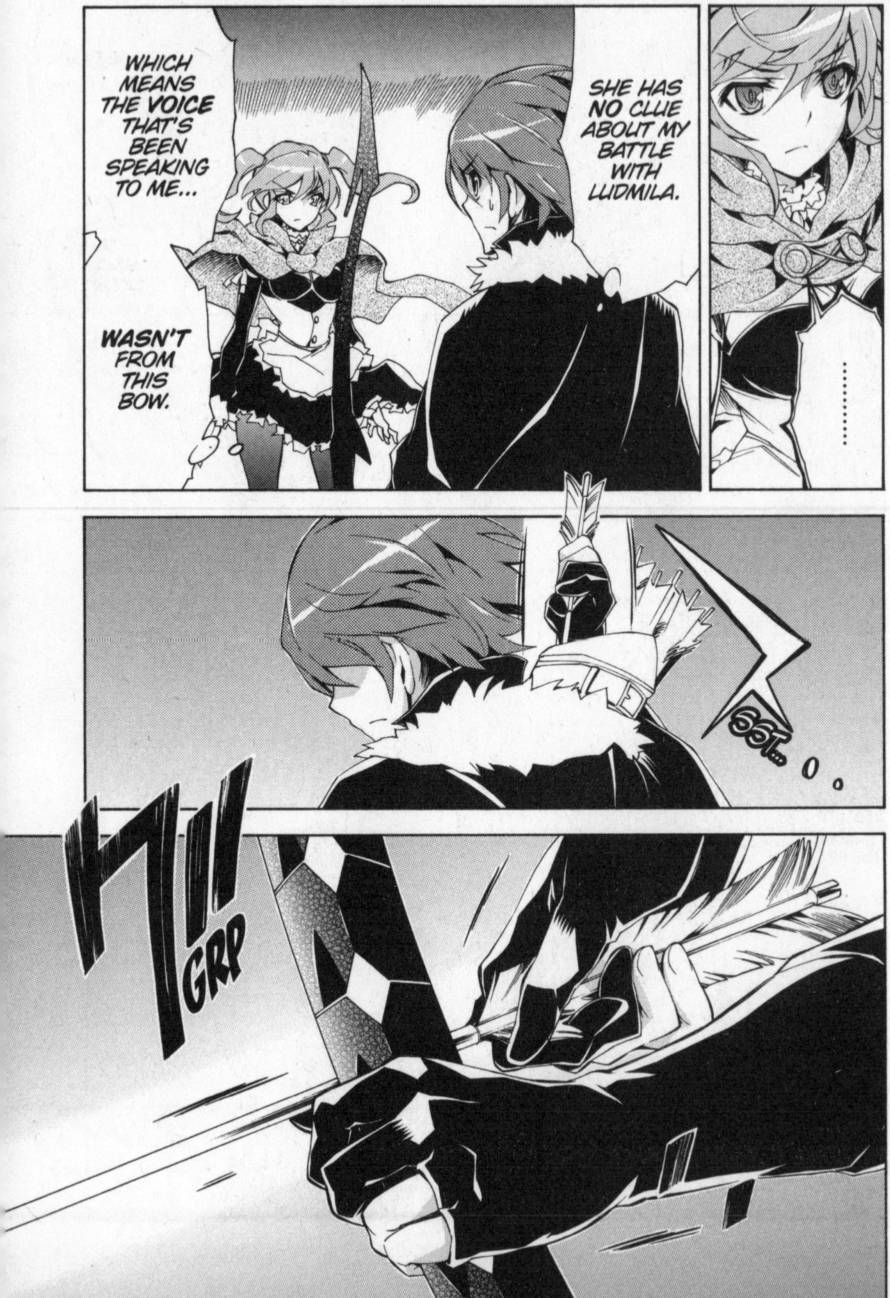
......
SHE HAS NO CLUE ABOUT MY BATTLE WITH LUDMILA.
WHICH MEANS THE VOICE THAT'S BEEN SPEAKING TO ME...
WASN'T FROM THIS BOW.
SST...
GRP

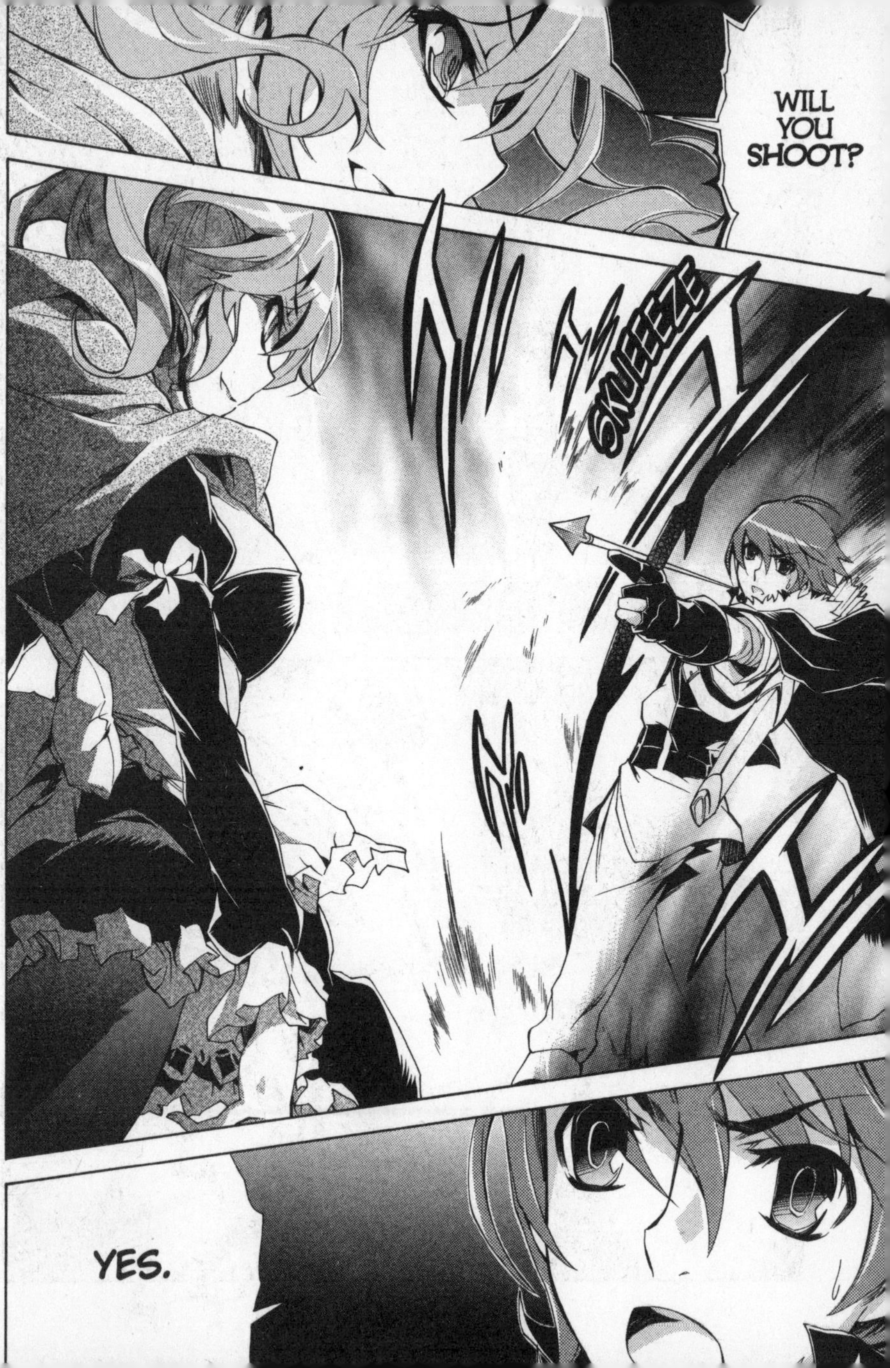
WILL YOU SHOOT?
SKWEEEEZE
YES.

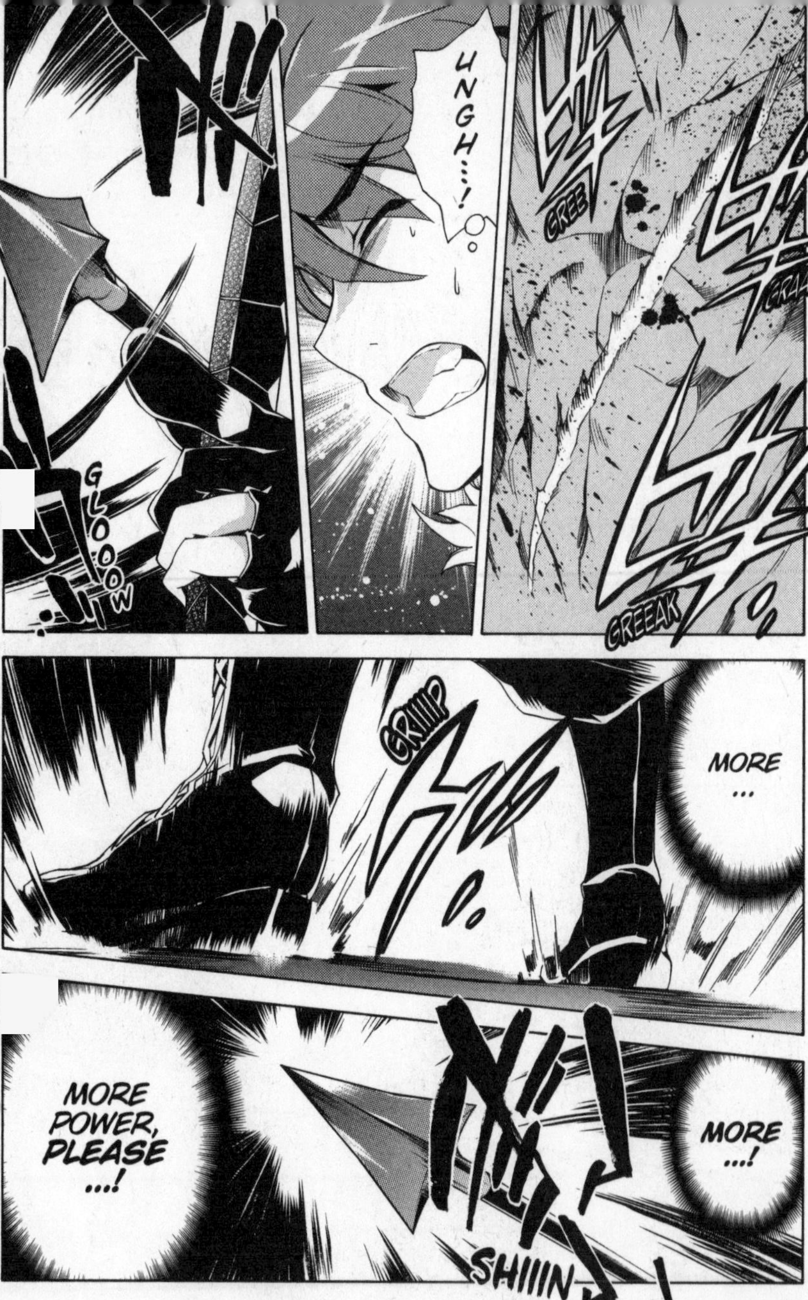
GRAAA
GREEB
GREEAK
UNGH...!
GLOOOW
MORE ...
GRIIIP
MORE ...!
SHIIIN
MORE POWER, PLEASE ...!

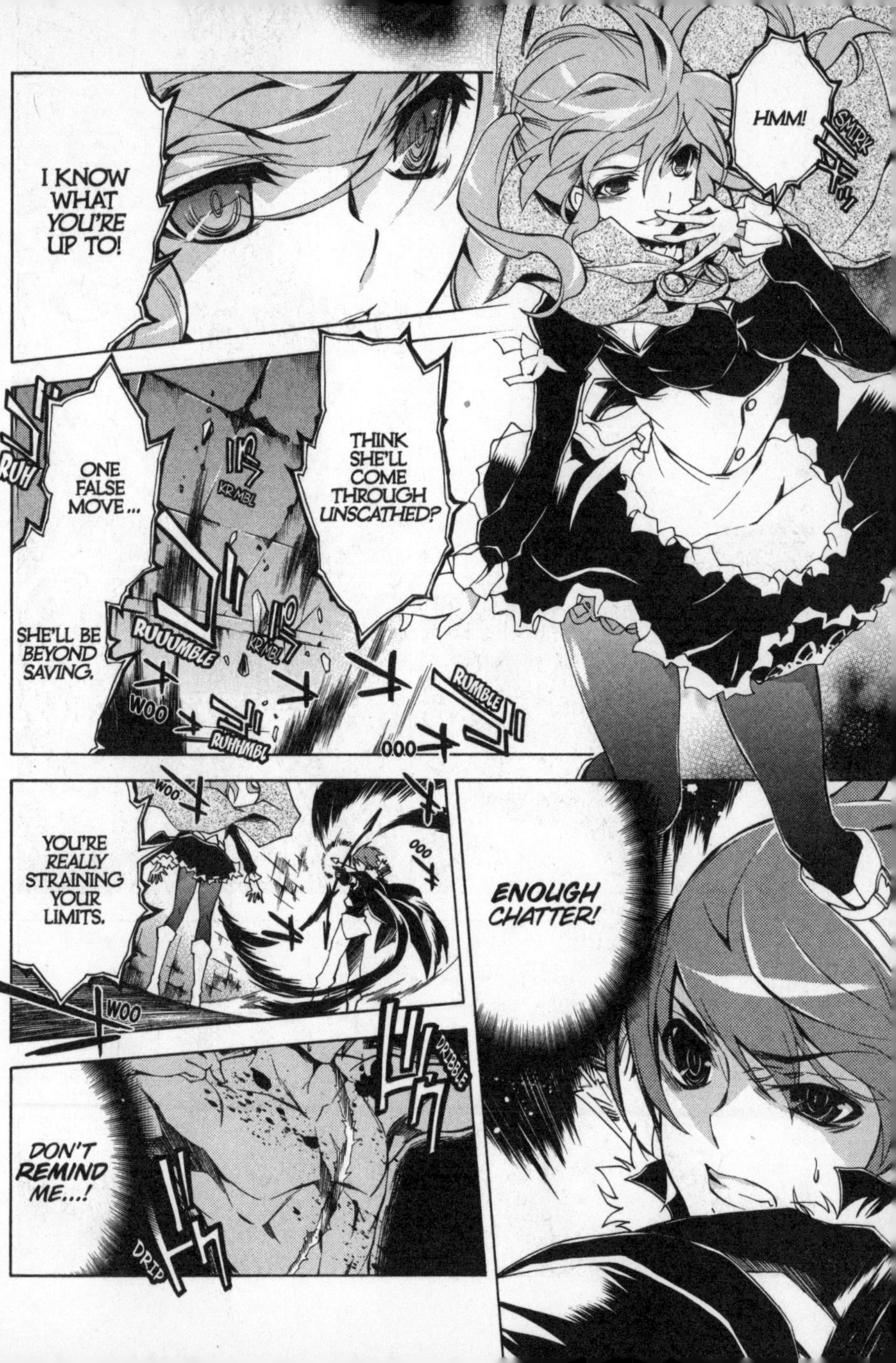
HMM!
SMIRK
I KNOW WHAT YOU'RE UP TO!
THINK SHE'LL COME THROUGH UNSCATHED?
RUH
ONE FALSE MOVE...
KRMBL
RUUUMBLE
KRMBL
SHE'LL BE BEYOND SAVING.
WOO
RUHHMBL
RUMBLE
OOO
ENOUGH CHATTER!
WOO
OOO
YOU'RE REALLY STRAINING YOUR LIMITS.
WOO
DRIBBLE
DON'T REMIND ME...!
DRIP

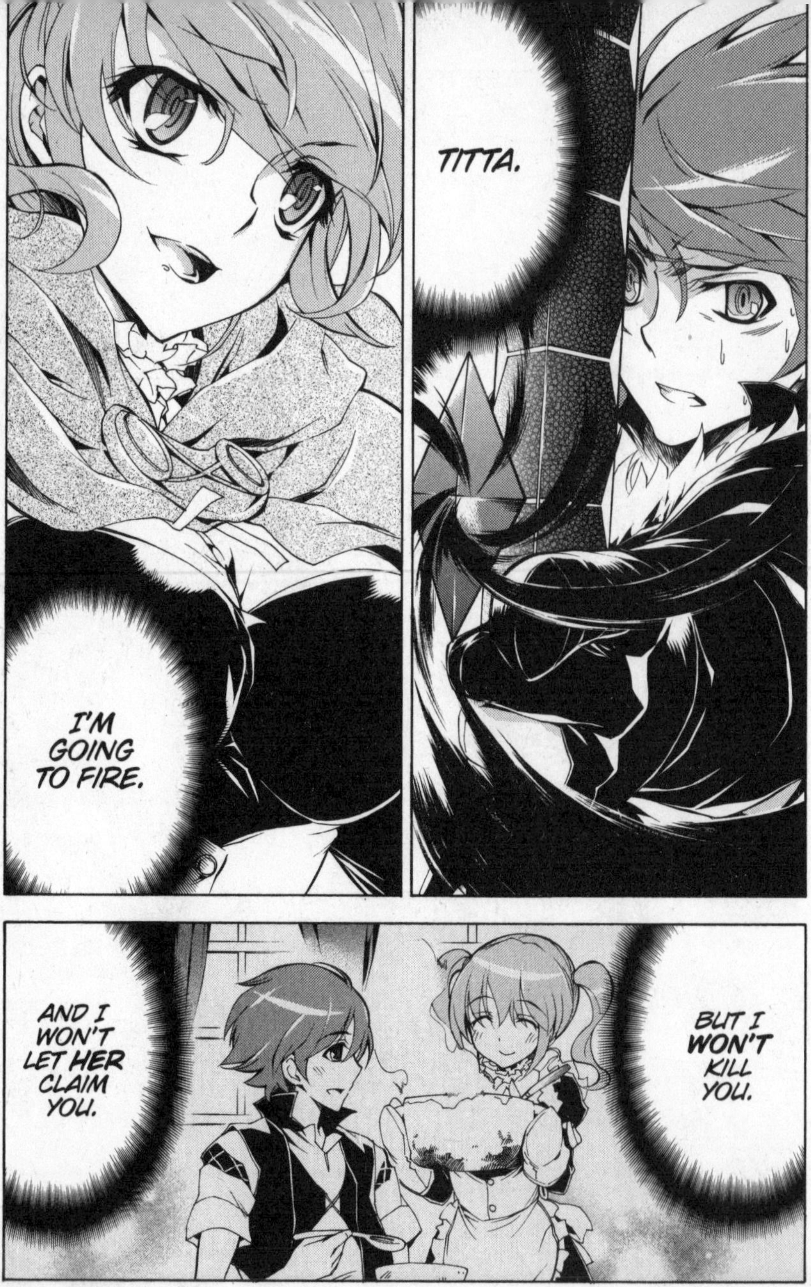
TITTA.
I'M GOING TO FIRE.
BUT I WON'T KILL YOU.
AND I WON'T LET HER CLAIM YOU.

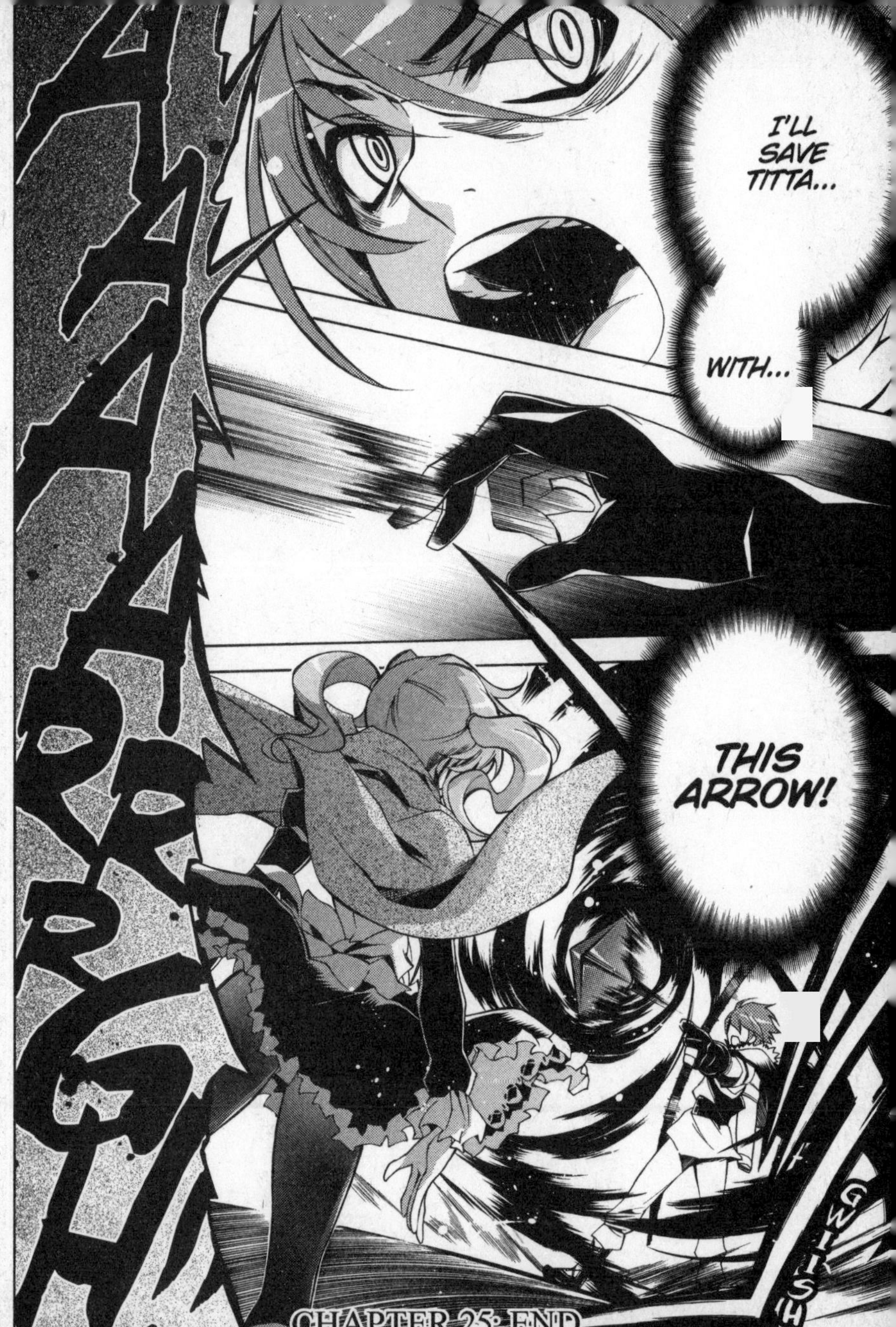
I'LL SAVE TITTA...
WITH...
THIS ARROW!
GWISH

CHAPTER 25: END

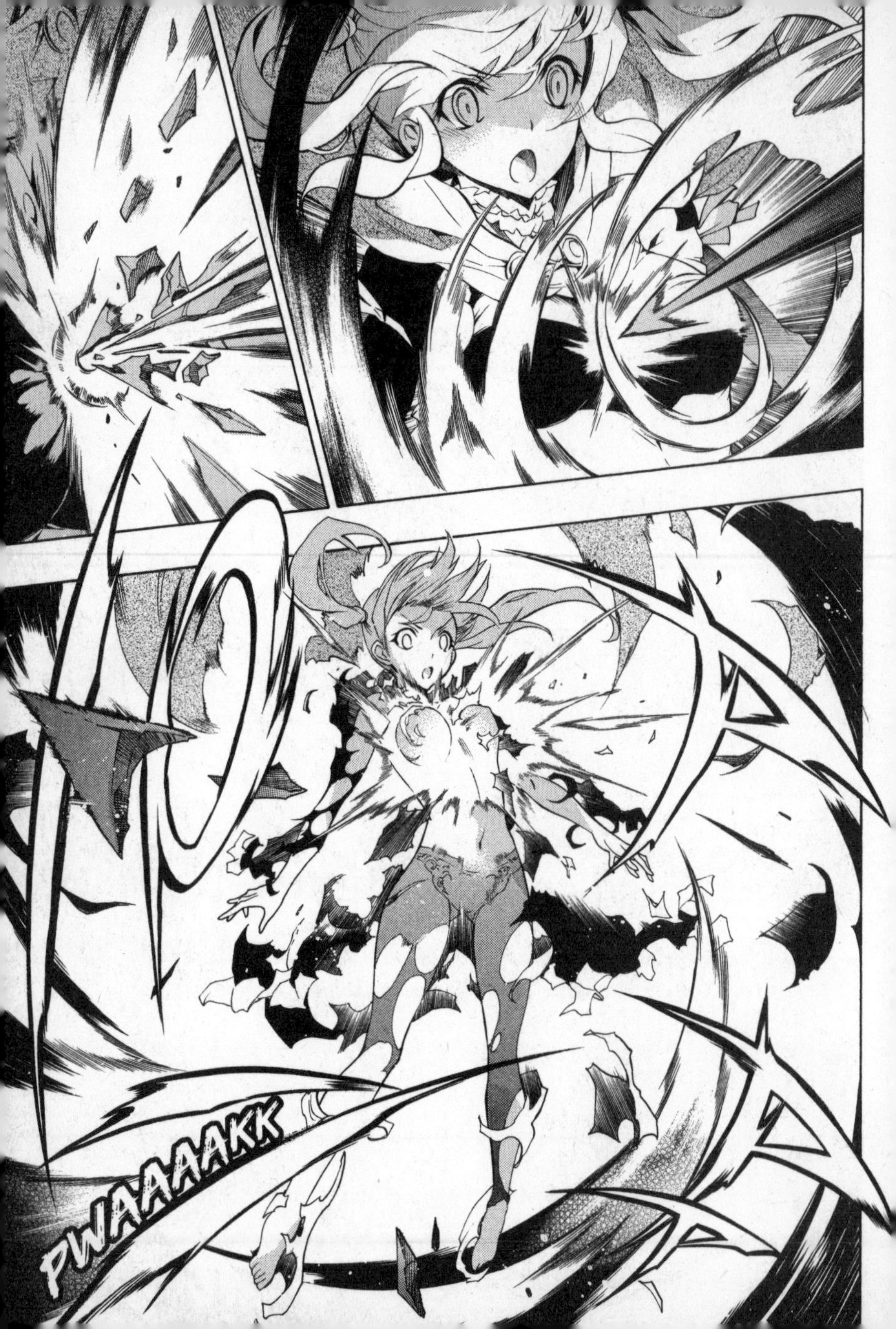
PWAAAAKK

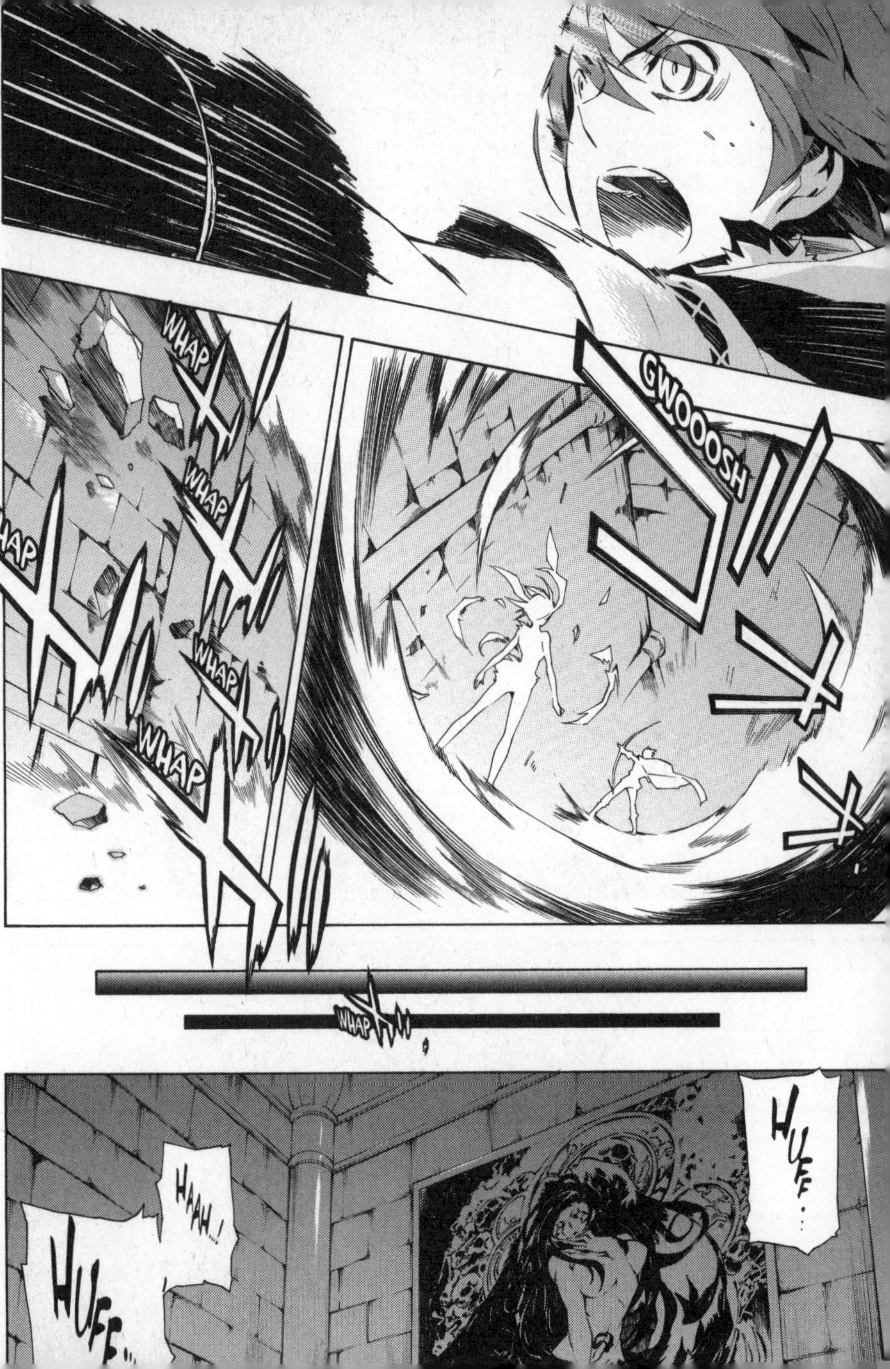
GWOOOSH
WHAP
WHAP
WHAP
WHAP
WHAP
WHAP
HUFF...
HAAH..!
HUFF...

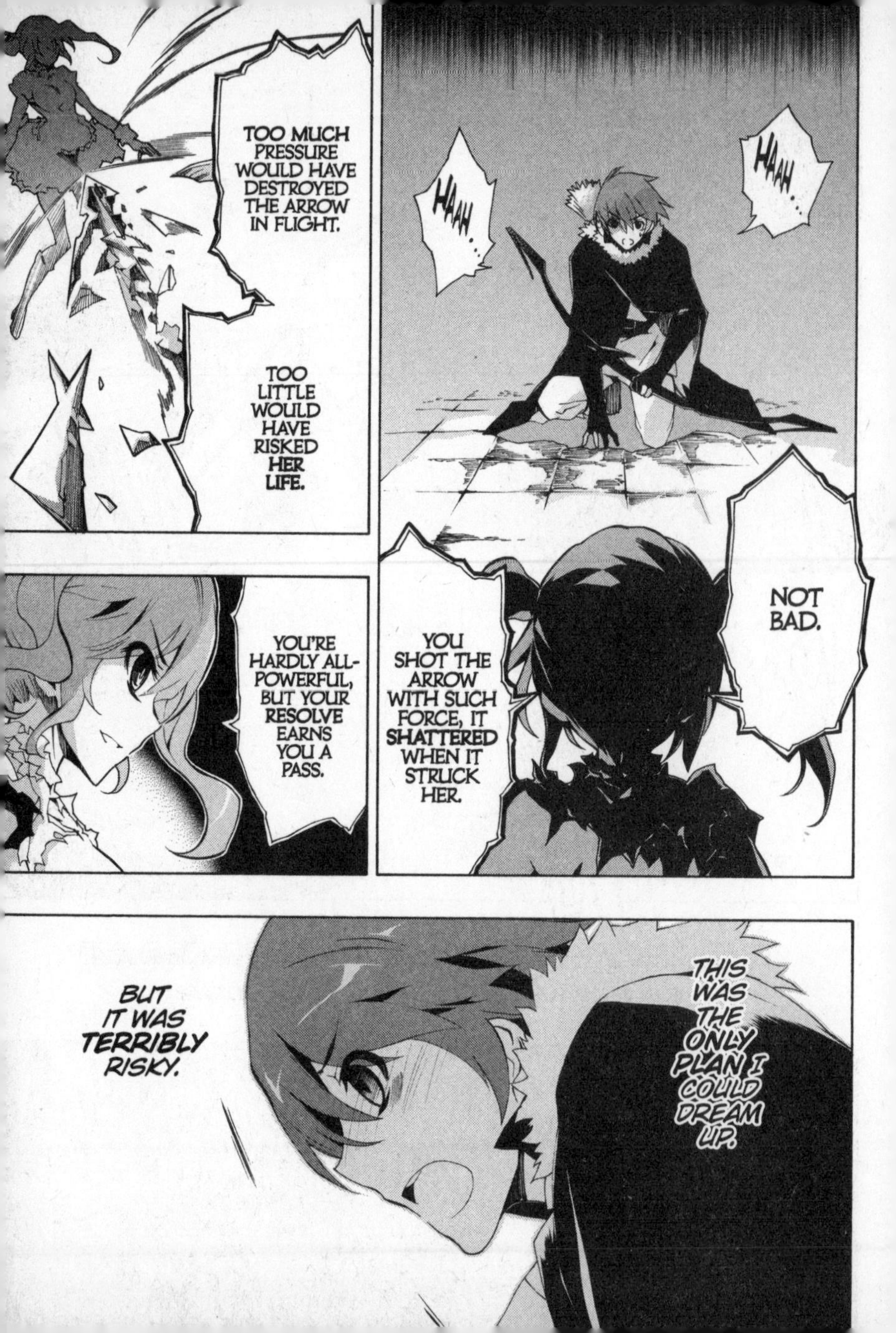
HAAH...
HAAH...
TOO MUCH PRESSURE WOULD HAVE DESTROYED THE ARROW IN FLIGHT.
TOO LITTLE WOULD HAVE RISKED HER LIFE.
NOT BAD.
YOU SHOT THE ARROW WITH SUCH FORCE, IT SHATTERED WHEN IT STRUCK HER.
YOU'RE HARDLY ALL-POWERFUL, BUT YOUR RESOLVE EARNS YOU A PASS.
THIS WAS THE ONLY PLAN I COULD DREAM UP.
BUT IT WAS TERRIBLY RISKY.

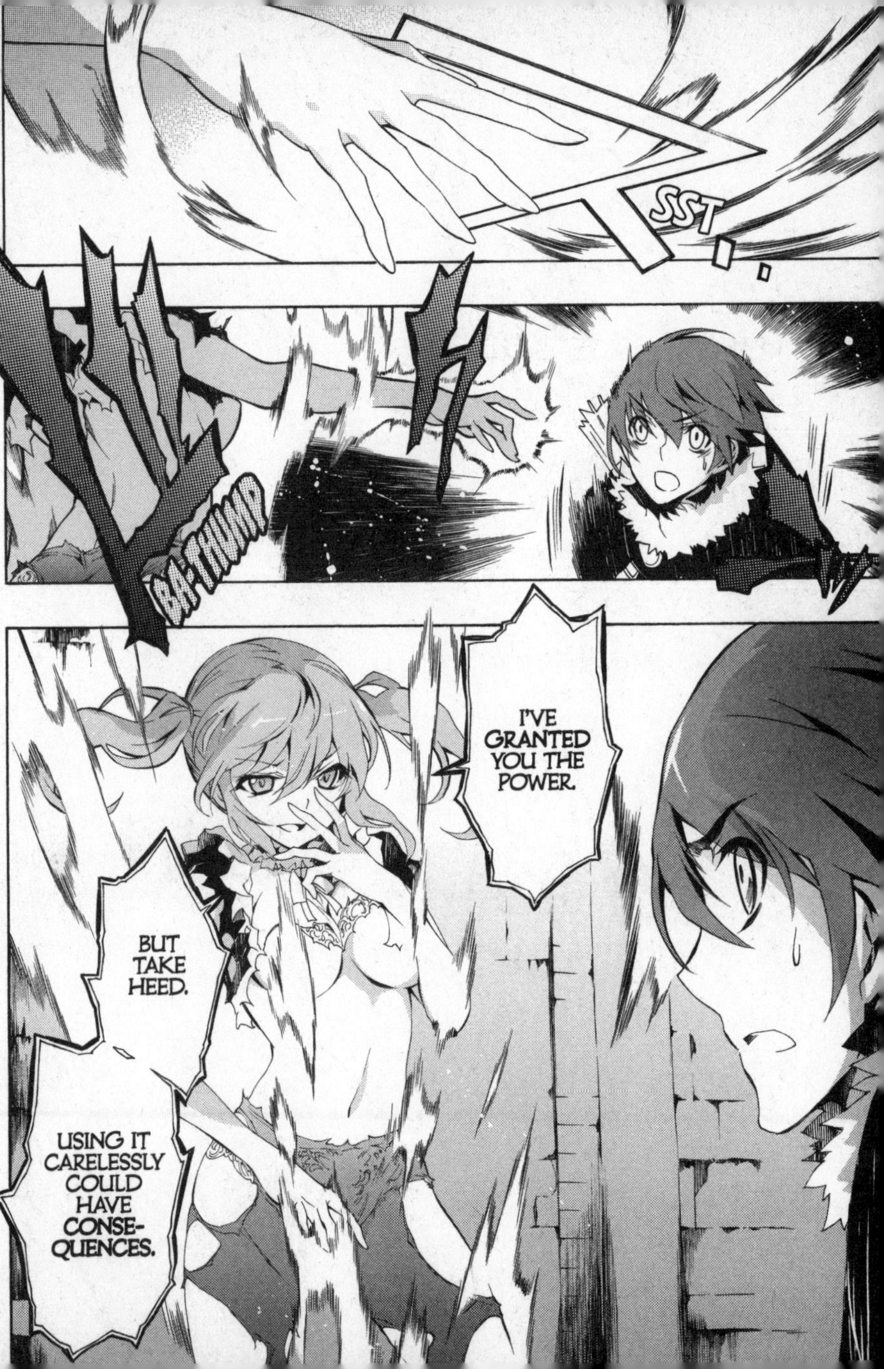
SST
BA-THUMP
I'VE GRANTED YOU THE POWER.
BUT TAKE HEED.
USING IT CARELESSLY COULD HAVE CONSE-QUENCES.

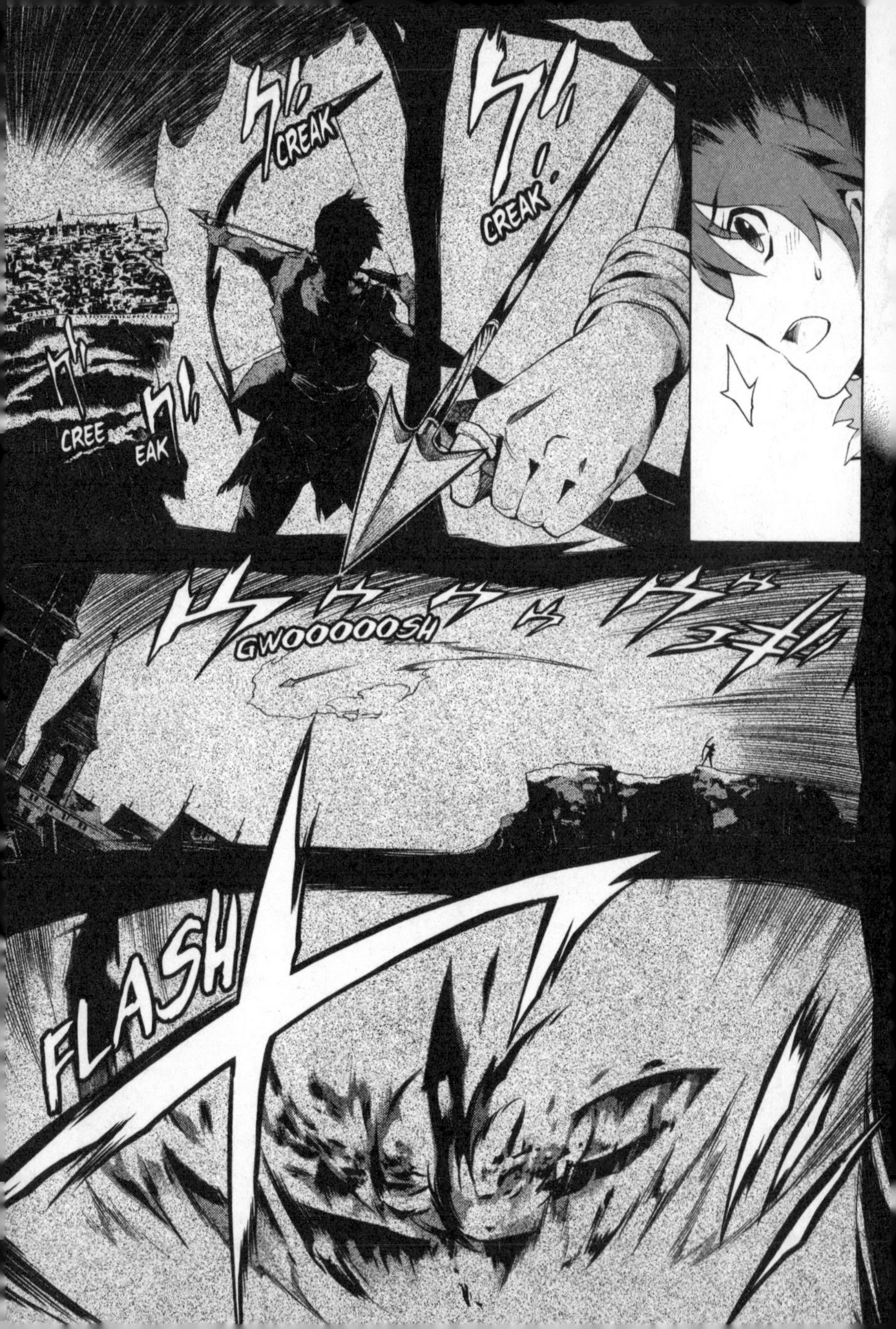
CREAK
CREAK
CREE
EAK
GWOOOOOOSH
FLASH

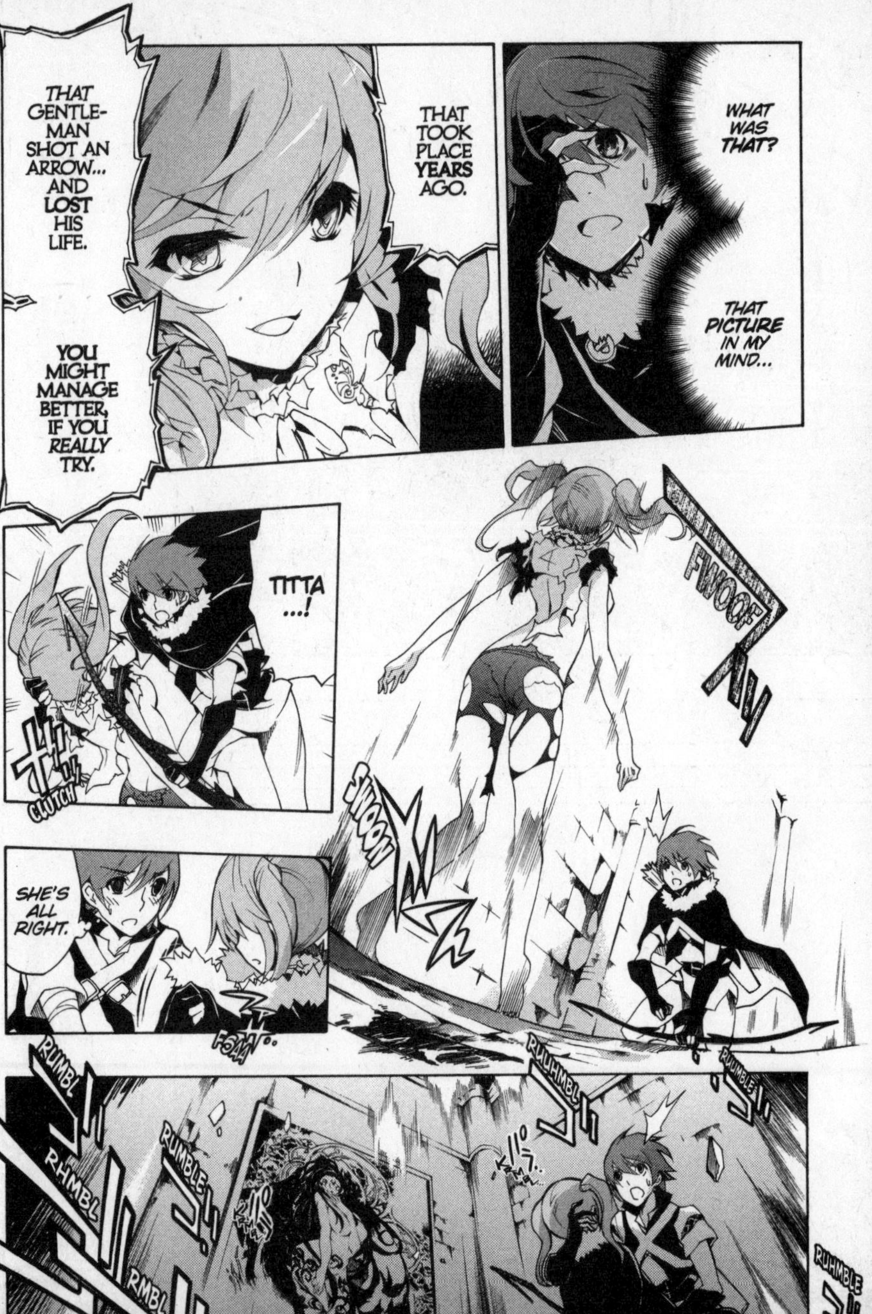
WHAT WAS THAT?
THAT PICTURE IN MY MIND...
THAT TOOK PLACE YEARS AGO.
THAT GENTLEMAN SHOT AN ARROW... AND LOST HIS LIFE.
YOU MIGHT MANAGE BETTER, IF YOU REALLY TRY.
FWOOF
SWOON
TITTA ...!
CLUTCH
SHE'S ALL RIGHT.
FSAA
RUMBLE
RUHMBL
RUMBLE
RHMBL
RUMBL
RMBL
RUHMBLE

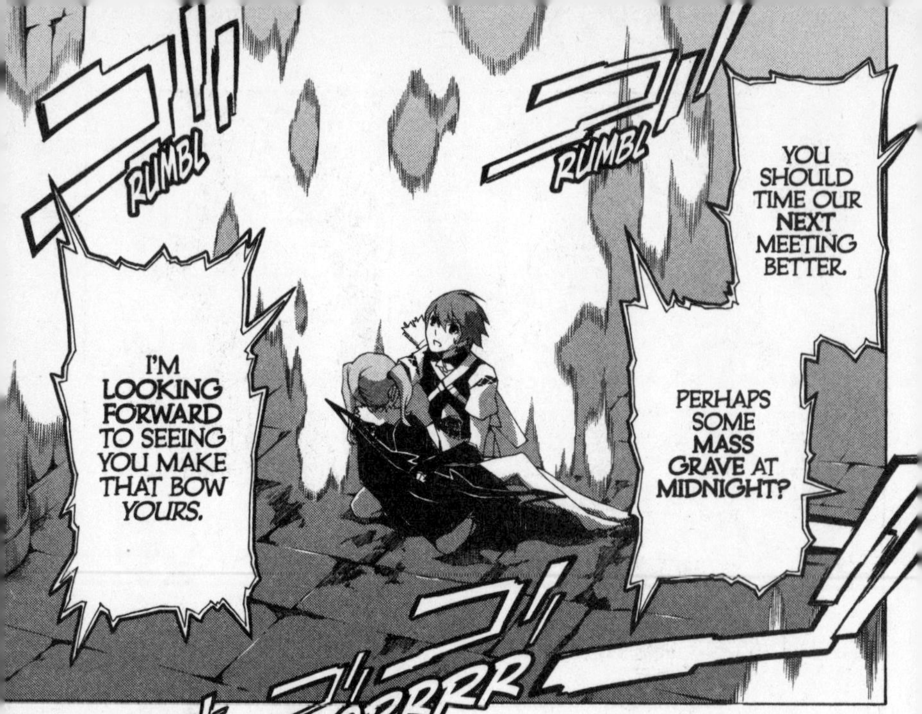
RUMBL
YOU SHOULD TIME OUR NEXT MEETING BETTER.
PERHAPS SOME MASS GRAVE AT MIDNIGHT?
RUMBL
I'M LOOKING FORWARD TO SEEING YOU MAKE THAT BOW YOURS.
ROORRRRR

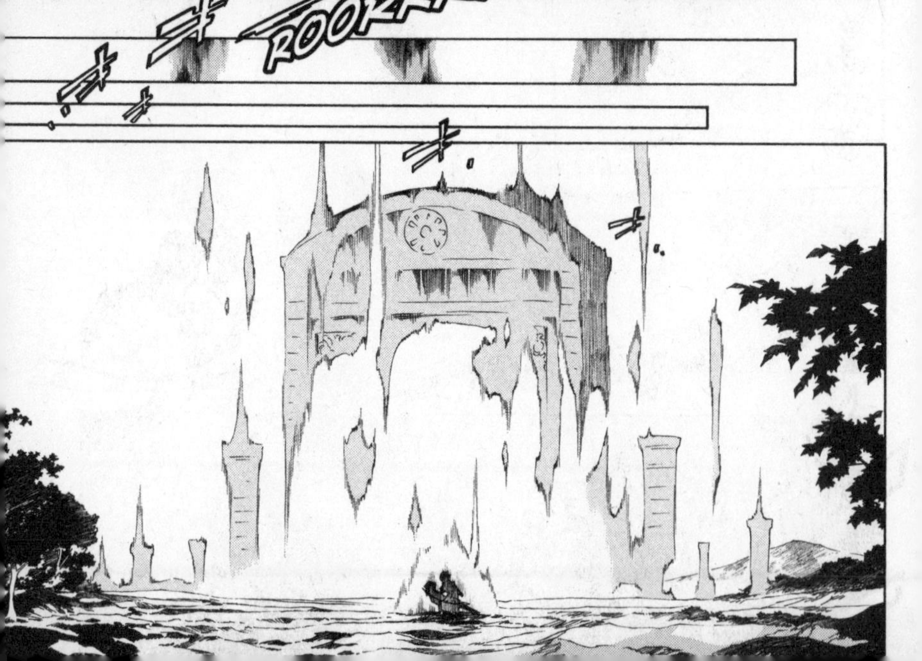

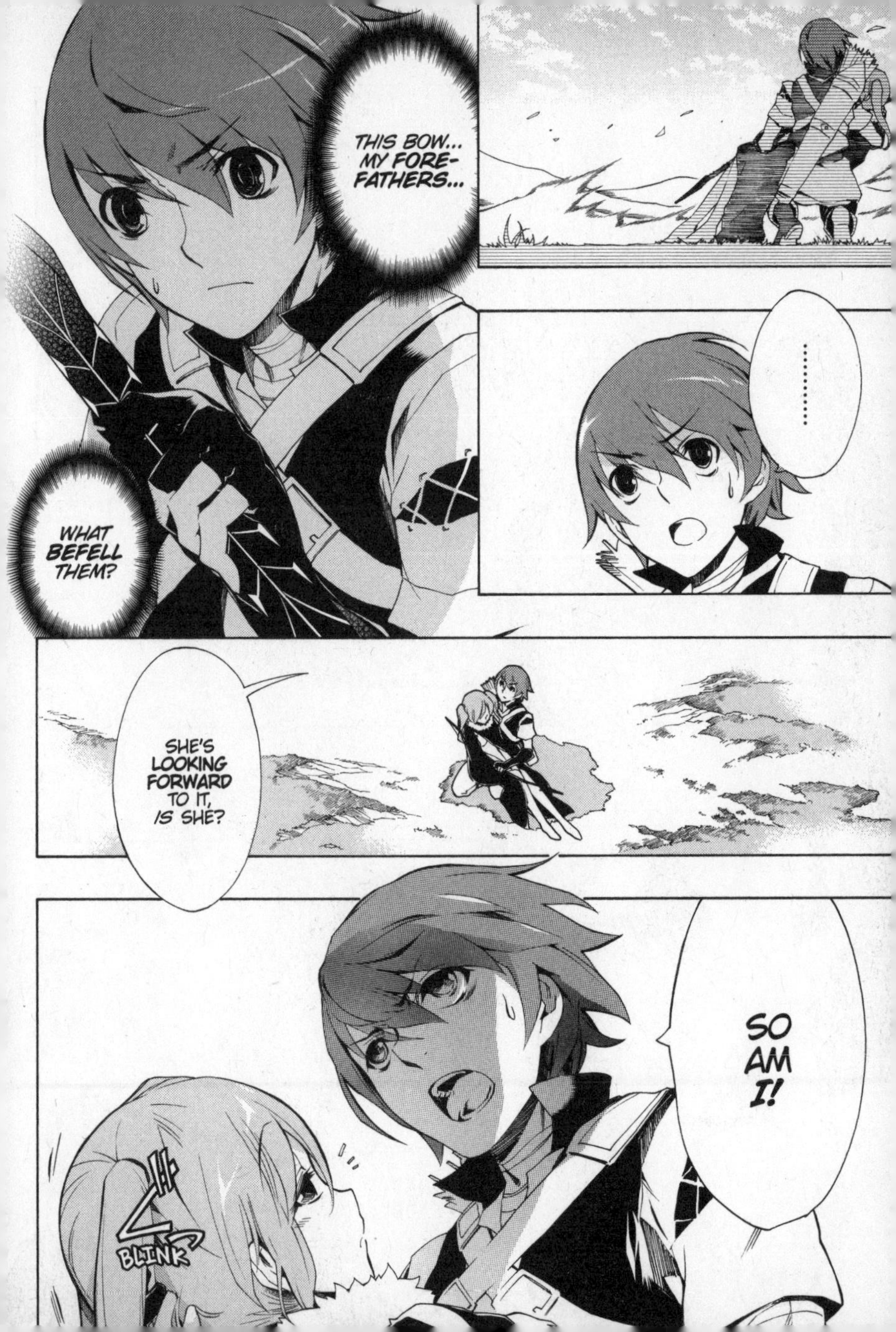
......
THIS BOW... MY FORE-FATHERS...
WHAT BEFELL THEM?
SHE'S LOOKING FORWARD TO IT, IS SHE?
SO AM I!
BLINK

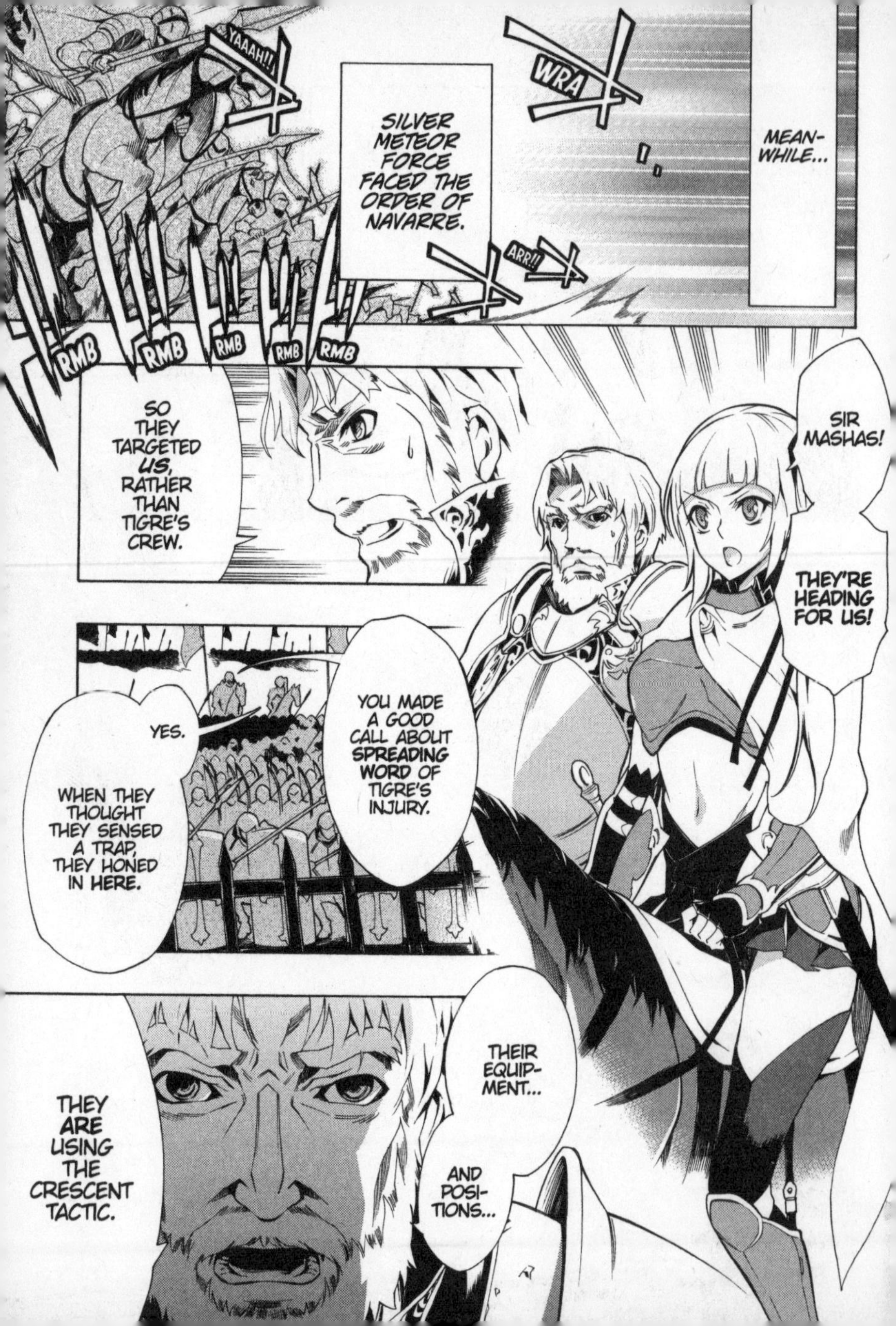
MEAN-WHILE...
WRA
ARR!!
SILVER METEOR FORCE FACED THE ORDER OF NAVARRE.
YAAAH!!
RMB
RMB
RMB
RMB
RMB
SIR MASHAS!
THEY'RE HEADING FOR US!
SO THEY TARGETED US, RATHER THAN TIGRE'S CREW.
YOU MADE A GOOD CALL ABOUT SPREADING WORD OF TIGRE'S INJURY.
YES.
WHEN THEY THOUGHT THEY SENSED A TRAP, THEY HONED IN HERE.
THEIR EQUIPMENT...
AND POSITIONS...
THEY ARE USING THE CRESCENT TACTIC.

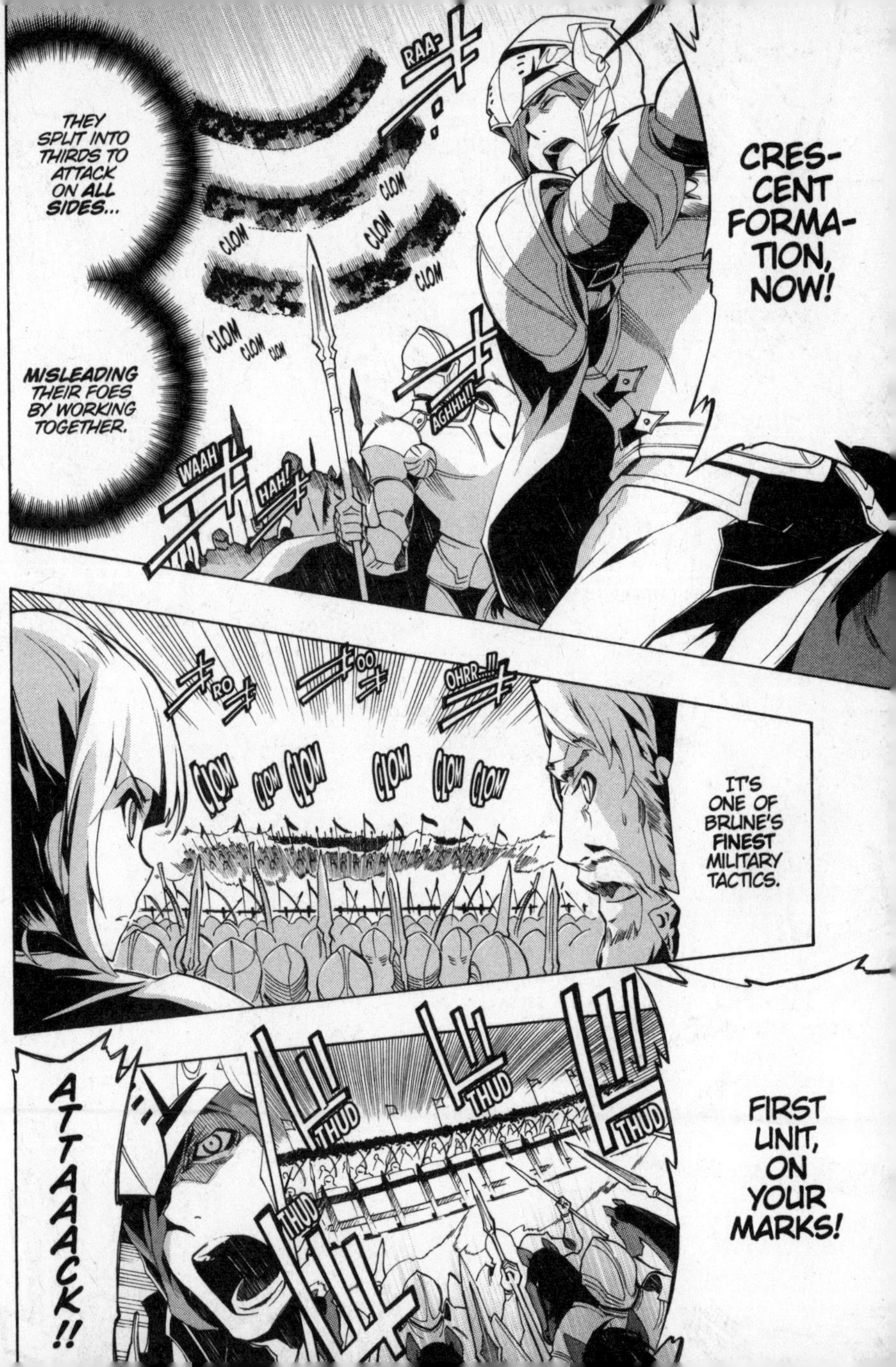
CRES-CENT FORMA-TION, NOW!
RAA-
THEY SPLIT INTO THIRDS TO ATTACK ON ALL SIDES...
CLOM CLOM CLOM
CLOM CLOM CLOM
AGHHH!!
MISLEADING THEIR FOES BY WORKING TOGETHER.
WAAH HAH!
IT'S ONE OF BRUNE'S FINEST MILITARY TACTICS.
OHRR...!!
OO
RO
CLOM CLOM CLOM CLOM CLOM CLOM
FIRST UNIT, ON YOUR MARKS!
THUD THUD THUD THUD
ATTAAACK!!

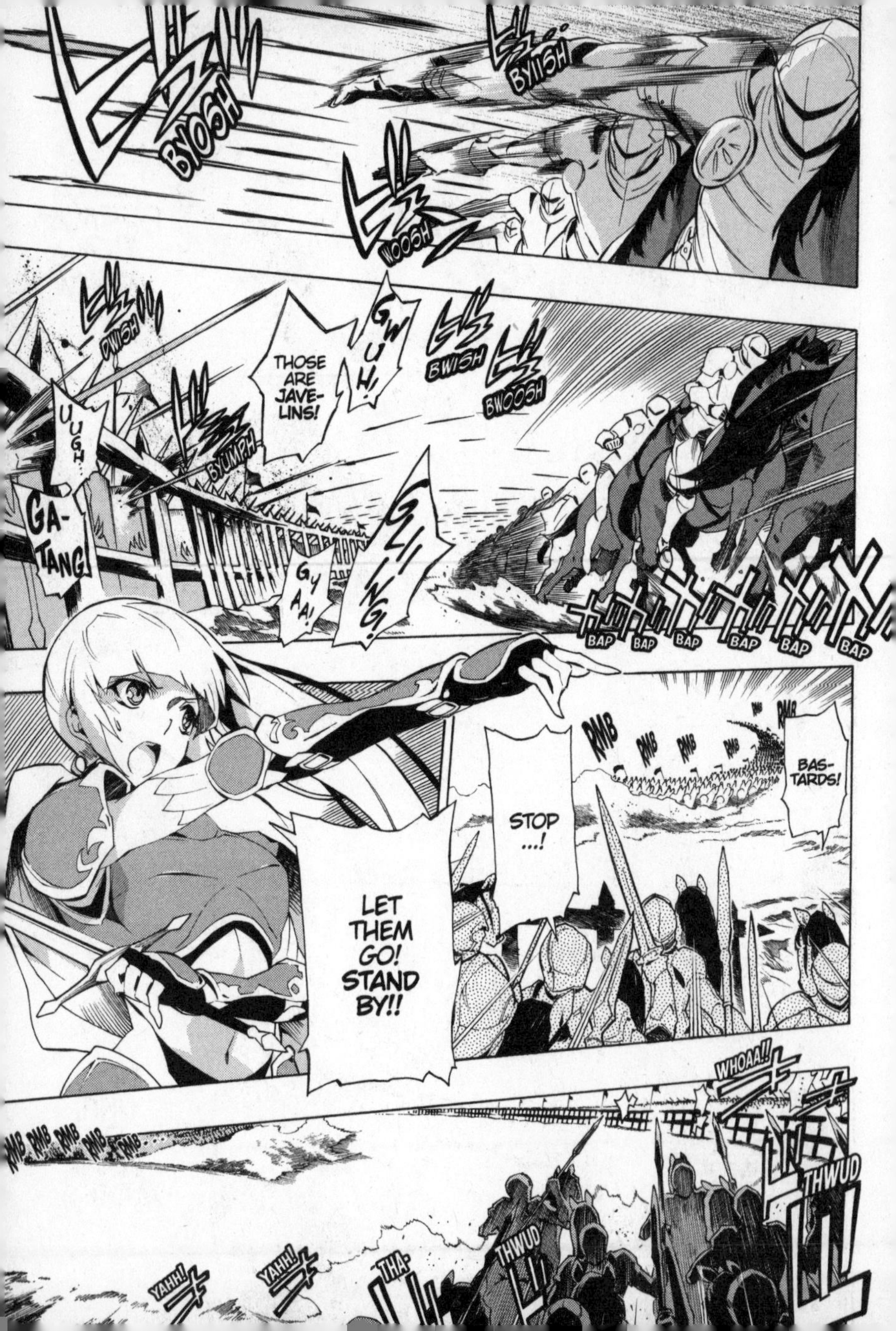
BYIISH
WOOSH
BYOSH
BWOOSH
BWISH
GWUH!
THOSE ARE JAVE-LINS!
DWISH
BYUMPH
UUGH...
GA-TANG!
GLIING!
GYAA!
BAP BAP BAP BAP BAP BAP
BAS-TARDS!
RMB RMB RMB RMB RMB RMB
STOP ...!
LET THEM GO! STAND BY!!
WHOAA!!
THWUD
THWUD
THA-
YAHH!
YAHH!
RMB RMB RMB RMB RMB

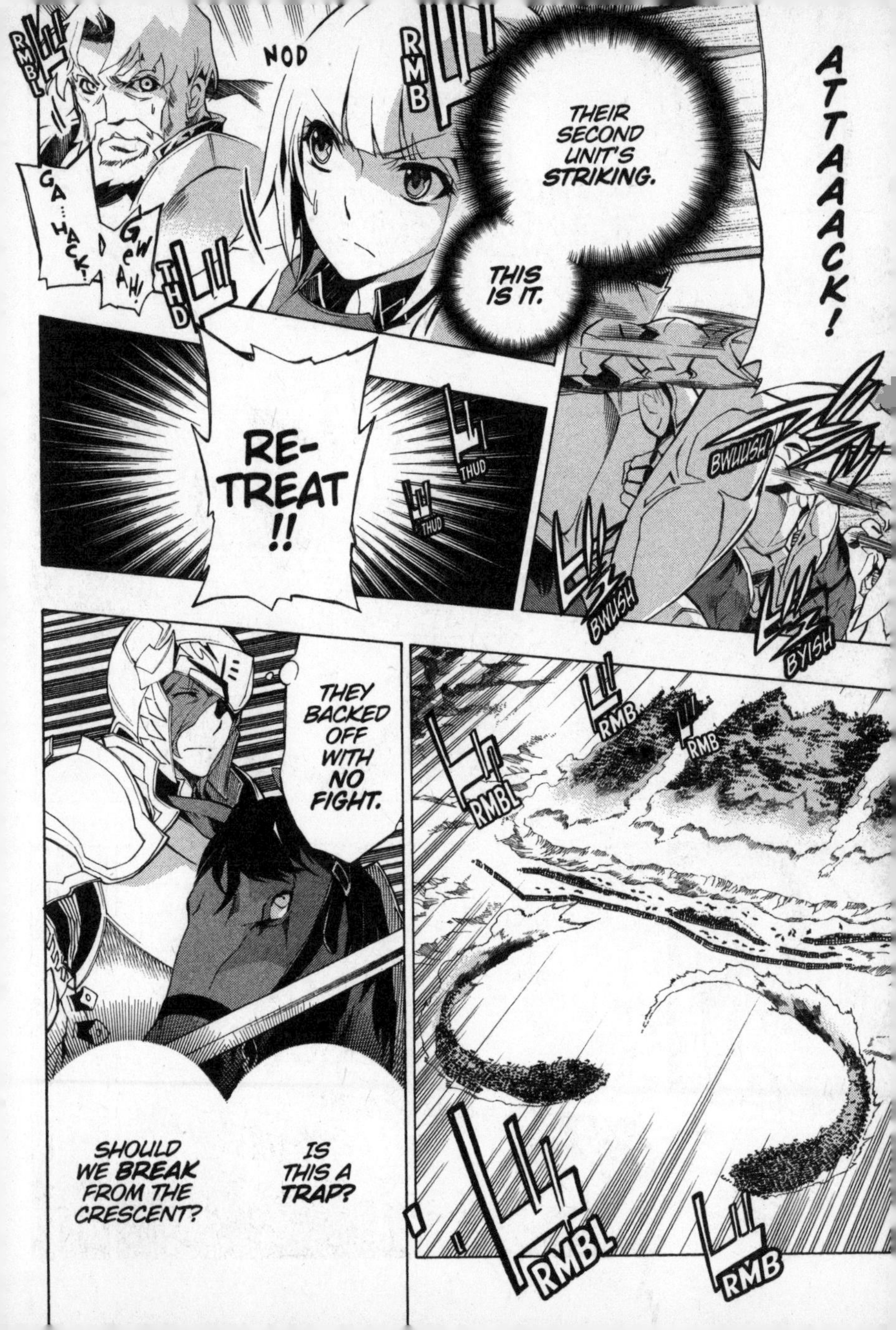
ATTAAACK!
THEIR SECOND UNIT'S STRIKING.
THIS IS IT.
RMB
NOD
RMBL
GA...HACK!
GWEAH!
THD
BWUUSH
BWUSH
BYISH
RE-TREAT!!
THUD
THUD
RMB
RMBL
RMB
RMBL
RMB
THEY BACKED OFF WITH NO FIGHT.
IS THIS A TRAP?
SHOULD WE BREAK FROM THE CRESCENT?

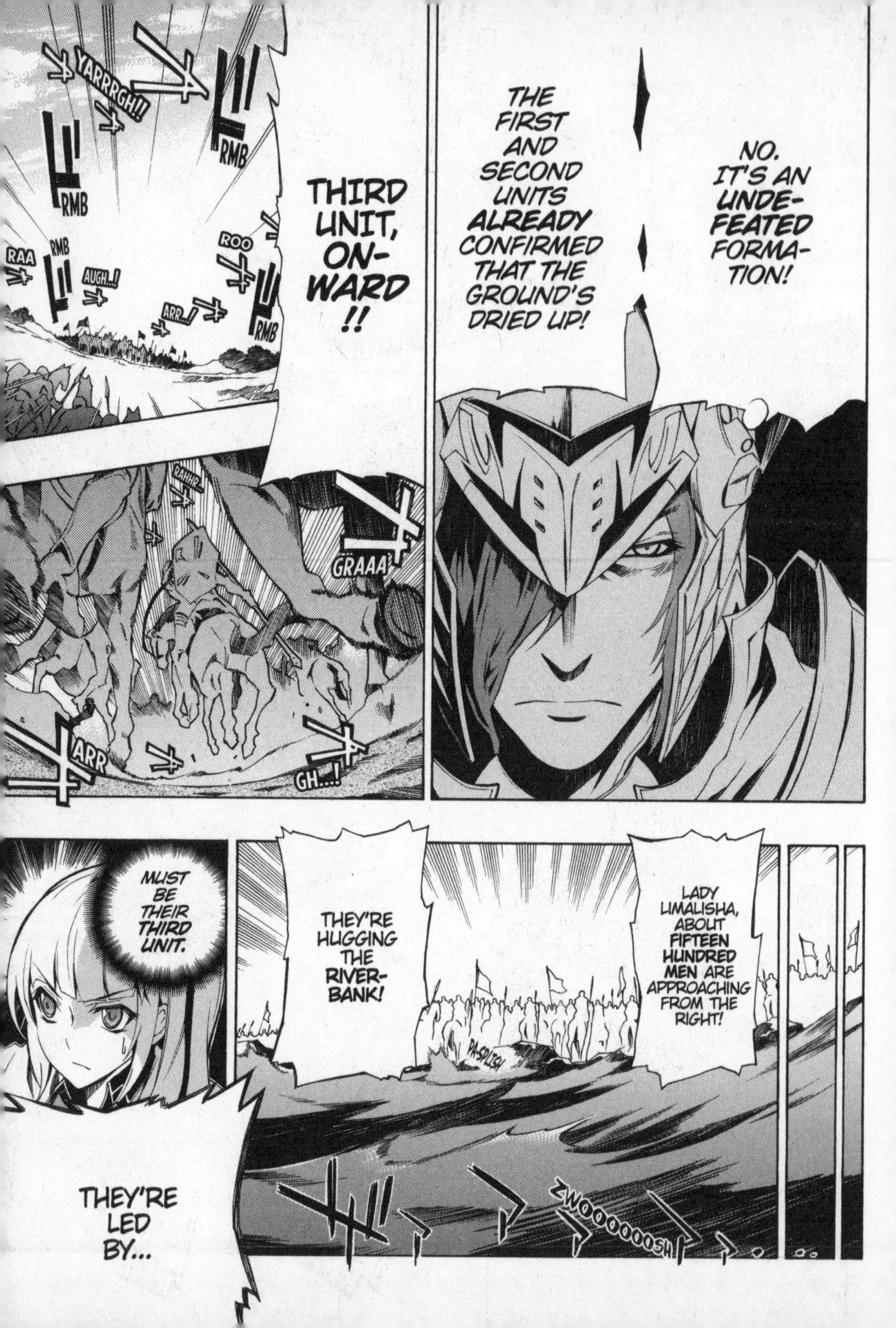
NO. IT'S AN UNDEFEATED FORMATION!
THE FIRST AND SECOND UNITS ALREADY CONFIRMED THAT THE GROUND'S DRIED UP!
THIRD UNIT, ONWARD!!
YARRRGH!!
RMB
RMB
ROO
RMB
RAA
AUGH...!
ARR...!
RMB
RAHHR...
GRAAA
ARR
GH...!
LADY LIMALISHA, ABOUT FIFTEEN HUNDRED MEN ARE APPROACHING FROM THE RIGHT!
THEY'RE HUGGING THE RIVERBANK!
PA-SPLISH
ZWOOOOOOOSH
MUST BE THEIR THIRD UNIT.
THEY'RE LED BY...

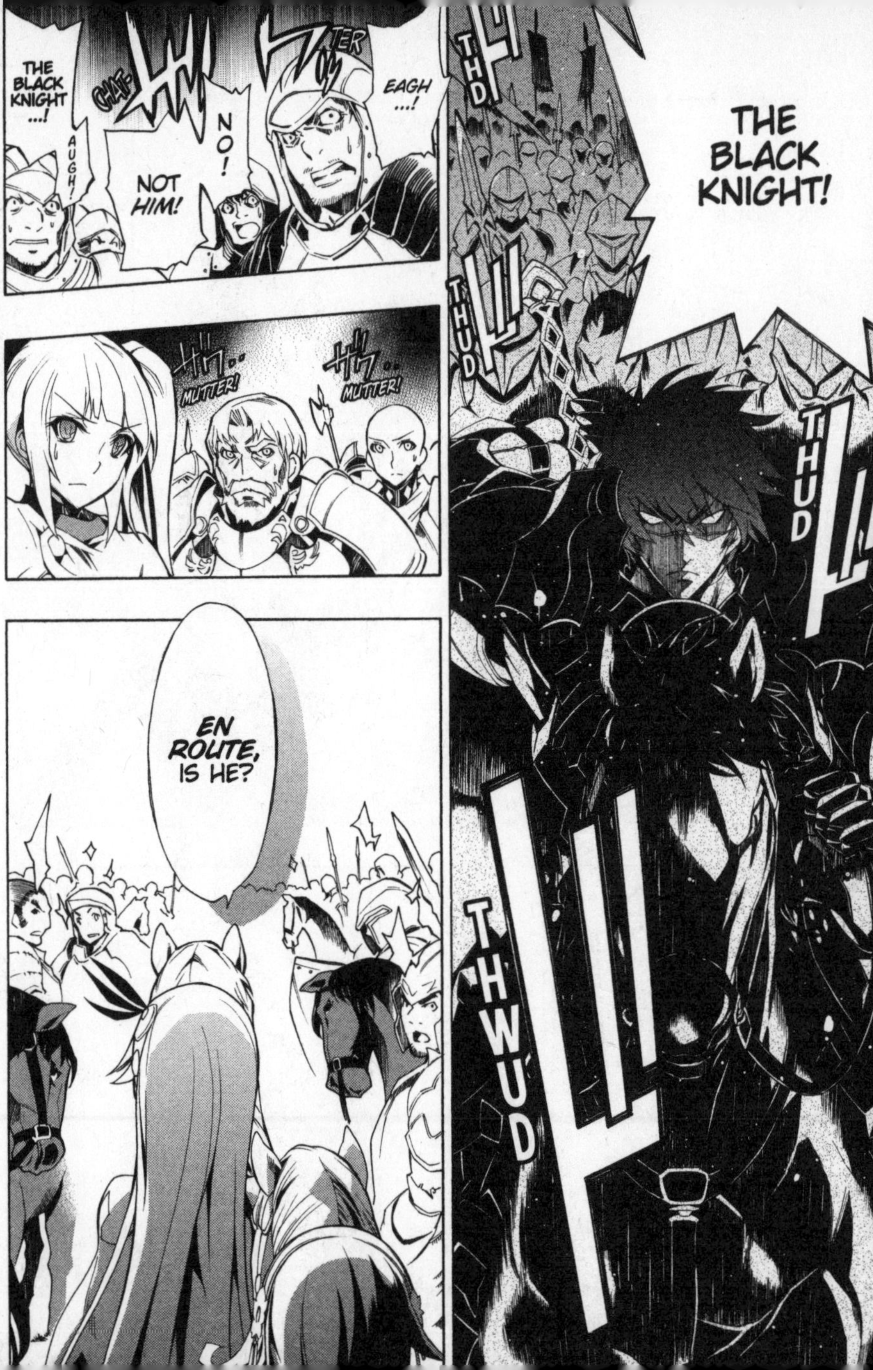
THE BLACK KNIGHT!
THD
THUD
THUD
THWUD
THE BLACK KNIGHT ...!
AUGH!
CHAF-
TER
NO! NOT HIM!
EAGH ...!
MUTTER!
MUTTER!
EN ROUTE, IS HE?

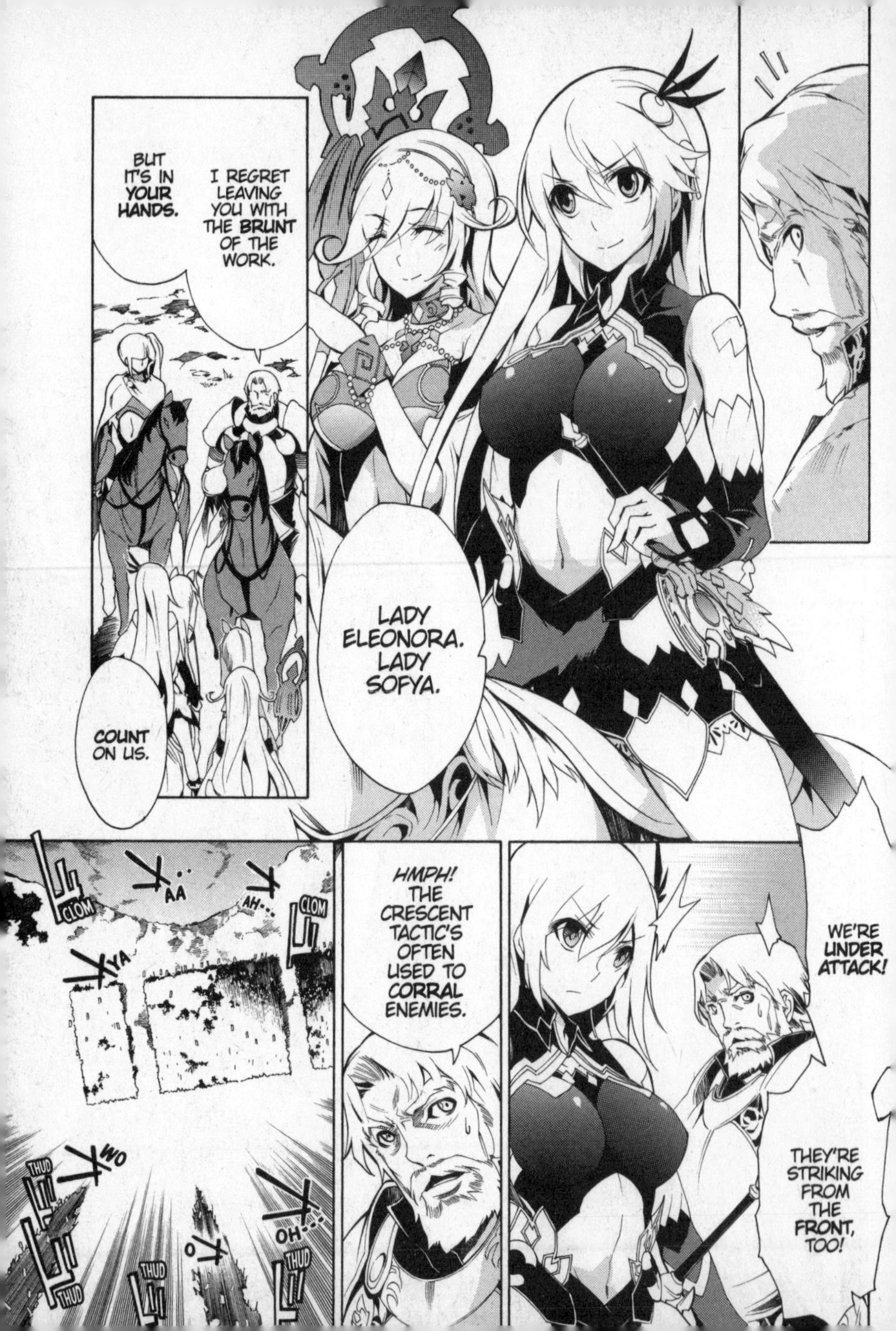
!!
LADY ELEONORA. LADY SOFYA.
I REGRET LEAVING YOU WITH THE BRUNT OF THE WORK.
BUT IT'S IN YOUR HANDS.
COUNT ON US.
WE'RE UNDER ATTACK!
THEY'RE STRIKING FROM THE FRONT, TOO!
HMPH! THE CRESCENT TACTIC'S OFTEN USED TO CORRAL ENEMIES.
AH...
CLOM
AA
CLOM
YA
OH...
THUD
O
WO
THUD
THUD
THUD

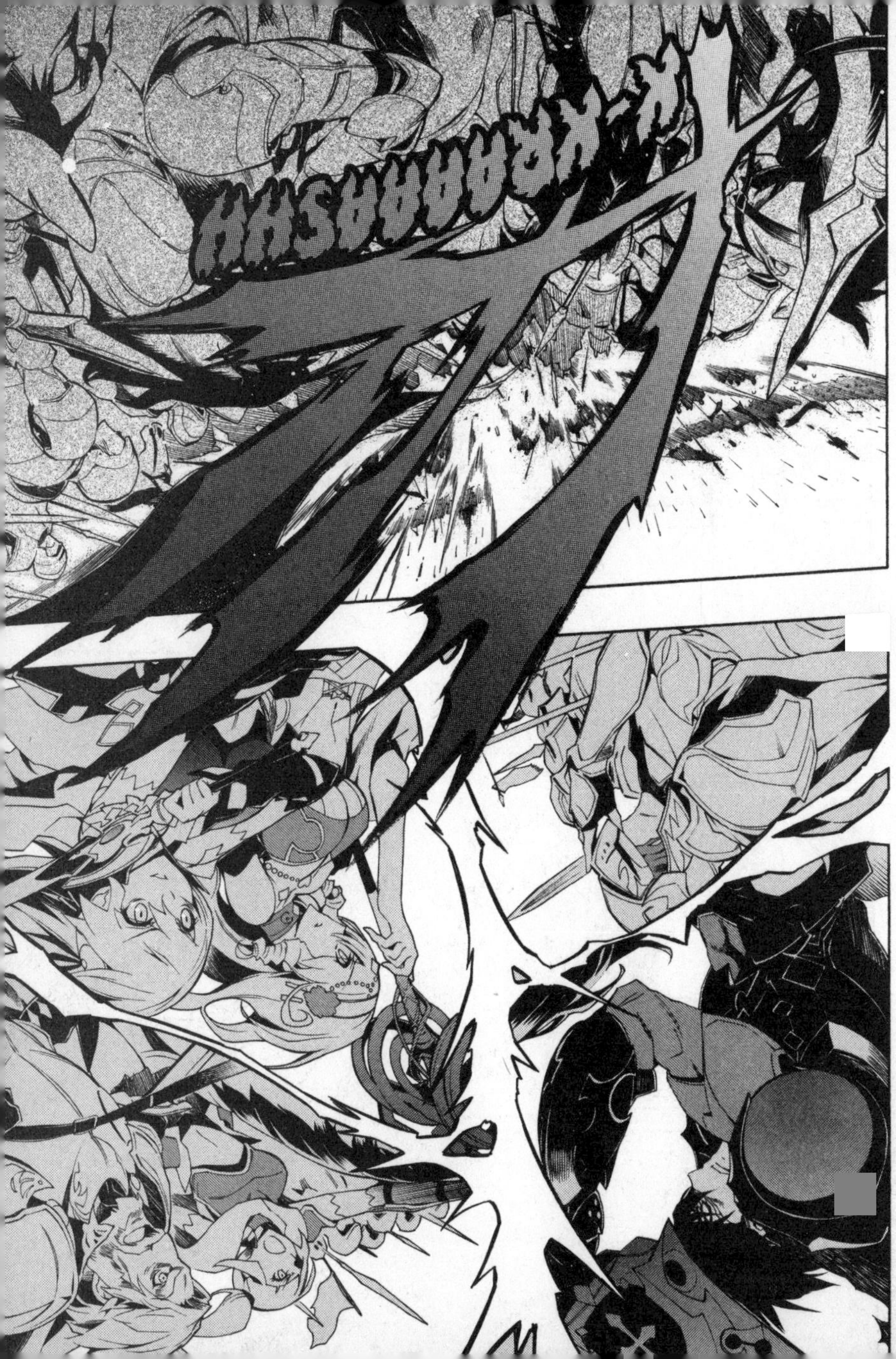

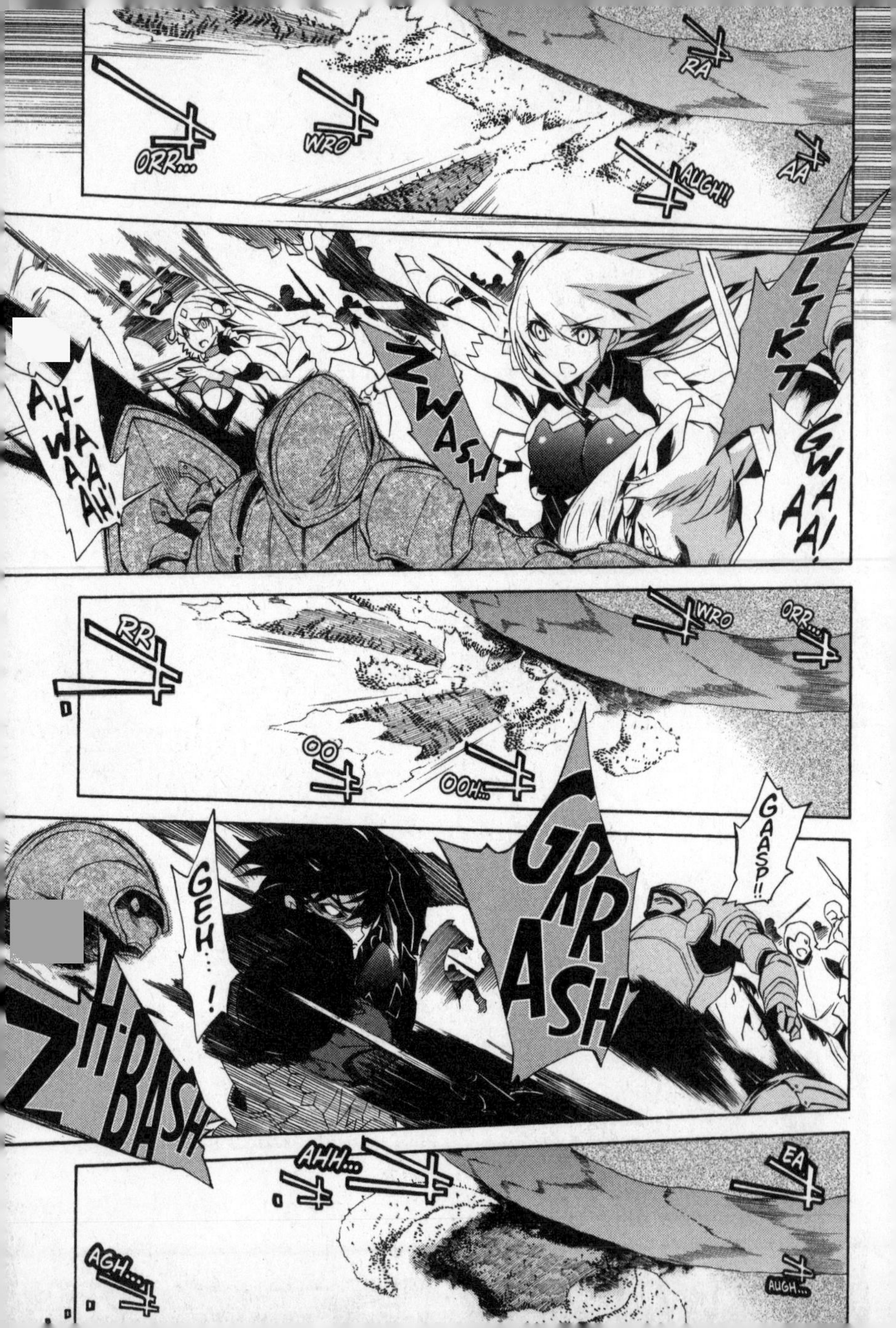
RA
AA
AUGH!!
WRO
ORR...
GWAAA!
ZLIKT
ZWASH
AH-WAAAAH!
ORR...
WRO
OOH...
OO
RR
GAASP!!
GRRASH
GEH...!
ZH-BASH
EA
AHH...
AUGH...
AGH...

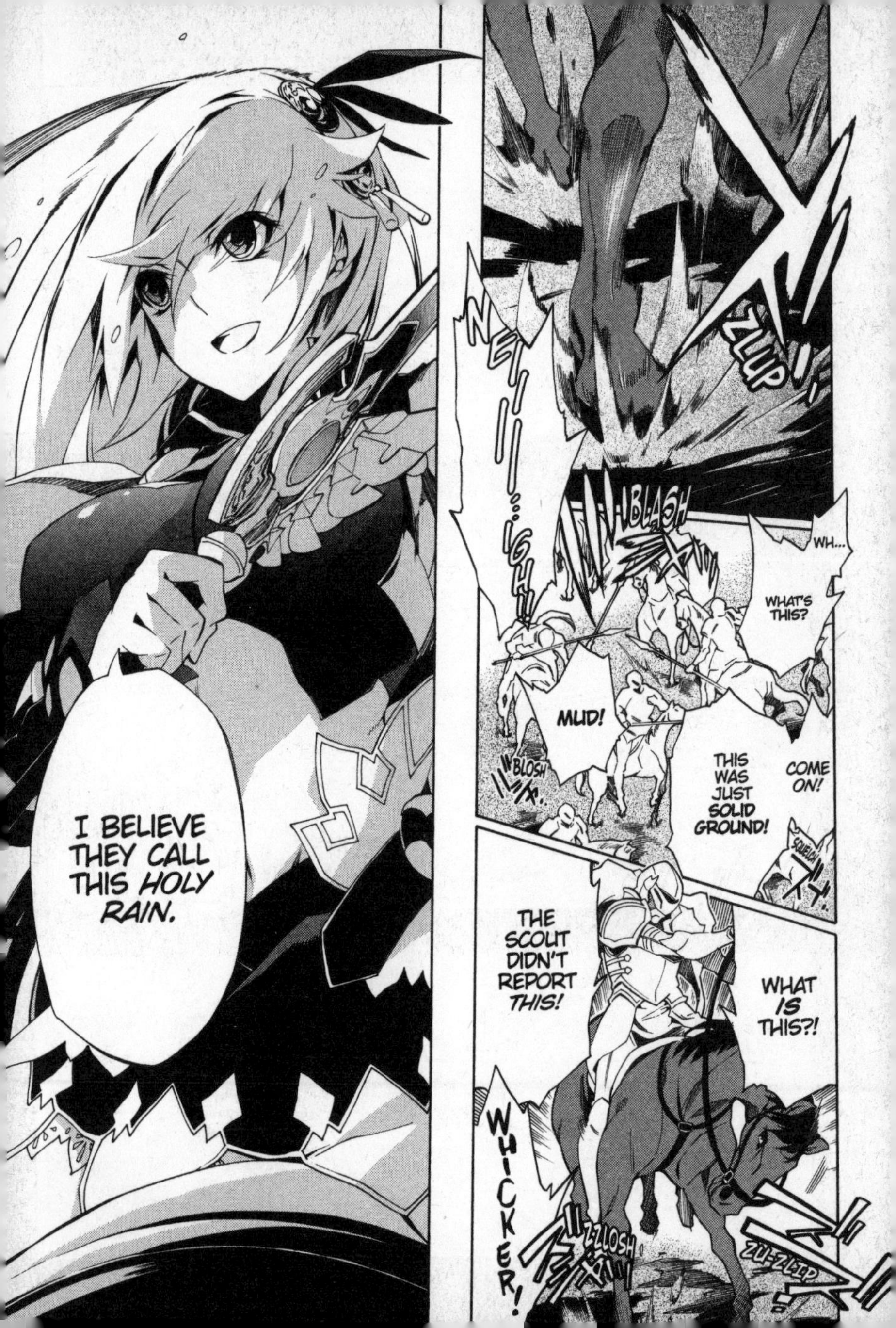
ZLUP
NEIIII...GH!!
BLASH
WH...
WHAT'S THIS?
MUD!
BLOSH
COME ON!
THIS WAS JUST SOLID GROUND!
SQUELCH
THE SCOUT DIDN'T REPORT THIS!
WHAT IS THIS?!
WHICKER!
ZZLOSH
ZU-ZLOP
I BELIEVE THEY CALL THIS HOLY RAIN.

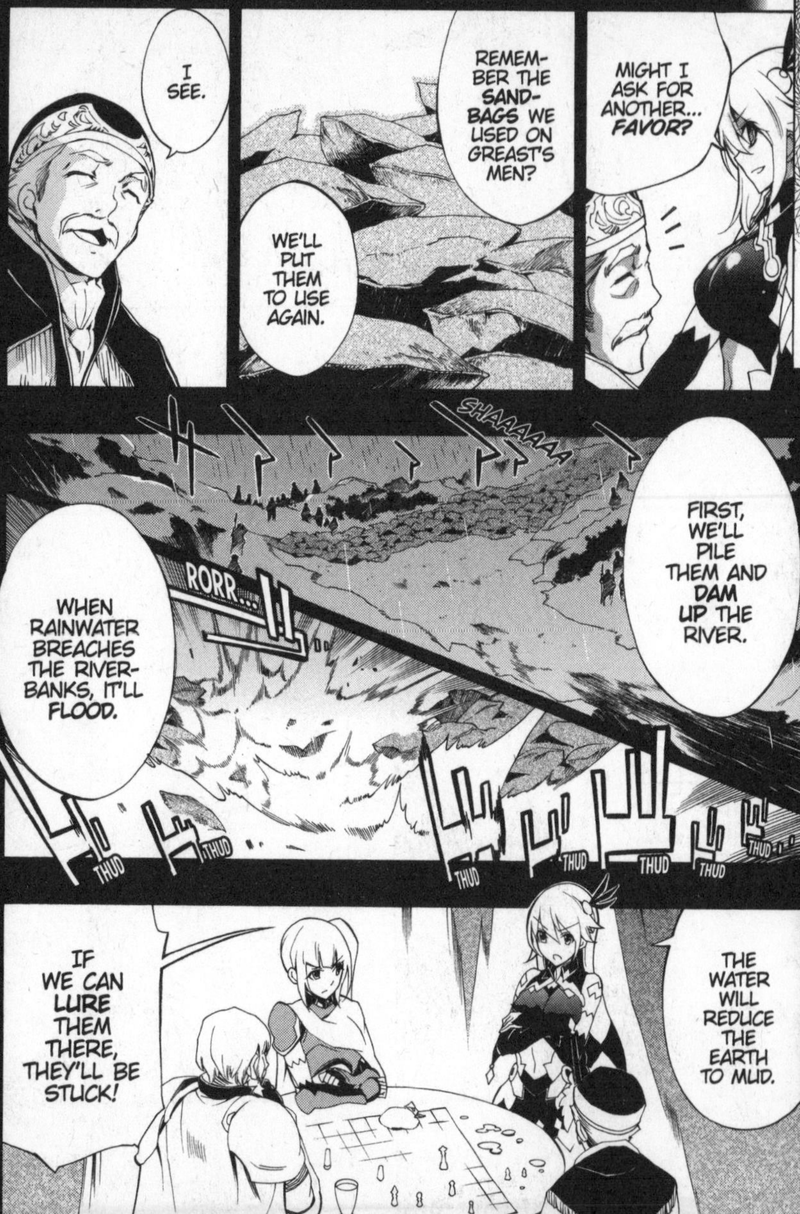
MIGHT I ASK FOR ANOTHER... FAVOR?
REMEMBER THE SANDBAGS WE USED ON GREAST'S MEN?
WE'LL PUT THEM TO USE AGAIN.
I SEE.
SHAAAAAAA
FIRST, WE'LL PILE THEM AND DAM UP THE RIVER.
RORR...
WHEN RAINWATER BREACHES THE RIVER-BANKS, IT'LL FLOOD.
THUD
THUD
THUD
THUD
THUD
THUD
THUD
THE WATER WILL REDUCE THE EARTH TO MUD.
IF WE CAN LURE THEM THERE, THEY'LL BE STUCK!

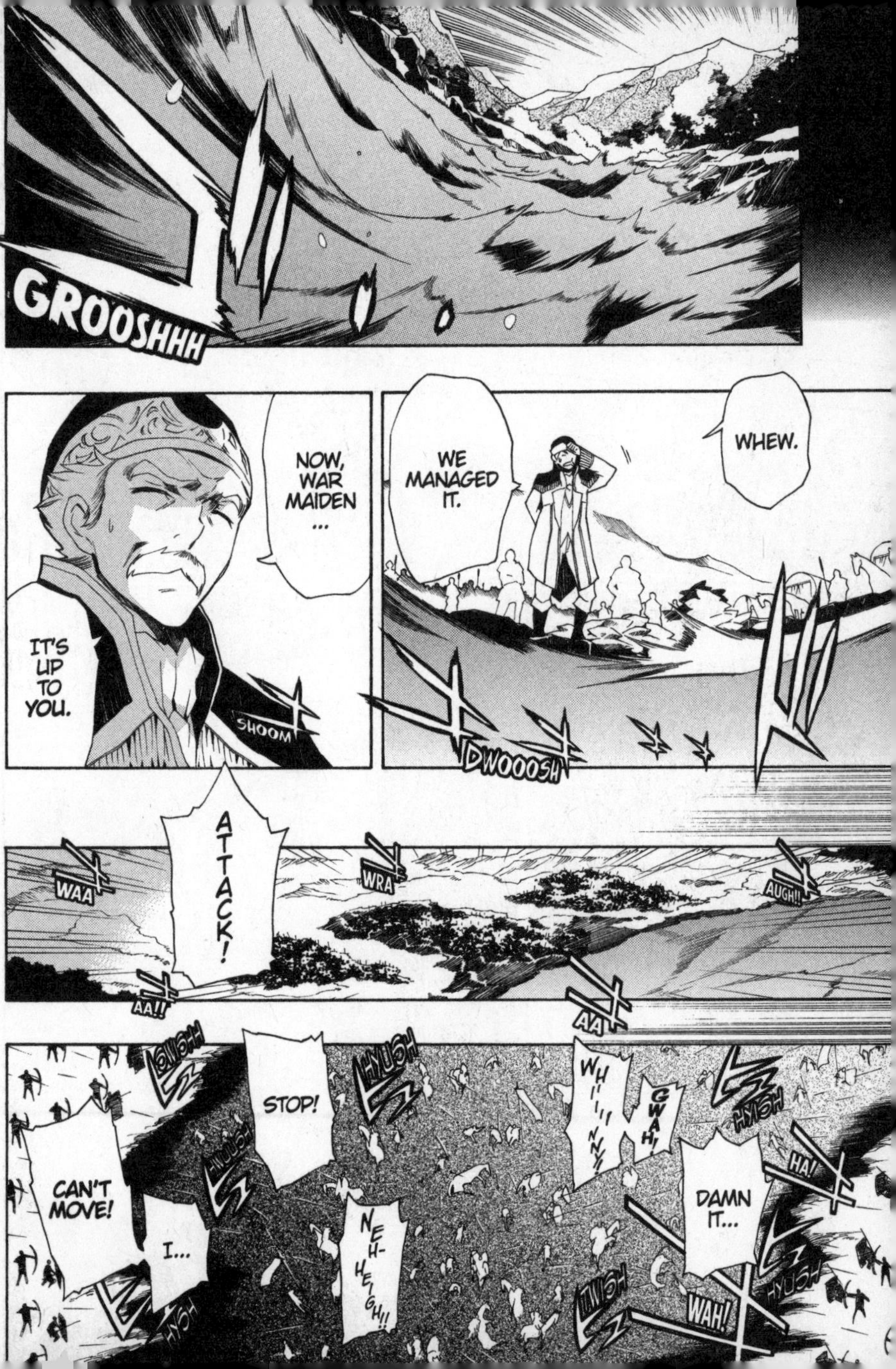
GROOSHHH
WHEW.
WE MANAGED IT.
DWOOOSH
NOW, WAR MAIDEN...
IT'S UP TO YOU.
SHOOM
ATTACK!
AUGH!!
WRA
WAA
AA!!
AA
HYUSH
DAMN IT...
HA!
GWAH!
WHI-I-I-NNY!!
STOP!
HYUSH
NEH-HEIGH!!
CAN'T MOVE!
I...
HYUSH
WAH!

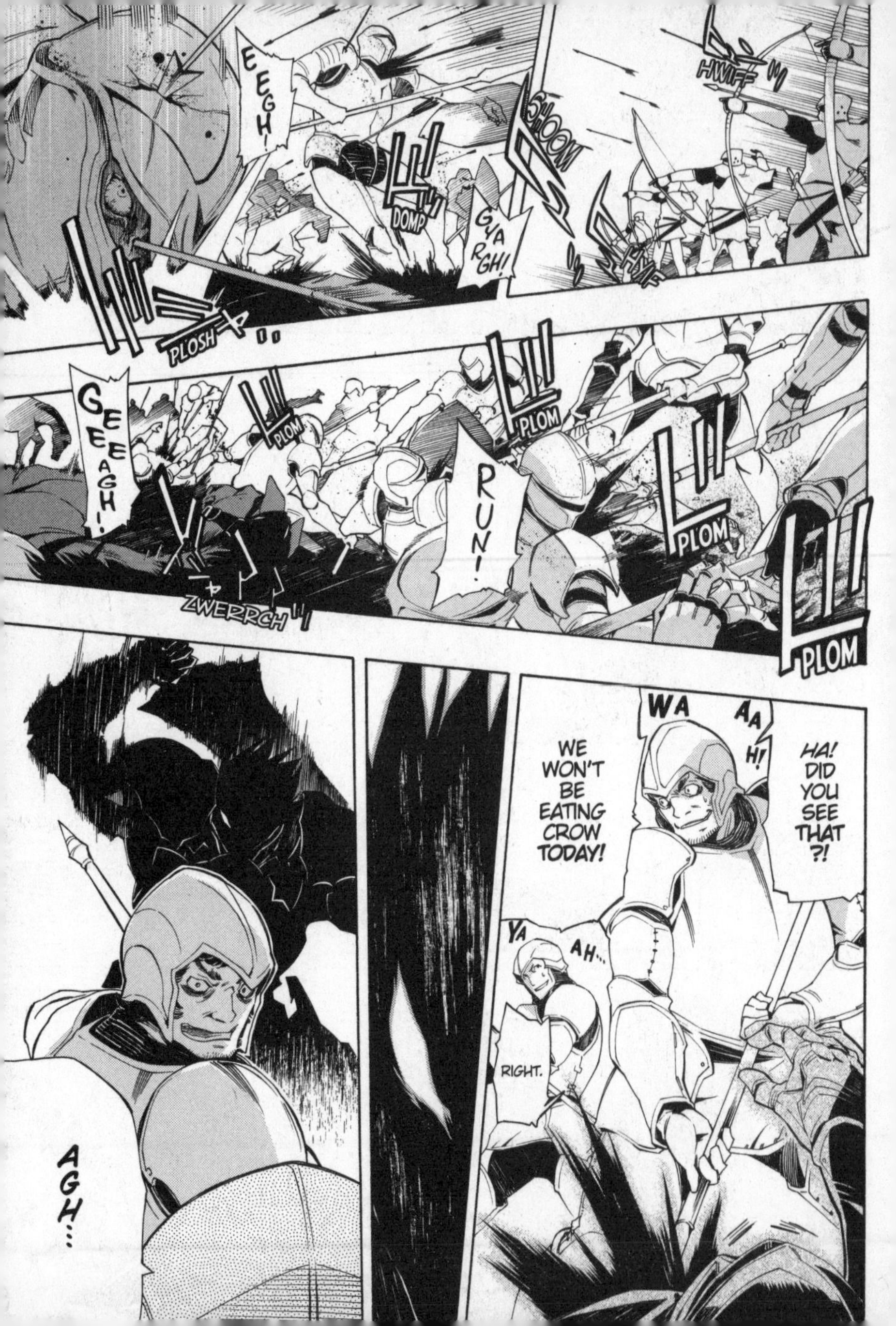
HWIFF
SHOOM
HYF
GYARGH!
DOMP
EEGH!
PLOSH
PLOM
PLOM
RUN!
PLOM
GEEEAGH!
ZWERRCH
PLOM
HA! DID YOU SEE THAT?!
WAAAH!
WE WON'T BE EATING CROW TODAY!
YA AH...
RIGHT.
AGH...

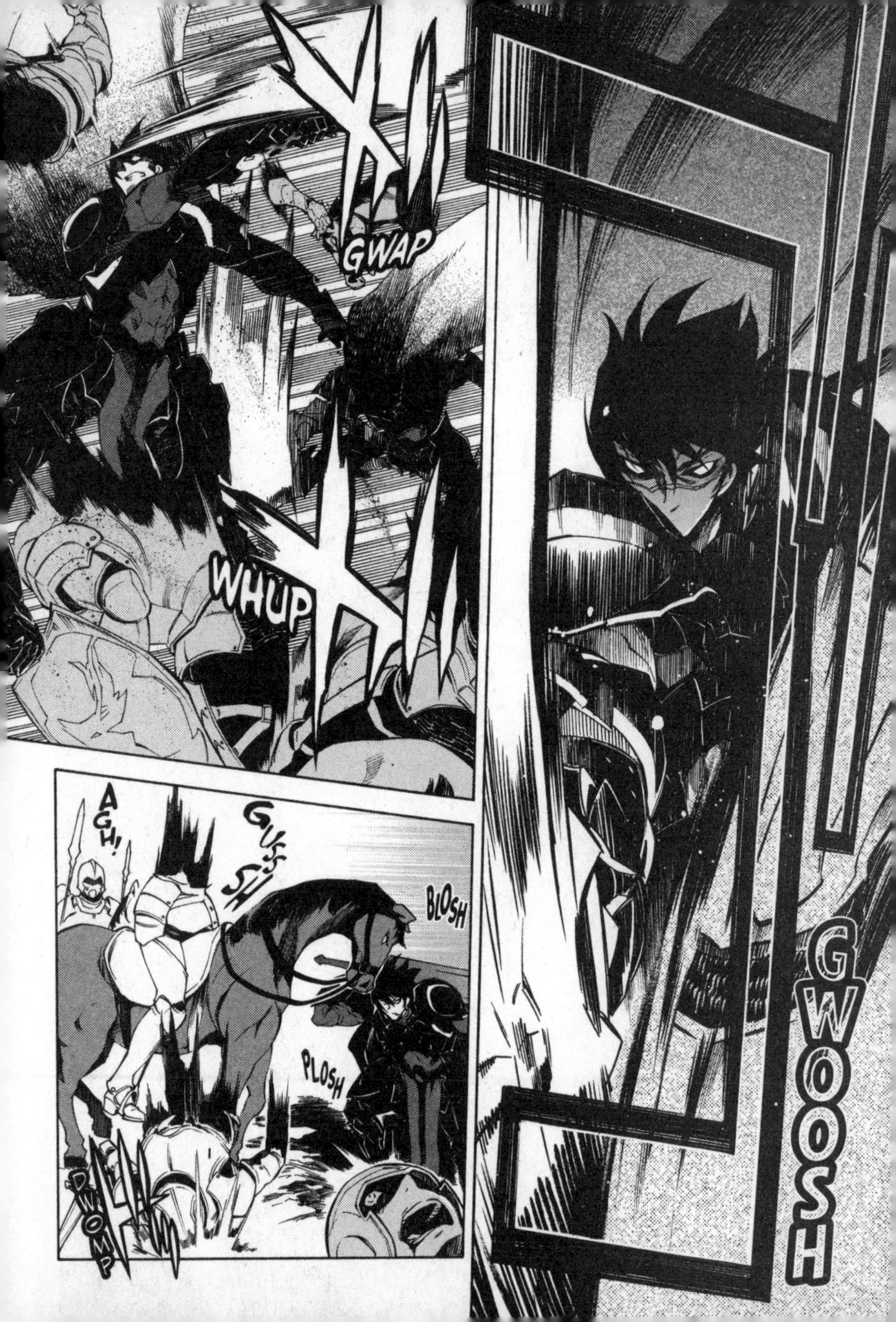
GWOOSH
GWAP
WHUP
BLOSH
GUSSSH
AGH!
PLOSH
DWOMP

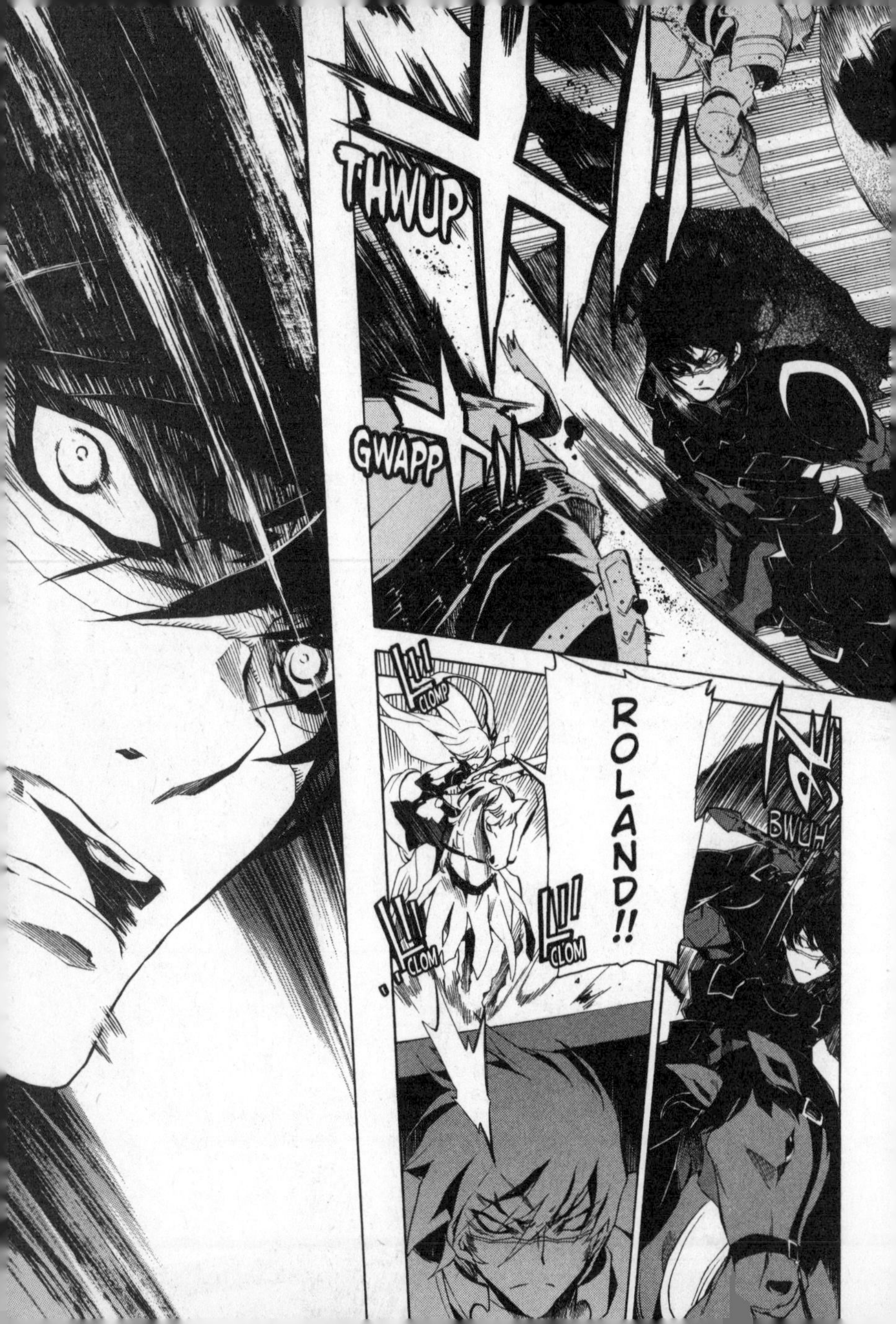
THWUP
GWAPP
BWUH
ROLAND!!
CLOM
CLOM
CLOMP

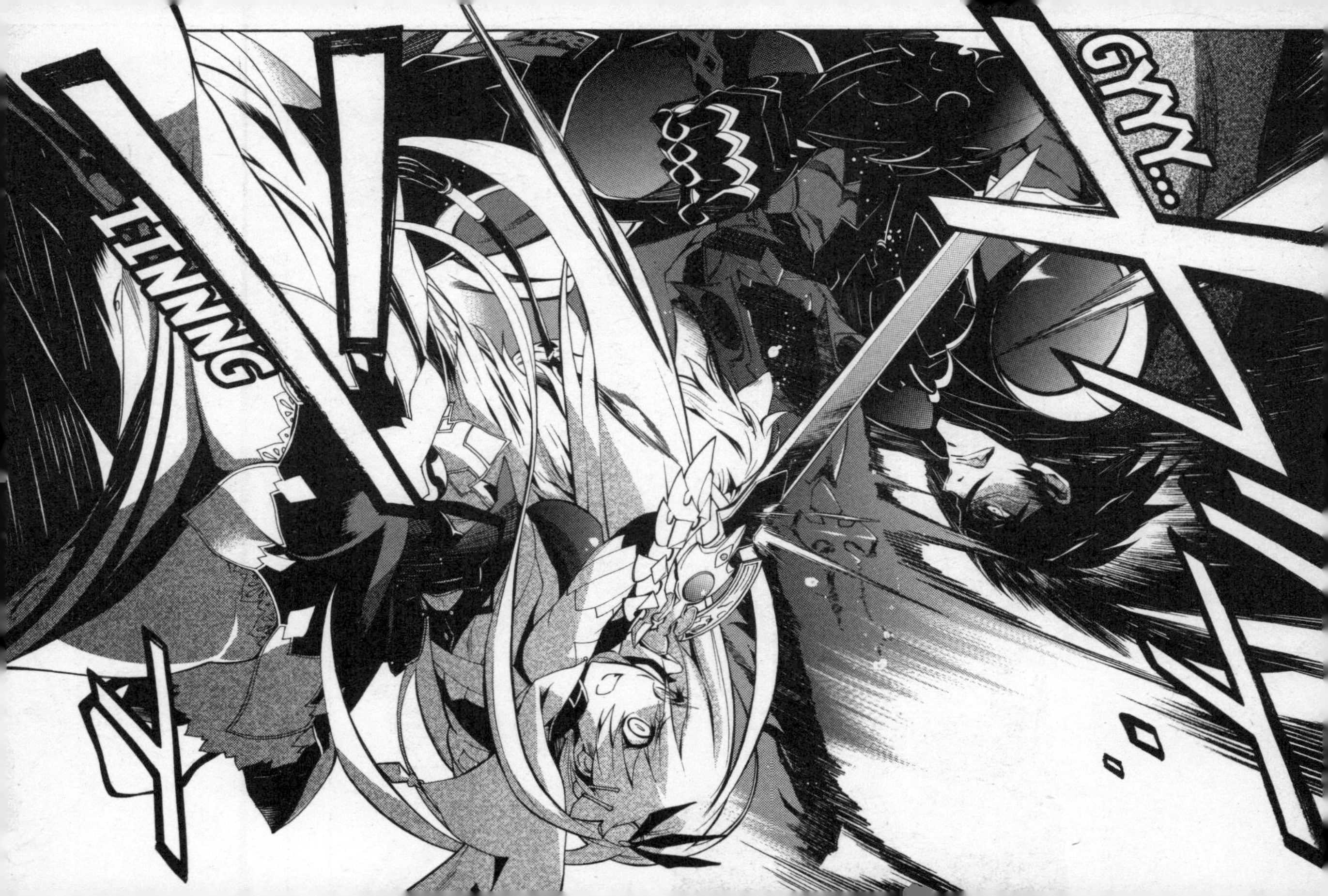
GYYY...
TINNNG

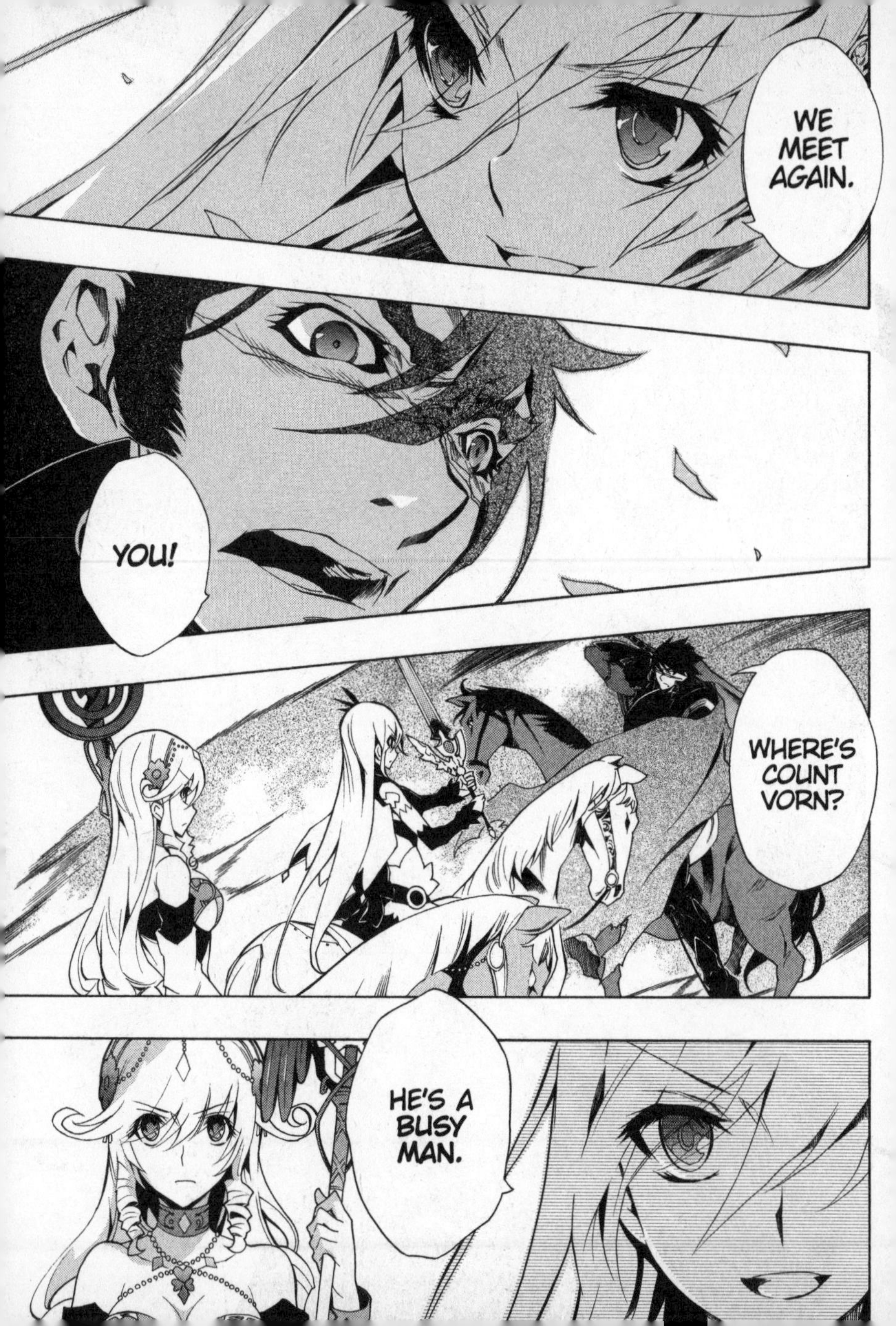
WE MEET AGAIN.
YOU!
WHERE'S COUNT VORN?
HE'S A BUSY MAN.

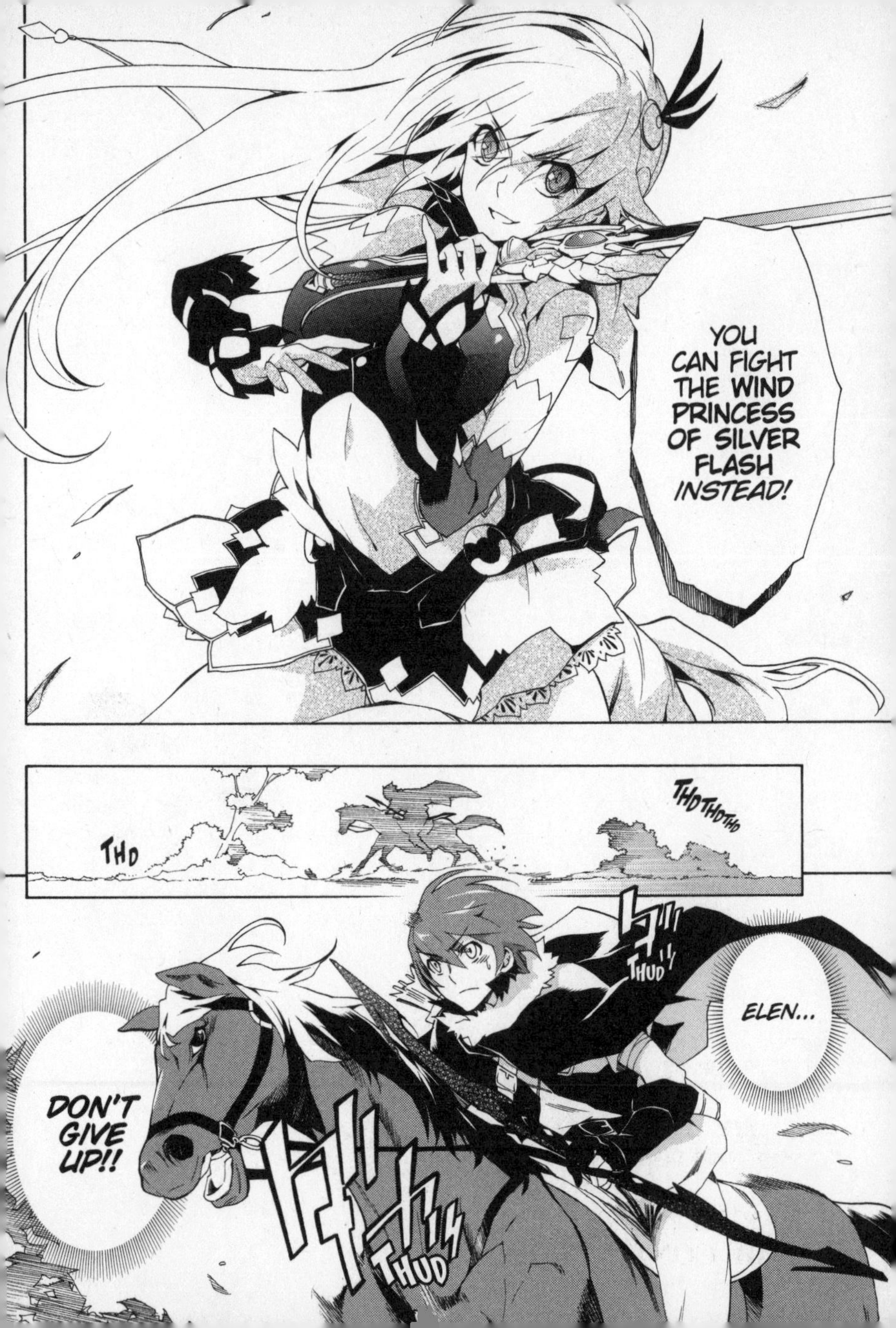
YOU CAN FIGHT THE WIND PRINCESS OF SILVER FLASH INSTEAD!
THDTHDTHD
THD
THUD
ELEN...
THUD
DON'T GIVE UP!!

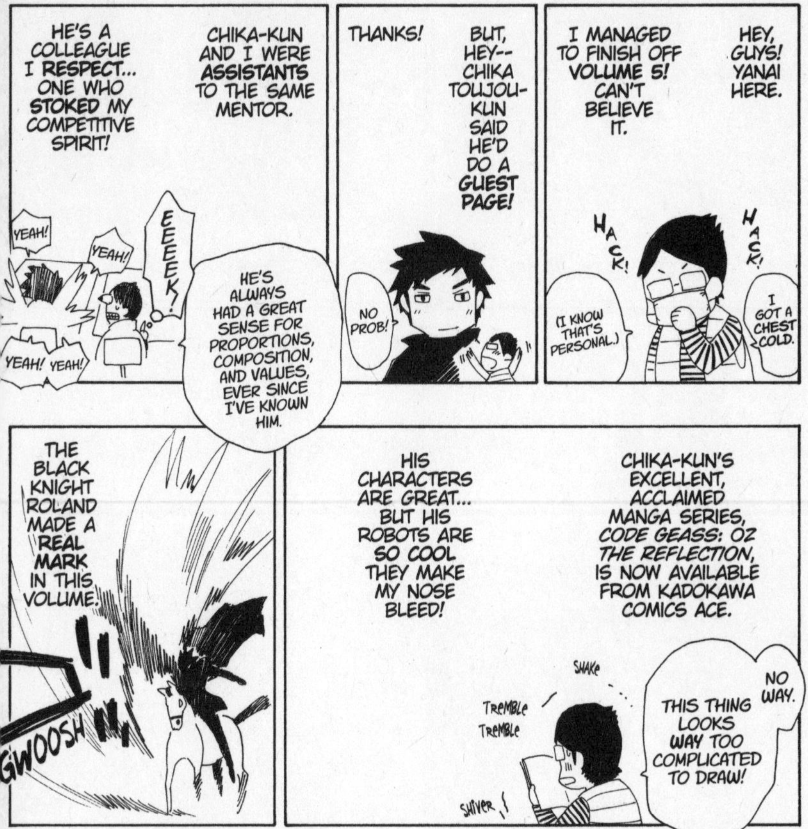
HEY, GUYS! YANAI HERE.
I MANAGED TO FINISH OFF VOLUME 5! CAN'T BELIEVE IT.
HACK!
HACK!
I GOT A CHEST COLD.
(I KNOW THAT'S PERSONAL.)
BUT, HEY-- CHIKA TOUJOU-KUN SAID HE'D DO A GUEST PAGE!
THANKS!
NO PROB!
CHIKA-KUN AND I WERE ASSISTANTS TO THE SAME MENTOR.
HE'S A COLLEAGUE I RESPECT... ONE WHO STOKED MY COMPETITIVE SPIRIT!
HE'S ALWAYS HAD A GREAT SENSE FOR PROPORTIONS, COMPOSITION, AND VALUES, EVER SINCE I'VE KNOWN HIM.
EEEEK!
YEAH!
YEAH!
YEAH!
YEAH!
CHIKA-KUN'S EXCELLENT, ACCLAIMED MANGA SERIES, CODE GEASS: OZ THE REFLECTION, IS NOW AVAILABLE FROM KADOKAWA COMICS ACE.
HIS CHARACTERS ARE GREAT... BUT HIS ROBOTS ARE SO COOL THEY MAKE MY NOSE BLEED!
NO WAY.
THIS THING LOOKS WAY TOO COMPLICATED TO DRAW!
SHAKE
TREMBLE
TREMBLE
SHIVER
THE BLACK KNIGHT ROLAND MADE A REAL MARK IN THIS VOLUME.
GWOOSH

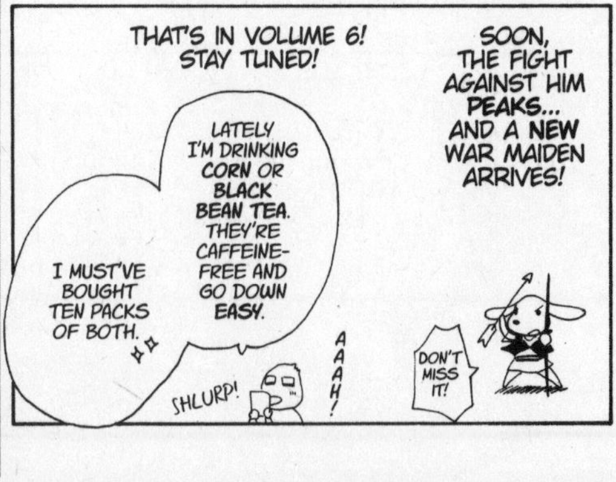
SOON, THE FIGHT AGAINST HIM PEAKS... AND A NEW WAR MAIDEN ARRIVES!
THAT'S IN VOLUME 6! STAY TUNED!
DON'T MISS IT!
LATELY I'M DRINKING CORN OR BLACK BEAN TEA. THEY'RE CAFFEINE-FREE AND GO DOWN EASY.
I MUST'VE BOUGHT TEN PACKS OF BOTH.
AAAH!
SHLURP!

· STAFF ·

Aoki-san, Matsuo-kun, Ishizawa-kun

· SPECIAL THANKS ·

Tsukasa Kawaguchi-sensei, Yoshi☆wo-sensei, Koutarou Yamada-sensei, Kiriyama-san, Hamada-kun, I-kura-san the manager...

and my **readers**!!

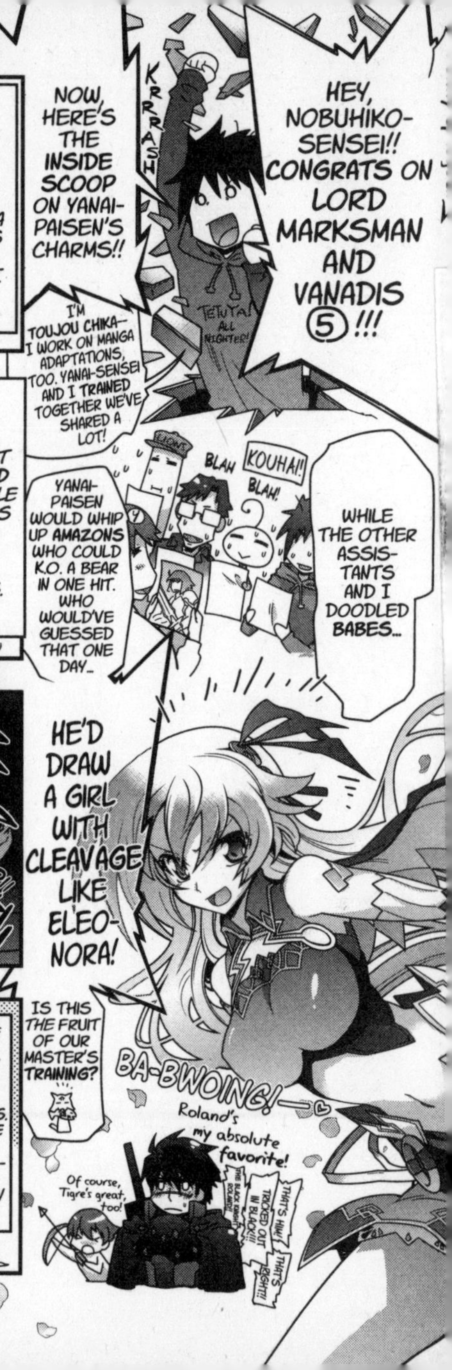
HEY, NOBUHIKO-SENSEI!! CONGRATS ON LORD MARKSMAN AND VANADIS ⑤!!!
KRRRASH
NOW, HERE'S THE INSIDE SCOOP ON YANAI-PAISEN'S CHARMS!!
TETUYA! ALL NIGHTER!
I'M TOUJOU CHIKA-I WORK ON MANGA ADAPTATIONS, TOO. YANAI-SENSEI AND I TRAINED TOGETHER WE'VE SHARED A LOT!
WHILE THE OTHER ASSIS-TANTS AND I DOODLED BABES...
KOUHAI!!
BLAH!
BLAH
YANAI-PAISEN WOULD WHIP UP AMAZONS WHO COULD K.O. A BEAR IN ONE HIT. WHO WOULD'VE GUESSED THAT ONE DAY...
HE'D DRAW A GIRL WITH CLEAVAGE LIKE ELEO-NORA!
IS THIS THE FRUIT OF OUR MASTER'S TRAINING?
BA-BWOING!
Roland's my absolute favorite!
THAT'S RIGHT!!
THAT'S HIM!! TRICKED OUT IN BLACK!!!
THE BLACK KNIGHT ROLAND!!
Of course, Tigre's great, too!

MEETING YANAI-PAISEN: A FOUR-PANEL MANGA

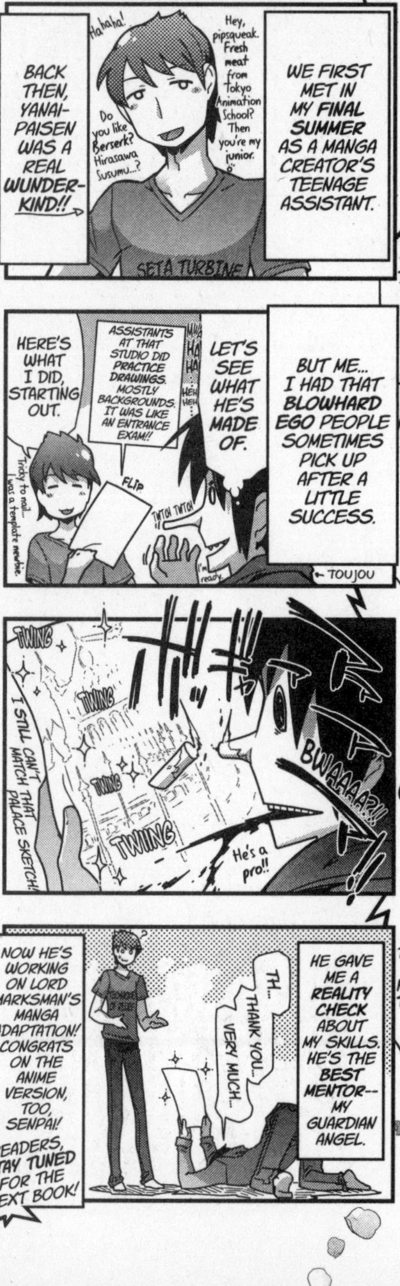
WE FIRST MET IN MY FINAL SUMMER AS A MANGA CREATOR'S TEENAGE ASSISTANT.
Hey, pipsqueak. Fresh meat from Tokyo Animation School? Then you're my junior.
Do you like Berserk? Hirasawa Susumu...?
Ha ha ha!
BACK THEN, YANAI-PAISEN WAS A REAL WUNDER-KIND!!
SETA TURBINE
BUT ME... I HAD THAT BLOWHARD EGO PEOPLE SOMETIMES PICK UP AFTER A LITTLE SUCCESS.
LET'S SEE WHAT HE'S MADE OF.
MWA HA HA
HEH HEH
TWITCH TWITCH
I'm ready.
← TOUJOU
ASSISTANTS AT THAT STUDIO DID PRACTICE DRAWINGS. MOSTLY BACKGROUNDS. IT WAS LIKE AN ENTRANCE EXAM!!
HERE'S WHAT I DID, STARTING OUT.
FLIP
Tricky to nail... I was a template newbie.
BWAAAA?!!
He's a pro!!
TWING
TWING
TWING
TWIING
I STILL CAN'T MATCH THAT PALACE SKETCH.
HE GAVE ME A REALITY CHECK ABOUT MY SKILLS. HE'S THE BEST MENTOR-- MY GUARDIAN ANGEL.
TH... THANK YOU... VERY MUCH...
NOW HE'S WORKING ON LORD MARKSMAN'S MANGA ADAPTATION! CONGRATS ON THE ANIME VERSION, TOO, SENPAI!
READERS, STAY TUNED FOR THE NEXT BOOK!

Lord Marksman
⚔─and Vanadis─➤

CHAPTER 26: END
TO BE CONTINUED...

魔弾の王と戦姫(ヴァナディース)

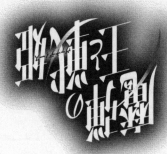